Images of Projects

Images of Projects

Mark Winter and Tony Szczepanek

GOWER

Published by
Gower Publishing Limited
Wey Court East
Union Road
Farnham
Surrey
GU9 7PT
England

Gower Publishing Company
Suite 420
101 Cherry Street
Burlington
VT 05401-4405
USA

www.gowerpublishing.com

Mark Winter and Tony Szczepanek have asserted their moral right under the Copyright, Designs and Patents Act, 1988, to be identified as the authors of this work.

British Library Cataloguing in Publication Data
Winter, Mark.
  Images of projects.
  1. Project management. 2. Planning--Technique.
  I. Title II. Szczepanek, Tony.
  658.4'04-dc22

  ISBN: 978-0-566-08716-5

Library of Congress Cataloging-in-Publication Data
Winter, Mark.
  Images of projects / by Mark Winter and Tony Szczepanek.
       p. cm.
  Includes bibliographical references and index.
  ISBN 978-0-566-08716-5
  1. Project management. I. Szczepanek, Tony. II. Title.
  HD69.P75W56 2009
  658.4'04--dc22

                                                                 2009003161

Mixed Sources
Product group from well-managed
forests and other controlled sources
www.fsc.org Cert no. SA-COC-1565
© 1996 Forest Stewardship Council
FSC

Printed and bound in Great Britain by
MPG Books Ltd, Bodmin, Cornwall.

How am I thinking about this?
How else could I think about it?

Peter Checkland

Thinking about thinking is not a common habit
but is an important part of the skill of thinking.

Edward de Bono

Brief Contents

Detailed Contents

PART 1   Introduction to *Images of Projects*

PART 2   Seven Core Images of Projects

[Images] create insight. But they also distort.
They have strengths. But they also have limitations.
Gareth Morgan

PART 3 Applying the Images in Practice

List of Figures

List of Tables

List of Abbreviations

APM	Association for Project Management
BCS	British Computer Society
BFG	The Big Food Group
BSR	Branch Specific Ranging
2CP	Context/Content/Process
CEO	Chief Executive Officer
CRMP	Centre for Research in the Management of Projects
CRPR	Complex Responsive Processes of Relating
DMAIC	Define/Measure/Analyze/Improve/Control
DSDM	Dynamic Systems Development Method
EPSRC	Engineering and Physical Sciences Research Council
ERP	Enterprise Resource Planning System
ESCO	Executive/Support/Communications/Operations
GDPM	Goal Directed Project Management
HIPs	Home Improvement Packs
IPT	Integrated Project Team
IJPM	International Journal of Project Management
JDI	Just Do It
LOCOG	London Organizing Committee of the Olympic and Paralympic Games
MBA	Masters in Business Administration
MD	Managing Director
MOD	Ministry of Defence
MOP	Management of Projects
MPA	Major Projects Association
MSP	Managing Successful Programmes
NHS	National Health Service
NPfIT	National Programme for IT
ODA	Olympic Delivery Authority
OGC	Office for Government Commerce
PFI	Private Finance Initiative
PID	Project Initiation Document
PM	Project Management
PMI	Project Management Institute
PMO	Programme Management Office
PRINCE2	Projects in Controlled Environments
PSO	People, Systems and Organization
PSO	Project or Programme Support Office
SIGs	Special Interest Groups
SLA	Situation-Learning-Action
SSM	Soft Systems Methodology
UCL	University College London
UMIST	University of Manchester Institute of Science and Technology

Acknowledgements

Starting from a belief that everything is connected in life, we wish to start by saying thank you to everyone who has had some 'input' to this book: our parents and other family members, past lecturers and ex-fellow students, ex-work colleagues and past students, and ex-fellow practitioners. In short, the 'ground' for this book stems from the 'input' of all these people. Also, this book could never have been written without the scholarly work and practical support of the various people mentioned below.

Firstly, *Images of Projects* has been inspired and informed by the work of five eminent contributors to the management field: Peter Checkland, Gareth Morgan, the late Donald Schön, Edward de Bono and Guy Claxton. A summary of their work appears in Appendix D. In short, without the pioneering and seminal work of these people and those before them, *Images of Projects* could never have been written.

Secondly, there are many other people whose ideas and perspectives have influenced our own ideas over the years, either through their own published work, or just through conversation or discussion: Erling Andersen, David Brown, Svetlana Cicmil, Terry Cooke-Davies, Brian D'Arcy, Richard Dodd, Roger Elvin, Damian Hodgson, Steve Kempster, David Lowe, John Mackness, Harvey Maylor, Peter Morris, Sue Morton, Jeff Pinto, John Poulter, Charles Smith, Janice Thomas, Lynn Webster, Brian Wilson, and Graham Winch. Also, each author has learnt much from the other over the years. Thank you to everyone here.

Thirdly, we would like to mention four people for their organizational support and encouragement in the writing of this book: Graham Winch and David Lowe both at Manchester Business School, and Kevin Dobson at Royal Liver Group and Norman Bell of the former Big Food Group. Thank you for your support.

Fourthly, our thanks go to the people at Gower Publishing who have helped considerably in the planning and production of this book, notably Gillian Steadman for typesetting both the text and diagrams, and to Jonathan Norman for his enduring patience and helpful guidance at all stages of the process – thank you.

Finally, we wish to thank our families for all their support and encouragement in the writing of this book. The hermit-like existence of writing a book often places huge demands on other family members, including the loss of weekends and other disruption to everyday life. For this, special thanks go to Helen for her unceasing and unconditional support in enabling this book to be written. Only you can ever know how much time and support you have given to this work. Thank you!

The world we have created is a product of our thinking;
it cannot be changed without changing our thinking.

Albert Einstein

Foreword

It is not surprising that 'project' is a popular word. To say that you have a project to do something carries a nice air of purposeful intent, and gives the impression that you know what you are doing, and are not simply thrashing about. For most people the broad understanding of the word is that it suggests a systematic approach to achieving some declared end, and that resources, timing and cost have been thought about.

Professionally, a substantial literature supports this activity: the literature of 'Project Management' (PM). The conventional wisdom in this literature is that objectives are carefully defined and then, working from these objectives, activities to achieve them are carried out, with attention paid to monitoring progress and checking on resource use. Various techniques are there to facilitate progress towards achieving the desired end. This is the same conventional wisdom as that found in the general management literature, where again the response to a human aim is organized as objective-seeking. So the weight and influence of this concept and its literature are immense.

However, the certainty often conveyed in the PM and management literature is fragile. As long ago as 1994 Professor Peter Morris, Head of the School of Construction and Project Management at University College London, argued in his book *The Management of Projects* that the concepts and techniques available to practitioners "are often inadequate to the overall task of managing projects". The key word here is 'overall', since organizing the achievement of any defined objectives in a human situation will require the consideration of a range of factors: financial, social, political, organizational and so on. This means that a focus only on the *technical* work of a project, neglecting the social and organizational context, will prove to be not rich enough to relate closely to real situations. This is why Peter Morris prefers the phrase 'The Management of Projects' to the reductionist phrase 'Project Management'.

Most experienced project managers are aware of these contextual considerations, just as most managers quickly learn that real-world complexity is never fully captured by the techniques presented in the management textbooks.

In this book Mark Winter and Tony Szczepanek address head-on and comprehensively the issue to which Professor Morris pointed. Their approach does not casually abandon the conventional wisdom of objective-seeking. Rather it subsumes it into a broader approach which cheerfully embraces the randomness, the chaos and the rich reflexivity which actually characterizes everyday real-life within complex projects. The core image at the heart of the book is in fact no less than a view of the social nature of everyday life, one derived from soft systems thinking. This sees social life itself as an unfolding flux of a stream of (changing) ideas and a stream of (only partially predictable) events, each stream influencing and helping to create the other. To define and carry out a project is then to craft a portion of this flux in a way which will create value. The authors address this crafting of the flux of events and ideas through the elaboration of seven perspectives from which the project may deliberately be viewed: social, political, as an intervention, as value creation, as development, as a temporary organization, as a change process. Part 3 of the book then describes the methodological uses of these perspectives and concludes with accounts of real-world examples of the methodology in use.

The approach advocated and illustrated here is based neither on abstract theoretical ideas as such, nor simply on raw unreflective experience in the field. Rather it is based on the *cyclic interaction* between ideas (theory) and experience (practice). This is an interaction in which each of these elements over time helps to create the other, ideas leading to experience which is itself the source of ideas.

This timely and refreshing reappraisal of PM will be helpful not only to practitioners and students studying in the field, but also to teachers. The greater sophistication of this account makes sense of practitioner experience and provides much-needed methodological grounding for further development in this increasingly relevant field.

Peter Checkland
Emeritus Professor of Systems
Lancaster University

Overview of *Images of Projects*

This is a book about projects but *Images of Projects* is not another college textbook and nor is it a quick reference guide that over simplifies or trivializes the subject. It is for people who intuitively know that the real-world is more complex than the textbook or one-week guide suggests, but also recognize that relying just on experience is not always the most effective approach. So, how can this book help? In the course of the next few pages, we seek to summarize the book's aim and rationale, the main ideas and how they can be used in different situations, the intended audiences and how the book is structured. Finally, in the Appendices section, we briefly summarize the main theoretical foundations of *Images of Projects* and how the ideas have been developed.

The Aim of *Images of Projects*

The aim of *Images of Projects* is to help people deal with the complex realities of projects in conjunction with their own knowledge and experience. Everyday experience in the world of projects shows that different people deal with situations in different ways and this book's approach is best illustrated by comparing it with other approaches that the reader might be familiar with:

> [Person A] "Listen, we really don't have time to think and talk about this, we just need to get on with the project and deliver what's in the brief."

> [Person B] "It's obvious to me, based on 20 years' experience of working on projects, that the best way of approaching this is to do what we did in the previous project."

> [Person C] "I've just been on a project management training course and I think we should follow the procedures specified in the methodology manual."

> [Person D] "As I see it, I suggest we look at the situation from various perspectives, agree the action needed, and then review the situation again for what to do next."

Images of Projects favours the approach of Person D and is an invitation to the reader to develop (or enrich) this kind of approach for dealing with the complex realities of projects in real situations. It rejects the approach of 'just do it', or the one 'best way' approach, or just 'follow the manual', and seeks instead to encourage a *pragmatic* and *reflective* approach, based on consciously seeing projects from *multiple perspectives*. There is a choice: people can either interpret everything from a fixed standpoint, or they can become skilled (or more skilled) in the craft of seeing and approaching the realities of projects from different perspectives. The purpose of *Images of Projects* is to help you develop (or enrich) this crucial skill. Moreover, the reason we favour this kind of approach is because there is strong *evidence* to support it, as we now show.

The Rationale Behind *Images of Projects*

It was John Maynard Keynes who suggested that people who described themselves as practitioners, proud not to be influenced by any kind of theory, often turned out to be the intellectual prisoners of the theoreticians of yesteryear. Whether we agree with this or not, it does remind us that all practical action is based on some knowledge or theory, irrespective of whether the practitioner is aware of the theory guiding their action, as shown by the model in Figure I. As the model shows, a practitioner's *knowledge* is rooted in their

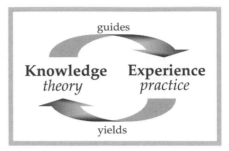

Figure I   The knowledge-experience cycle

experience of the world, and their experience in the world is guided by their own personal knowledge. This might seem obvious perhaps, but the important point is whether or not the practitioner is *aware* of the theory guiding their action, for it is this connection between knowledge and experience (that is, the top arrow in Figure I) that is central to the main argument of this book, as we now briefly explain.

Why not 'JUST DO IT'?

Experience shows that to do any project, one must have an *image* of that project, and also an *underlying image* of projects upon which that image is based. Once again, this might seem obvious, but the key point is whether or not the practitioner is aware of the images that guide their thinking, for it is these images that drive what gets done on projects, and these images might not always be useful. For example, for an IT-related initiative, if the underlying image is an IT project, then what gets done is an IT project, and yet this might not be the most useful way of seeing the project; in fact, many organizations no longer recognize the idea of an IT project, and only focus now on projects such as business projects involving IT; in short, change the image and what gets done is a different kind of project. In this book, we call this the *image-action connection* and it is so important that we devote the first chapter to explaining it in more detail. It also explains why the 'just do it' approach is so inherently flawed.

No one 'best way' of seeing projects and programmes

In response to person B's approach, this book also takes the view that there is no one 'best way' of seeing all projects and programmes, and the evidence for this can be seen in Table I. Actually the list in Table I is not as long as it might seem, as some of the examples could be synonymous or strongly linked: for example, a production project could also be a cost reduction project, and a construction project could be part of a regeneration programme. Nevertheless, what the list shows is the breadth of project work now being carried out

Action learning projects	IT-related projects and programmes
Action research projects	Leadership development programmes
Building projects	Learning and development programmes
Building development programmes	Maintenance projects
Business change projects	Management development programmes
Business development projects	Manufacturing projects
Business improvement programmes	Marketing campaigns
Business research projects	Merger programmes
Business transformation programmes	New product development projects
Charity projects	Offender rehabilitation programmes
Civil aerospace projects	Organizational change programmes
Civil engineering projects	Organizational development programmes
Community development projects	Performance improvement projects
Conservation projects	PFI projects (e.g., school refurbishment)
Construction projects	Policy development projects
Consultancy projects	Process improvement projects
Cost reduction projects	Production projects
Cultural change programmes	Professional development programmes
Defence aerospace projects	Property development projects
Drug rehabilitation programmes	Public-private partnerships
Education programmes	Quality improvement projects
E-government programmes	Regeneration projects
E-learning programmes	Research and development projects
Enquiry-based learning projects	Research projects and programmes
Energy conservation projects	Service development programmes
Environmental improvement projects	Service improvement projects
Environmental protection projects	Six Sigma projects
Factory relocation projects	Social enterprise programmes
Health improvement programmes	Staff development programmes
Health service development programmes	Strategic initiatives
Heritage preservation projects	Strategy implementation programmes
HR development programmes	Strategic reviews
Infrastructure projects and programmes	Sustainable development projects
Infrastructure programmes	Systems development projects
Integrated solutions projects	Systems engineering projects
International aid programmes	Training programmes
International development programmes	Urban regeneration programmes

Table I   Projects and programmes everywhere!

across different sectors and industries, and hence why the idea of a one 'best way' type approach is simply impractical. Also, a few words of caution are needed here: seeing and organizing work as 'projects' has various consequences, and adopting a project approach might not always be the most sensible way of approaching a particular situation or task. In short, the word 'project' is not just a label for real-world action, it also represents a particular *way of seeing* the world, and as this book will explain, a way of seeing is also a *way of not seeing*, in the sense that there are other perspectives that could be more relevant, for example 'intervention' rather than 'project'. Hence, to suggest that projects can be seen everywhere reflects a certain perspective, which might not always be appropriate. That said, the amount of work now being carried out through projects and programmes is very significant and for this we need to mention one other point about person B's approach. Their experience might well be 20 years, but it might also be '1 year's experience 20 times' as they say. Clearly, there is no substitute for real experience, but like all things, it has its limitations and relying solely on experience-based knowledge is not always the most effective approach. As Sue Pearce and Shelia Cameron point out in their book *Against the Grain:*

> *different managers will respond to situations in ways influenced by **different** experiences, **different** beliefs and values, and **different** models of the world. Even where such experiences, beliefs and models are shared, as may be the case in organizations with a strong culture, they may be based on the past, and not totally appropriate to a present which is dramatically different.*[1]

This, then, just leaves person C's approach which relies more on the training manual than personal knowledge and experience. As the final part of our rationale, the focus here is on the usefulness of mainstream project management tools and techniques.

Usefulness of mainstream PM tools and techniques

According to Professor Peter Morris in his excellent book *The Management of Projects* published in 1994, *'Modern project management emerged between the 1930s and the 1950s ... [and] despite its long development, the concepts and techniques now available to the general practitioner, however advanced and specific they may be, are often inadequate to the overall task of managing projects.'*[2] Since then, new concepts and techniques have been developed in areas such as programme management and risk management; however, there still remains a core image of projects that dominates many PM publications and many industry training courses run for practitioners. The detail of this core image is beyond the scope of this introduction, however, the gist of some of the main ideas are shown in Figure II, which we use to conclude the main argument of this book.

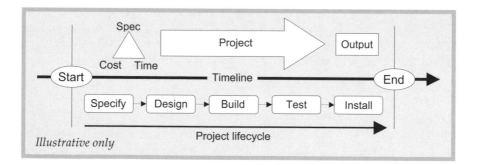

Figure II   The mainstream image of projects

With its origins in engineering and construction, the mainstream image of projects in Figure II is essentially a *production* view of projects, that focuses on a certain product, system or facility, to be created, engineered or improved. Of course, this does not mean it's the 'wrong' view to adopt, only that it represents a particular *image* of projects, rather than an all-encompassing theory as many of the college textbooks and other publications seem to imply. It is also much less applicable to other projects and programmes such as organizational change projects and education programmes. As Peter Morris points out in *The Management of Projects*, it is a limited view in that it fails to take account of '*strategy, technology, finance, politics, the environment and so on.*'[3] This was confirmed in 2006 by the UK Government-funded research initiative called *Rethinking Project Management*, which highlighted a crucial shift now taking place in the world of projects. In short, whilst the mainstream image is about *product creation* – producing something to specification, cost and time – the focus now is no longer just on doing this, but increasingly that of *value creation* through projects and programmes, which is a much broader concept than that shown in Figure II. In other words, the concern now is no longer just about *doing projects right*, but *doing the right projects*,[4] which is a much more strategic view, and one that Peter Morris has been continually arguing for in broadening the subject of project management:

> *we would do better to enlarge the subject to the broader one of the **'management of projects'**, including specifically [topics such as strategy, finance, and politics etc] than to keep to the more narrowly defined areas of **'project management'** as it has typically been conceived and taught.*[5]

In industry terms, this broader view now covers three levels of management activity: *project management* (the management of single projects), *programme management* (generally seen as the management of multiple projects) and *portfolio management* (generally seen as the management of whole portfolios of projects and programmes). Clearly, this is a much broader focus than the traditional view of project management and there is no one model or image that can cover all three of these levels. Indeed, this was another key finding of *Rethinking Project Management* which concluded:

> *the need for multiple images to inform and guide action at all levels in the management of projects, rather than just the classical lifecycle model of project management.*[6]

Moreover, the research also identified the need for '*practitioners who can learn, operate and adapt effectively in complex project environments through experience, intuition and the pragmatic application of theory in practice.*'[7] This essentially is the sort of approach being taken by person D in our opening example, and is the kind of approach that we seek to develop in the rest of this book. To begin this process, the next section briefly introduces the main ideas in *Images of Projects*, followed by brief sections on how the book is organized and how different readers might make use of the book.

The Main Ideas in *Images of Projects*

Firstly, this book draws its inspiration from Gareth Morgan's best-selling book called *Images of Organization*, which takes the view that *'organizations and organizational problems can be seen and understood in many different ways'*.[8] We take the same view of projects, and also start from the same position that Morgan starts from in thinking about organizations, as shown by his words below and our words in square brackets:

ORGANIZATIONS ARE MANY THINGS AT ONCE!
[SO TOO ARE PROJECTS!]

They are complex and multifaceted.
[So too are projects.]

They are paradoxical.
[So too are projects.]

That's why the challenges facing managers and practitioners are often so difficult.[9]
[For example, project managers.]

Known internationally for his work, Gareth Morgan has written extensively in the field of organizations and management, and has consulted widely with organizations across the world. His *Images* concept is neatly summarized by Derek Pugh and David Hickson in their book *Writers on Organizations*:

> *everyone in an organization has in mind an implicit picture of that organization, a mental image of what it is like. Morgan contends not only that an organization is seen differently by different people, but that it can be seen in different ways by any one person. If multiple images of an organization are used, much greater understanding is gained, for organizations are many things at once, so multiple images envisage more of what is going on. They can reveal new ways of managing and designing organizations.*[10]

In essence, this is the *Images* concept and it is our contention that the same idea can be applied to projects, and the easiest way to express this is to simply adapt the words in the extract above:

> *everyone involved in a project has in mind an implicit picture of that project, a mental image of what it is like. We contend not only that a project is seen differently by different people, but that it can be seen in different ways by any one person. If multiple images of a project are used, much greater understanding is gained, for projects are many things at once, so multiple images envisage more of what is going on. They can also help in managing projects in conjunction with one's own knowledge and experience.*

Moreover, the core idea of *Images of Projects* is applicable at all levels, from small-scale projects through to major programmes and strategic portfolios; however, from this point on, we restrict this discussion to individual projects and programmes in order to briefly summarize the main ideas, starting with this book's root image of projects.

A root image of projects

By 'root' image, we mean this book's general concept of a project that can be used as a starting point for making sense of any particular project or programme. In broad terms, we define a project or programme as *temporary purposeful action,* but do not specify what the action should be concerned with. To start with, then, we view all projects as *temporary* action that lasts days, weeks, months or years; also, they are *purposeful* in that they involve people and organizations with aims and objectives, linked to differing interests and agenda; and finally they are about *action* in that they involve people all continually interacting together and doing things in an ever-changing flux of events unfolding through time – see Figure III.

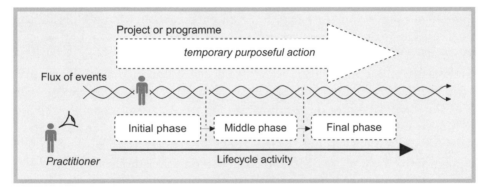

Figure III   This book's root image of projects

Clearly, this is a much broader concept than the mainstream image in Figure II, but notice we still use the lifecycle idea, for whilst the reality is always an unfolding flux of events, it is still very useful to think of any project or programme as passing through a number of different 'phases' or 'stages'; and for this, we use a simple three-phase model that can be applied to any of the examples in Table I. Finally, notice in Figure III that the practitioner is also shown to indicate that everyone involved in a project or programme has their own mental image of the action being carried out.

Seven core images of projects

Building on the root image in Figure III, *Images of Projects* offers seven core images for engaging with the complex realities of projects. For the practitioner shown in Figure III, they are images that can be used in conjunction with one's own knowledge and experience, and these images are shown in Figure IV below.

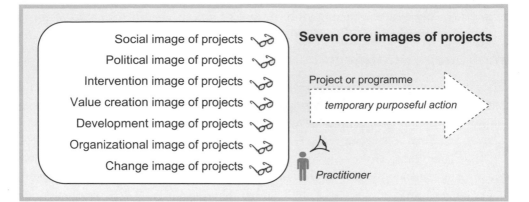

Figure IV   Seven core images of projects

Very importantly, these images are *not* alternatives between which a choice has to be made, and nor is our list meant to be all-encompassing. Like Morgan's images, each one is a way of seeing projects from a particular perspective, but we make no assumption that they are the *only* images that can be used in practice. That said, all seven images can be applied to most projects, and some of them (for example, the social and political images) can be used in any situation; hence, why we call them *core* images for use with the root image shown in Figure III. Also, whilst this book offers a particular image for each perspective, there is no assumption that this is the 'right' image to use for that perspective. In this book, we use them because experience has shown them to be *useful* in real situations. However, this is not to say that additional or alternative images could not be used to inform or guide a particular perspective. For example, this book's social process image is based on the idea of seeing projects as an ever-changing flux of events, but this is not the only social process perspective that could be taken. Also, whatever images are used, they are not recipes or prescriptions, they are prompts for seeing, thinking and talking about projects in real situations, as the next section shows.

Applying the images in practice

Firstly, applying the images in practice depends on the practitioner's role and their own organizational context. For example, whilst a project sponsor might use the social and political images to help make sense of a situation, a team leader might use some of the other images. In other words, different images will be relevant to different people in different situations. Irrespective of this aspect, however, there are three quite distinct ways of using the images in practice which are illustrated in the following three independent examples:

"It seems to me the project is much more about developing the internal service operation than about implementing a new IT system, and if we were to adopt this view of the project, then the whole approach would be very different, including how the staff could be involved."

"Given the complexity of the situation, a structured review is needed to find an acceptable way forward for the project. And in carrying out this review, we need to look at the situation from various perspectives in order to reach an accommodation about the action needed."

[Person A] "From a development perspective, here are two possible concepts ..."
[Person B] "It seems to me, from a change angle, the first one is more achievable ..."
[Person C] "I agree, but politically, it might still be necessary to do the second ..."

Although these examples might seem similar, they illustrate three different types of use: the first illustrates the *selective use* of the images, by which we mean the use of certain images in particular situations for sensemaking purposes, and/or as a guide to action; the second is an example of *structured use,* which refers to a more systematic use of the images in a formal review for example; and the third is an illustration of *shared use,* where the images can be used collectively as a sort of common language with which to think and talk about projects. Moreover, the first example shows how the images can be used purely in the 'background' as it were, without the other people in the situation knowing that a framework is being used; in this case, the practitioner is simply using the development image to offer a different perspective on the project. In other situations, however, like the third example, the framework can be used much more openly as a way of prompting and steering discussions.

Now, some readers might say that they already think about projects from different perspectives, based on experience and intuition, and no doubt this is true. But consider once again our three examples: the people in the situations above are *consciously* thinking from multiple perspectives, rather than just relying on experience and intuition; in other words, as well as experience, they are deliberately using different images and frameworks to help think and talk about their particular projects. And it is *this* that can make an important difference in real situations: in short, the deliberate use of images and frameworks can direct attention to aspects of projects and programmes that might not otherwise be *thought* about, and hence can influence the *action* that follows, and the eventual *results* that might be achieved.

In summary, **Images of Projects** *is simply an invitation to practitioners to do what they already do, but to do so more consciously, with the aid of some images and frameworks, as and when required.*

9

Philosophy of Approach

Just as all organizations and projects are many things at once, *Images of Projects* is also many things at once, or rather several things at once, because of the several different contributions that this book seeks to make. Rightly or wrongly, *Images of Projects* has been written with several audiences in mind and the reason for this is that we wish to break out of the conventional categories of academic texts and practitioner guides to offer a book that aims to be both *useful* to the reader and *reflective* in its approach. In our view, too many books are published in the management literature that are either written in very esoteric terms, or in superficial terms that trivialize the subject. In this book, we seek to take a more balanced approach: on the one side, we take the view that projects are complex and we need more sophisticated ways of thinking about them, and on the other, we strive to approach this in a practical and accessible way. Hence, the book also has a particular structure as we now explain.

The Book's Structure and Chapters

Images of Projects is organized into three parts: Part One consists of two chapters that provide a more detailed overview of the book's main ideas, starting with the image-connection in Chapter 1, followed by a detailed summary in Chapter 2. In Part Two, the focus is then on the seven core images and each one is covered in a separate chapter, from Chapters 3 to 9. Also, because the main audience is practitioners, the structure and approach to Part Two follows a particular format which is explained at the start. Then, in Part Three, we return to using the images in practice focusing on the three types of use: Chapter 10 covers selective use, Chapter 11 covers structured use and Chapter 12 covers shared use. In the last two chapters, Chapters 13 and 14, we also show how the ideas have actually been used in practice to reinforce the ideas in previous chapters. Finally, it is important to note that all the chapters follow a particular pattern: each one begins with a real example to illustrate the main ideas for that chapter, and in some chapters more than one example is used. Brief descriptions of all the projects and programmes featured in the book are provided in Part Two.

Intended Audiences and Advice On Use

First and foremost, *Images of Projects* is written for *practitioners* working on any kind of project or programme in any sector, in any role and at any level. Although some formal knowledge of project management is useful, this is not a prerequisite; much more important is a willingness to be challenged and an openness to new ideas and new ways of thinking. Also, different readers are likely to find some of the images more relevant than others and some may even find themselves disagreeing with certain ideas and may want to add their own ideas. This is the way it should be, for the aim is not to prescribe how projects *should* be seen, but rather to encourage an open dialogue embracing many different perspectives. Moreover, for this audience, the book is deliberately written in a way that enables the reader to reflect upon their own ideas and perspectives in relation to the seven core images, with a view to enriching and developing their own knowledge of projects.

Secondly, *Images of Projects* is also written for *student practitioners* by which we mean practitioners on any kind of management programme, or programmes in other fields such as urban planning or international development. In the management field, this includes short executive programmes, certificate and diploma programmes, MBA programmes and MSc programmes, and for these readers, the book can be used more systematically to develop one's knowledge of all the images and how to apply them in real situations. For course instructors too, the book can also be used to support any project management course, including final-year undergraduate courses that take a more advanced perspective on projects.

Finally, *Images of Projects* also seeks to make a contribution to the developing field of projects and in this regard we hope it will be of interest to *researchers* working in universities and other institutions around the world. It builds directly on the main findings of the *Rethinking Project Management* initiative (2004–06) and contains a brief summary at the end about the underlying research approach.

For these three audiences, the table below offers some suggestions for how different readers might orientate themselves towards the book.

Chapter	Practitioners					Student practitioners					Researchers				
Chapter 1															
Chapter 2															
Chapter 3															
Chapter 4															
Chapter 5															
Chapter 6															
Chapter 7															
Chapter 8															
Chapter 9															
Chapter 10															
Chapter 11															
Chapter 12															
Chapter 13															
Chapter 14															
Appendices	A	B	C	D	E	A	B	C	D	E	A	B	C	D	E

Part 1
Introduction to Images of Projects

Choice of attention area, choice of entry point, choice of factors, these are all part of the first stage of thinking.

Edward de Bono

Chapter One

Why not "JUST DO IT"?
The Image-Action Connection

Introduction

In the early 1990s when the lead author started teaching on executive programmes, he was introduced to what he thought was a new management approach called JDI. *"We don't have time to think"* said one delegate in an MBA class, *"We use an approach called JDI"*. Curious to know what this was, the author naively replied, *"That's interesting, I've not come across that before, what is JDI?"* Of course, once the delegate said what the letters stood for, the author then realized it was not a new approach and the class were highly amused! But the MBA delegate also said that from his experience this *was* the approach to projects within his organization and it was very ineffective in his view. Moreover, many of the other delegates agreed and said JDI was the dominant approach in their organizations too. So, what is wrong with JDI as an approach to projects? Apart from some obvious practical reasons, the approach is misguided in two respects: firstly, thinking and doing are not two separate domains, as it suggests, and it also fails to recognize something fundamental about all projects. Whilst all projects are clearly about *action* and working to timescales and so on, such action is always based on an *image* of what needs to be done, and it is this *image-action connection* that has very important implications, as this chapter shows using the following real example.

Illustrative Example

Equipment Direct Project

The Hampshire Coalition of Disabled People, in partnership with Hampshire County Council and the NHS, are embarking on an exciting and innovative project, which will greatly improve access to equipment for disabled people. The project will provide disabled people in Hampshire with improved access to and greater choice in equipment services. Funded by a Government 'Invest to Save' grant it will pioneer the development of the country's first Internet-based equipment service, *Equipmentdirect.org.uk*. The new service will use the latest website technology to give disabled people more choice and faster access to a wider range of equipment for daily living direct from independent suppliers or through specialist social and health care services.[1]

What sort of project is this?

To answer the question of what sort of project is the *Equipment Direct Project*, there are many possible answers to this question, just like there are different ways of seeing the old woman/young woman picture. Consider the following answers for instance:

    👓 **An IT system development project**

    👓 **An IT-enabled change programme**

    👓 **A process improvement project**

    👓 **A service development project**

    👓 **A quality of life improvement project**

    👓 **A cost reduction project**

    👓 **A research and development project**

The important point is not that the *Equipment Direct Project* can be seen or categorized in different ways, but rather that each answer is a different *image* of the project with its own implications for *action*. In other words, each answer is a different perspective on the project and each perspective suggests different activities that might need to be carried out. For example, seeing the project as an IT system development project would lead to a different set of activities to say those associated with viewing it as a service development project, or a quality of life improvement project. In all cases, the main focus of the project is different: the first perspective focuses on the development of an IT system, the second focuses on the development of a new service, and the third focuses more broadly on improving the quality of life for disabled people. Clearly, all three perspectives could be linked if we were to explore this further, but this is not the main point of the example, as we now explain.

The Image-Action Connection

The message here might seem obvious perhaps, but the point is very important for any project as the *Equipment Direct Project* shows: if the image is that of an 'IT project' for instance, then no matter how much resource is put into it, the project will be organized and managed as an IT project. Once this image is fixed at the start, it drives the action of the project, unless of course the image changes at some later date. A counter argument here could be that most of the answers listed above are really just synonyms or labels for the same project, and that *"it's obvious really what the project is about"*. Unfortunately however, this rather misses the point about the *image-action connection* and the importance of understanding how this fundamentally affects the work of projects. Moreover, what is obvious to one person may be less obvious to another, and here again the implications for action could be important. For instance, just the difference between project and programme, as in the first two images of the *Equipment Direct Project*, could have significant implications for how the work is organized and managed. Moreover, any individual image may also invoke different ideas about the work that needs to be done: for example, one person's image of an IT system development project could be quite different to someone else's image of an IT system development project. In summary, no matter what kind of image it might be, each has its own implications for action, and being mindful of how this works in both directions is also very important, as shown by the diagram in Figure 1.1. As the diagram shows, the *image-action connection* is another version of the *knowledge-experience cycle* used in the Overview. Basically, any image is knowledge

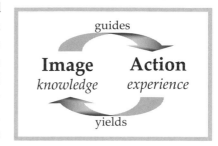

Figure 1.1   The image-action connection

acquired from experience, as represented by the lower arrow in Figure 1.1, and it is this knowledge that guides action in the world, as shown by the top arrow, but without people being necessarily aware of this. Also, as the next section shows, this continues until there is a need to change this knowledge or image in the light of new experience.

Sector example: projects and programmes involving IT

A good example which illustrates the importance of the image-action connection is the area of IT-related projects, where many organizations are now moving away from the traditional image of an IT project, to business projects involving IT, or business transformation programmes for instance, as shown in the three examples below.

*[Sainsburys] are investing ... £1bn in new systems ...
this isn't an IT programme – it's a business transformation programme, and
that's such an important distinction.*[2]

*[GlaxoSmithKline] requires that all IT projects are really
business projects with an IT element.*[3]

*[Birmingham City Council] don't have IT projects,
we have business transformation projects.*[4]

The reason it's such an important distinction for Sainsburys, for example, is because it has important implications for how the programme is organized and managed. In other words, the *image* of a transformation programme is different to the image of an

IT programme, or an IT project, and this is the message behind the other examples too. They have different implications for action which are highly significant from a project management perspective. Indeed as a UK Government Report stated in 2000:

Thinking in terms of 'IT projects' is itself a primary source of problems. Delivering IT is only ever part of the implementation of new, more effective, ways of working. A change of approach is needed.[5]

UK Government Report, 2000

What is particularly interesting about the statement above is the implied link to the image-action connection, namely that *'thinking in terms of 'IT projects' is itself a primary source of problems.'* In short, it is the very *image* of an 'IT project' which is seen as one of the main problems with the *action* of projects involving IT; change the *image* and the *action* should change with it.

As an aside, what is rather alarming about the statement above is that despite it being one of the top findings published by the UK Government in 2000, recent reports continue to highlight major problems with projects and programmes involving IT. In January 2008, for example, The Guardian Newspaper reported that *'the cost to the taxpayer of abandoned Whitehall computer projects since 2000 has reached almost £2bn.'*[6] Moreover, it also seems many publications since 2000 continue to take as given, unknowingly it seems, the very concept of an 'IT project', which previous research has shown to be one of the main problems. Two examples of this can be seen below.

This study, conducted by a group of Fellows of The Royal Academy of Engineering and British Computer Society (BCS), seeks to improve the understanding of how complex IT projects differ from other engineering projects, with a view to identifying ways to augment the successful delivery of IT projects.[7]

Royal Academy of Engineering and BCS Report, 2004

Anyone involved in or affected by IT projects could benefit from this [text] including users, buyers and directors. ... the point of [this text] is to improve the management of IT projects, where there have been cases of huge losses caused by project failure.[8]

Project Management for IT-Related Projects, BCS, 2004

Fortunately, as our earlier industry examples show, current thinking about projects and programmes involving IT is now changing, and more recent publications are now calling for this shift of perspective, as shown in the example below:

executives need to stop looking at IT projects as technology installations and starting looking at them as periods of organizational change that they have a responsibility to manage.[9]

Harvard Business Review, November 2006

Returning to the main point, namely the significance of the image-action connection, it is important to emphasize that the same phenomenon applies to all projects and programmes and not just IT-related projects, in that *all* purposeful action is based on some image, or images of what needs to be done. As Peter Senge, author of *The Fifth Discipline* points out:

none of us can carry an organization in our minds – or a family, or a community. What we carry in our heads are images and assumptions.[10]

In summary, the most significant point of all about the UK Government's statement opposite is the implication that *how people think* about projects and programmes is fundamental to their success. In other words, how people *initially* perceive and think about projects, or situations involving projects, is hugely important, simply because it determines the *subsequent* thinking and action that is carried out. And yet this first 'stage' in thinking is never explicitly recognized in mainstream publications in project management and many practitioners also seem unaware of this crucial first 'stage'. This really is fundamental and it is this 'stage' that forms the main focus of this book, based on the following model of thinking developed by Edward de Bono.

First- and Second-Stage Thinking

Generally regarded as one of the world's leading experts on the subject of thinking, Edward de Bono is the author of many books and one of them *Lateral Thinking for Management* contains a very insightful model that is highly relevant to projects. Before we look at this however, consider the following problem:

A man pushing his car stopped outside a hotel.
As soon as he got there, he knew he was bankrupt.
Why?

For those not familiar with the 'man pushing his car' problem, the answer is that he was playing *Monopoly*, which of course is not the most likely answer people would give to this problem. Since people are more in contact with conventional size cars and hotels (re: the *experience* part in Figure 1.1), they often try to solve the problem with this imagery in mind rather than the imagery of a toy car and plastic hotel (re: the *knowledge* part). So, why this example? The reason is simple: it neatly illustrates the two 'stages' of thinking that Edward de Bono describes in the box below.

First-stage thinking and second-stage thinking

Most people are aware of the second stage of thinking. The first stage is taken for granted and often assumed not to be there at all. The second stage is concerned with the techniques of logic and mathematics [for example] … Logical and mathematical techniques are never applied directly to a situation. They can only be applied when that situation has been divided into concepts, features, factors, effects, and other perceptual parcels. These perceptual parcels are not themselves created by the application of any special techniques, but by the natural patterning processes of mind with all their limitations and arbitrariness. We assume that these starting concepts are correct … in other words, we assume that thinking only starts at the second stage.

It is in the first stage of thinking that the concepts and perceptual parcels are put together. … Choice of attention area, choice of entry point, choice of factors, these are all part of the first stage of thinking. And such choices will predetermine the final result of the thinking process. … In the first stage of thinking, the emphasis is not on the manipulation of concepts but on the concepts themselves. [This is where] one forms and re-forms concepts, cuts across them, introduces new concepts, and so on.[11]

Edward de Bono

To help summarize these two 'stages', de Bono also labels them the 'perception stage' and the 'processing stage', with the second stage being totally dependent on the first. Of course, in reality, the actuality of thinking is much more complex, but as a model for understanding *how we think*, this is a very insightful model in our view. It shows more than anything else the importance of the first 'stage', in that no amount of effort in the second stage can make up for deficiencies in the first. If the initial perceptions or ideas are wrong or deficient, then no amount of 'processing' can ever change this; for example, in the *Monopoly* exercise, if the perception is that of a conventional car and hotel, then no amount of processing will *ever* solve this problem. Only by 'returning to stage 1' and changing the imagery can this problem be solved. And the message for projects is even stronger, because unlike the *Monopoly* exercise which has a 'right' answer, there is no right answer in situations involving projects. Thus, how they are initially perceived, or *'divided into perceptual parcels'* in Edward de Bono's words, becomes very important, as the last section now explains.

First-Stage Thinking About Projects

In essence, the message here for projects is that if people's first-stage thinking doesn't connect with the actual complexity of a situation, then no amount of second-stage thinking, aided by any of the tools in mainstream project management, can ever make up for this. And notice by first-stage thinking, we do *not* mean the first stage of a project, as in the first stage of the lifecycle (for example, project initiation), but the first 'stage' in *thinking* about a project or situation, and it is this crucial 'stage' that is the concern of this book. As de Bono states, there are *'very good techniques for the second stage of thinking [for example, the techniques of maths and finance and so on] ... but we have no techniques at all for the first stage.'*[12] Of course, since writing this in 1971, de Bono himself has developed techniques such as the Six Thinking Hats®, but the main thrust of his point is still relevant, particularly in the field of projects, as we argue in the extract below adapted from de Bono's words opposite:

> *[mainstream PM techniques focus on] the second stage of thinking. The first stage is taken for granted and often assumed not to be there at all. The second stage is concerned with techniques such as critical path method, PERT, Gantt charts, risk registers, work breakdown structures, and earned value etc ... [but these] are never applied directly to a situation. They can only be applied when a project or programme has been named and framed with objectives, desired outcomes, deliverables and other perceptual parcels. [Mainstream PM techniques] assume that these starting concepts are correct ... in other words, [they] assume that thinking only starts at the second stage.*

Against this background, then, this is why we have written this book: to provide the practitioner with a framework of images to help with 'first-stage thinking' in project environments. Clearly, there is no substitute for experience-based knowledge, but relying solely on experience is not always the most effective approach, which is why we offer the framework of images in this book. Also, so far in this chapter we have only focused on a single image of projects as a guide to action, but in real situations multiple images are needed, and this is the framework that we turn to next.

All theories of organization and management are based on implicit images ... that persuade us to see, understand, and imagine situations in partial ways. ... Limit your thinking and you will limit your range of action.

Gareth Morgan

Chapter Two

Images of Projects:
A Pragmatic Framework

Introduction

Having explained the importance of the image-action connection, we turn now to this book's central idea, namely that of consciously working with multiple images to help deal with the complex realities of projects. Imagine a scenario in which the *Equipment Direct Project* used in the previous chapter has just been approved and the task now is to identify the action needed for moving the project forward; how might this be done? One could argue this is a difficult question to answer, since it depends on the actual situation and the people involved. This is largely true of course, but the question can still be posed at a general level: How, *in principle,* might the action be identified? In working with multiple images, a pragmatic approach could be to explore the insights and implications from a number of relevant perspectives, and then from these, craft a feasible set of actions to help move the project forward. And this is what we do in the next section with a worked example to illustrate the first part of this process, before introducing the images framework as a whole, and how it can be used in practice. Also, in doing this, we invite the reader to consider the following set of images in relation to their own perspectives, and how this way of thinking compares with the reader's own approach to thinking about projects.

Illustrative Example

Equipment Direct Project

The Hampshire Coalition of Disabled People, in partnership with Hampshire County Council and the NHS, are embarking on an exciting and innovative project, which will greatly improve access to equipment for Disabled People. The project will provide disabled people in Hampshire with improved access to and greater choice in equipment services. Funded by a Government 'Invest to Save' grant it will pioneer the development of the country's first Internet-based equipment service, *Equipmentdirect.org.uk.* The new service will use the latest website technology to give Disabled People more choice and faster access to a wider range of equipment for daily living direct from independent suppliers or through specialist social and health care services.

From what PERSPECTIVES might we view this project?

Social perspective

To begin the process, we would probably start by seeing the *Equipment Direct Project* as a *social process* involving various individuals, groups and organizations. This would then lead us to consider aspects such as the events, decisions and actions leading up to the current situation (that is, the social history of the project so far), how the various people and organizations have interacted up to now (for example, the meetings held to date) and what they perceive to be the main issues with the project. Other aspects that might also be considered would be the language used in project documentation and the informal social networks that seem to be operating in and around the project.

Political perspective

Linked to the social process image, we would also look at the *Equipment Direct Project* as a *political process*, by which we mean the individuals, groups and organizations all pursuing their own interests and agenda in the unfolding process. Seeing it from this perspective would lead us to ask questions such as: Whose interests are being served by this project? And, since not all interests and agenda are stated publicly, another question to ask could be: What might be the agenda behind this? Also, another important aspect of the *Equipment Direct Project* would be the power and influence of the people involved and how this might affect things from this stage on.

Intervention perspective

Given the nature of the project, we would also probably see it as an *intervention process* aimed ultimately at improving the daily living experience of disabled people. And a key consideration here could be the current framing of the project: Is it the right project to be doing? From an intervention point of view, is it just about improving access to equipment services, or is it also about improving the services themselves? In other words, has the current situation been sufficiently understood before deciding on what project(s) need to be carried out? In short, those involved might well agree that an intervention is needed, but what to do could still be unclear.

Value perspective

Another way of seeing the project is to also think of it as a *value creation process* where the concept at present (we would say) is about creating value for disabled people, that is, improved access to equipment services and greater choice of equipment. Adopting this perspective might also lead us to consider other desired outcomes which could be reduced operating costs and the development of a blueprint for use in other areas. Further considerations might then flow from these such as the criteria needed for measuring these outcomes and the mechanisms needed for tracking their delivery.

Development perspective

Another image that clearly applies to the *Equipment Direct Project* is the *development process* image, which would lead us to consider aspects such as what needs to be developed and by what date and within what budget? For example, those involved could decide to organize the project as a set of linked workstreams aimed at developing the service operation, the website and the people who will provide the new service; and hence, some possible deliverables could be new procedures, trained staff, a new Internet-based system, supplier contracts and service level agreements and so on. Other important aspects from this perspective could be service operation KPIs, system performance requirements, development risks and the use of relevant tools.

Organizational perspective

In applying this perspective, the sorts of aspects that would be considered here are roles and responsibilities, team structure, governance arrangements and so on. But this is not all, for in taking this perspective, the image used in this book is that of projects as *temporary organizations*, which means deliberately seeing a project as being like a conventional organization, only it is temporary rather than semi-permanent. This might be another useful image to apply to the *Equipment Direct Project* and might lead us to consider aspects such as financial and commercial aspects, support functions and marketing/communications. Also, the organizational entity itself might be better viewed as a *programme* rather than a *project*, in which case the 'operations' part could be organized as a set of linked workstreams rather than a set of projects for instance.

Change perspective

Finally, another important way of seeing the *Equipment Direct Project* is to think of it also as a *change process*, which for this project would be a very important perspective. For example, this would lead us to consider aspects such as the rationale for change, the scope of the planned change and the perceived readiness for change amongst the various people and organizations involved, notably the disabled people and those involved in delivering the new service. Also, what will the changes mean for other related services? Is there a need to link this project to other relevant projects? Such questions clearly have important implications for the project.

To engage with complexity, we need perspectives which admit the possibility that more than one thing can be true at once.

Arthur Battram

Images of Projects **Framework**

Underlying the example just provided is a framework of seven images for engaging with the complex realities of projects and it is this framework that we now focus on. As already mentioned, the inspiration for *Images of Projects* is Gareth Morgan's book *Images of Organization* which is why we begin with a brief introduction to the *Images* concept and how it can be applied to projects in the same way that it can be applied to organizations. The main assumption here is that the social reality of projects is fundamentally no different to the social reality of organizations, and hence the *Images* concept is just as applicable to projects. Also, a number of key principles for applying the *Images* concept are covered here, together with how the framework of images can be used with other frameworks and models. Later in the chapter, we introduce three distinct ways of using the framework in real situations, but first it is important to explain the *Images* concept itself.

Introduction to the IMAGES concept

The *Images* concept is based on the view that *'organizations and organizational problems can be seen and understood in many different ways'*[1] which Morgan illustrates using the picture shown in Figure 2.1. Underlying this view and the *Images* concept are various ideas from social theory, philosophy and psychology, but these ideas are beyond the scope of this book. Suffice to say there is a serious philosophy behind the *Images* concept about the nature of the social world and how it differs to the natural world, and hence why it needs to be approached differently by *seeing and thinking differently*. Interested readers are encouraged to explore the intellectual foundations of the *Images* concept by consulting Gareth Morgan's two books *Images of Organization* and *Imaginization*.

Source: *Images of Organization* by Gareth Morgan (2nd Edition), p.352. Sage Publications. Reproduced with kind permission

Figure 2.1 Different ways of seeing organizations

For our purposes, this section is just a brief introduction to the *Images* concept and how it can be applied to projects. So, returning to Figure 2.1, just as Gareth Morgan offers a set of images for engaging with the complex realities of organizations – based on the view that *organizations and organizational problems can be seen and understood in many different ways* – this book offers its own set of images for engaging with the complex realities of projects, based on the view that *projects can also be seen and understood in many different ways*.

As Gareth Morgan states and we state in square brackets:

ORGANIZATIONS ARE MANY THINGS AT ONCE!
[SO TOO ARE PROJECTS!]

They are complex and multifaceted.
[So too are projects.]

They are paradoxical.
[So too are projects.]

***That's why the challenges facing managers
and practitioners are often so difficult.***[2]
[For example, project managers.]

As we stated in the Overview, Gareth Morgan has written extensively in the field of organizations and management and has consulted widely with many organizations across the world. His *Images* concept is neatly summarized by Derek Pugh and David Hickson in their book *Writers on Organizations:*

> *everyone in an organization has in mind an implicit picture of that organization, a mental image of what it is like. Morgan contends not only that an organization is seen differently by different people, but that it can be seen in different ways by any one person. If multiple images of an organization are used, much greater understanding is gained, for organizations are many things at once, so multiple images envisage more of what is going on. They can reveal new ways of managing and designing organizations that were not apparent before.*[3]

In essence, this is the *Images* concept, and to operationalize the concept Morgan offers eight metaphorical images (for example, organizations as machines and organizations as brains and so on) for seeing and thinking about different aspects of organizations. And each image is a certain way of seeing with its own strengths and limitations. Some of the images may complement others in situations, some might be extremely insightful and others may prove less helpful, or not be relevant at all. However, the important point is not what images are used (although this is clearly important), but rather the principle of consciously working with multiple perspectives, as Morgan points out below:

> *there can be no single theory or [perspective] that gives an all-purpose point of view. There can be no "correct theory" for structuring everything we do. The challenge facing modern managers is to become accomplished in the art of using [multiple perspectives]: to find appropriate ways of seeing, understanding, and shaping the situations with which they have to deal.*[4]

In applying the *Images* concept to the world of projects, the contention of *Images of Projects* is the same as *Images of Organization,* and the easiest way to express this is by simply adapting the extract used on the previous page:

> *everyone involved in a project has in mind an implicit picture of that project, a mental image of what it is like. We contend not only that a project is seen differently by different people, but that it can be seen in different ways by any one person.*

> *If multiple images of a project are used, much greater understanding is gained, for projects are many things at once, so multiple images envisage more of what is going on. They can also help in managing projects in conjunction with one's own knowledge and experience.*

In summary, the contention of *Images of Projects* is that just like organizations there is no one 'best way' to view projects (despite what proponents of the latest methods or tools might claim), and hence a key challenge for practitioners is to become skilled in the art of using multiple images for dealing with the complexity of projects in real situations. A practitioner can either interpret everything from a fixed standpoint, or they can become skilled (or more skilled) in the craft of seeing, understanding and shaping projects from multiple perspectives. The purpose of the *Images of Projects* framework shown opposite is to help you develop (or enrich) this crucial skill. And to help with this, we need to elaborate more now on the *Images* concept rather than the seven images shown opposite, which are covered in Part 2.

Key principles in working with multiple images

To elaborate more on the *Images* concept, listed below are some principles to keep in mind when applying the images in practice and the next few pages explain these principles in more detail.

❖ BOTH/AND rather than EITHER/OR

❖ Seen AS rather than IS or ARE

❖ No RIGHT set of images or perspectives to use in situations

❖ Choose perspectives RELEVANT to the perceived situation

❖ PROMPTS for thinking rather than prescriptions for action

❖ Not the RIGHT image (eg. social) but a RELEVANT image

❖ Think PERSPECTIVE rather than discipline or subject area

Table 2.1   Key principles in working with multiple images

Images of Projects
A Framework of Pragmatic Perspectives

IMAGE 1: Projects as Social Processes

Covers aspects such as the flux of events, the people and organizations involved, social networks, culture and tribalism, and language and metaphor.

Social Perspective 👓

IMAGE 2: Projects as Political Processes

Covers aspects such as interests and agenda, hidden agenda, power and influence, political tactics (e.g., influence tactics) and people's attitudes to politics.

Political Perspective 👓

IMAGE 3: Projects as Intervention Processes

Concerned with seeing projects as interventions and covers aspects such as the perceived situation to be improved and the type of intervention.

Intervention Perspective 👓

IMAGE 4: Projects as Value Creation Processes

*Concerned with the value and benefit of projects, programmes and portfolios. Value as **not** just wealth creation, but also other kinds of value and benefit.*

Value Perspective 👓

IMAGE 5: Projects as Development Processes

Concerned with what needs to be developed, how, when, where and by whom etc. Development as not just product development but also people development etc.

Development Perspective 👓

IMAGE 6: Projects as Temporary Organizations

Concerned with seeing projects as being like whole organizations, and hence covers aspects such as structure, finance, governance, leadership and marketing.

Organizational Perspective 👓

IMAGE 7: Projects as Change Processes

Concerned with seeing projects as change processes, and hence covers aspects such as the context and rationale for change, and the perceived scope and content.

Change Perspective 👓

Not only are projects seen differently by different people, but they can also be seen in different ways by any one person.

Table 2.2   Images of projects framework

1. BOTH/AND rather than EITHER/OR

Very importantly, the different images listed on the previous page are *not* alternatives between which a choice has to be made. Applying this principle to the example of the *Equipment Direct Project*, means the project can be viewed *both* as an intervention process *and* as a temporary organization, and *not* that it should be seen *either* as an intervention *or* as a temporary organization. Moreover, the same project can also be seen as *both* a value creation process, *and* as a development process, and so on and so forth. In other words, projects and programmes are many things at once and it is this reality that means the principle is always *both/and* rather than *either/or*. As Arthur Battram says in his book *Navigating Complexity*, to engage with complexity *'we need perspectives which admit the possibility that more than one thing can be true at once'*.[5]

2. Seen AS rather than IS or ARE

Some PM books assert that *'a project IS a temporary production process'* whilst others assert that *'all projects ARE change processes'*, or that *'all projects ARE change projects'* (*capitals added*). Whilst these ideas might be helpful, they are simultaneously unhelpful in that they suggest or imply this is THE way to think about projects. The problem with these sorts of statements stems from the words IS and ARE which have the effect of 'closing off' other ways of thinking and other potentially useful insights which can only flow from taking other perspectives. A more pragmatic approach (and more defensible philosophically) is to think in terms of AS rather than IS or ARE, in the sense that different projects and programmes can be seen AS temporary production processes, but can also be seen AS change processes, and AS value creation processes, and AS temporary organizations and so on. Adopting this approach is much less prescriptive and can also have a profound effect on the subsequent work of a project or programme.

3. No RIGHT set of images or perspectives to use in situations

Two further points to make about working with the images is that there is no 'right' set of images to use in practice and nor is our list of seven images an exhaustive list. Like Morgan's eight images of organization, the seven images of projects represent seven pragmatic perspectives for engaging with the complex realties of projects; however, we make no assumption that they are the *only* images that can be applied in real situations. Experientially, the seven core images are known to be *useful*, but this does not preclude the use of other images and concepts, including Morgan's own framework for engaging with the organizational aspects of projects.

4. Choose perspectives RELEVANT to the perceived situation

If one accepts the idea that there is no 'right' set of images or perspectives, then a key implication of working with multiple perspectives is the need to make choices about which perspectives to use in particular situations. How might this be done? In practice, a useful principle to adopt here is to select perspectives which are thought to be *relevant* to the particular situation under consideration, as opposed to looking for the 'right' perspectives or the 'right' approach. Just like the difference between 'as' and 'is', the difference between 'relevant' and 'right' is a crucial distinction, mainly because the concept of 'relevance' invites the question of "relevant to what exactly?" By this we mean the choice of perspectives should always depend on the perceived situation and hence a useful question to ask is: What could be some relevant perspectives to look at it from? In short, one of the key characteristics of this book's pragmatic approach to projects is its emphasis on being *situation-driven* rather than *method-driven*.

5. PROMPTS for thinking rather than prescriptions for action

Another key point to make about the seven core images is that they are not models or frameworks to be applied prescriptively, as in 'following' a method for example; they are simply prompts for seeing, thinking and talking about projects in real situations. To use a distinction from *Against the Grain* by Sue Pearce and Sheila Cameron, they are *prompts for thinking* rather than *prescriptions for action*, which is a crucial distinction when it comes to using the images in real situations.[6] In other words, they are devices for *making sense* of projects, for *reflecting* on various aspects, for *conceptualizing* action possibilities, and for generally *prompting* group discussions in the everyday flux of events. In essence, they are devices for 'first-stage thinking'.

6. Not the RIGHT image but a RELEVANT image

Associated with each perspective is a particular core image that we have developed, but there is no assumption here that each of the images in Part 2 is the 'right' image to use for that perspective. In this book, they are seen as relevant images because experience has shown them to be *useful* in various situations. However, this is not to say that additional or alternative images could not be used to inform or guide a particular perspective. For example, this book's social image of projects is based on the idea of seeing projects as an ever-changing flux of events, but this is not the only social process perspective that could be taken. And similarly with the change perspective, the image used in this book is that of planned change because of its relevance to organizational change projects, but there are many other models of change that could be used.

7. Think PERSPECTIVE rather than discipline or specialism

The final principle to keep in mind when applying the different images is the need to think 'perspective' rather than 'discipline' or 'specialism'. Consider the following examples: change management, quality management, benefits management, risk management and so on; whilst such phrases are useful for certain purposes, they also create the impression that the world is divided into lots of separate disciplines, specialisms, and processes all operating 'out there' in the world. In this book, we argue that the actuality of a project or programme is just *one* process, a social and political process, rather than lots of processes, which seems to be the image in most of the mainstream literature on project management. Clearly, the idea of doing change management one day, risk management another and benefits management on another day, is just plain nonsense. A more useful approach is to think perspective rather than process or discipline, for example 'change perspective' rather than 'change management', just as we did for the *Equipment Direct Project*. In that example, we asked not what should the change management plan be for that project, but what are the main considerations from a change perspective? And also how should these considerations be integrated with the insights and implications from the other perspectives? To illustrate this further, consider the two contrasting images in Figure 2.2.

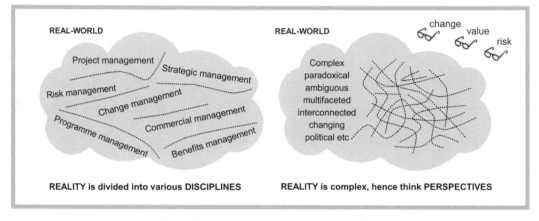

Figure 2.2   Two contrasting images of reality

In summary, most people accept without question that the world is not divided into disciplines and yet the language of management tends to suggest that it is. As Figure 2.2 shows, a key assumption of the *Images* concept is that the real world is inherently complex, paradoxical, ambiguous, multifaceted, interconnected and so on, which is why the concept is that of using multiple images to help engage with this complex reality. And not only this, each image has its own strengths and limitations, or as Morgan cleverly puts it, each image is both a *way of seeing* and a *way of not seeing,* in the sense that all images not only illuminate and reveal, they also conceal and hide.

> *[Each image] can create powerful insights that also become distortions, as the way of seeing ... becomes a way of **not** seeing ... There are no right or wrong theories in management in an absolute sense, for every theory illuminates and hides.*[7]

Gareth Morgan

Links with other frameworks and tools

So far we have introduced seven core images and seven principles for engaging with the complex realities of projects. In some situations, only one or two of these images or perspectives might be 'called upon', say in a discussion or conversation perhaps, whilst in other situations, most or all of the images could be used to help carry out a structured review for example. An example here could be a stage review, the aim of which could be to carry out a review of a project or programme before allowing it to proceed to the next stage; such a review would clearly need to draw on a number of different perspectives and those involved might also use a number of frameworks and tools to help carry out the task, as we now show.

By frameworks and tools, we mean any of the frameworks, models and techniques in areas such as project management, change management, operations management, strategic management, organizational development and so on, any number of which can be used with the images in this book. In short, it is useful to think of this in *what-how* terms: for example, if *what* someone needs to do is review project X from various perspectives, then *how* they might do this is by using some relevant frameworks from elsewhere; the perspectives direct attention to *what* needs to be reviewed and the frameworks provide help with *how* this might be done. This can be shown using the example again of the *Equipment Direct Project:* as our earlier section showed, we have already answered the question of *what* perspectives we might look at the project from to help identify the action needed, and the question now is *how* might we support these perspectives with some other relevant tools? Rather than list examples for each perspective, we can show this quite easily by using one example tool called the *Change Process Model* shown in Figure 2.3. Applying this model to the *Equipment Direct Project* might prompt the following questions:

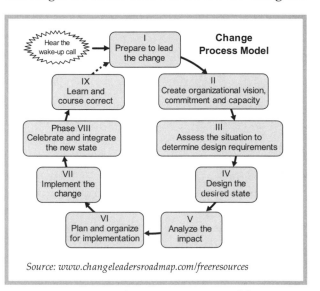

Figure 2.3   A change management model

- Re: the wake-up call – do those involved recognize the need for change?
- Re: phase I – who will lead the change and do they have the leadership capability?
- Re: phase II – is there a case for change and has this been adequately made?
- Re: phase III – has the current situation been sufficiently understood?

- Re: phase IV – has the desired state been defined beyond the IT requirements?
- Re: phase V – how should the users of the service (disabled people) be involved?
- Re: phase VI – is there a need to pilot the new service before implementation?

As our example shows, we have listed only seven questions and we have could have listed more, noting as well that these questions arise from using just one model from one perspective. Generally, not only is it important to consider using such models, because of the potential insights they can yield, it is also important to consider *how* they will be used in real situations. Also, this is an aspect we touched on earlier and it is important to emphasize it again here: although not usually expressed this way, management models and frameworks are more usefully seen as *prompts for thinking* rather than *prescriptions for action*, which is why we chose the *Change Process Model* as our example model. For example, here is what Dean and Linda Anderson say about their model in their book *Beyond Change Management*:

> the detail, logic and structure of the Change Process Model might create the impression that it is a cookbook for how to succeed at transformation. ... There is no cookbook for transformational change. Anyone using [it] must remember that it is a thinking discipline, not a prescription for action. ... Remember, the Change Process Model, in all its comprehensiveness, is simply designed to support you as you consciously ask which of its many activities are critical for your transformation's success. ... In any given transformation effort, we suggest that you consider all of what is offered in the model and then select only the work that is appropriate to your change effort.[8]

In other words, the role of the *Change Process Model* is not to prescribe what *should* be done for all projects and programmes, but to prompt various questions about what *might* be done within particular projects and programmes, for which the answers will always be dependent on the particular situation under consideration. Understanding this point, that all such models and frameworks are more usefully seen and used as prompts rather than prescriptions, is hugely important. As a guiding principle, it represents a totally different mindset to the conventional mindset of seeing a model or framework as a prescription for action, or something that has to be followed step by step as if it were a method or technique. To use a toolkit analogy, models such as the *Change Process Model* and other management frameworks are seen here as tools for thinking essentially, and when seen and used this way, they can play a helpful role as Sue Pearce and Sheila Cameron point out in their book *Against the Grain*:

> [management models] may offer few advantages over models based on experience ... [however], if used as prompt rather than prescription, some of them at least **can** broaden your perspective and help you to cope with the complexities around you.[9]

Sue Pearce and Sheila Cameron

Link with the Mainstream Image of Projects

Before we look at the different ways in which the *Images of Projects* framework can be used in real situations, it is important to briefly consider how the ideas in this book relate to the mainstream image of projects. By mainstream we mean the traditional concept of a 'project' in mainstream project management publications such as college textbooks, practitioner books, body of knowledge guides, methodology manuals and so on. Consider the following four definitions for instance:

> *A project involves a group of people working to complete a particular end product, or to achieve a specific result, by a specified date, within a specified budget and to meet a specified standard of performance (quality).*[10]

> *[A project is] an endeavour in which human, material and financial resources are organized in a novel way, to undertake a unique scope of work, of given specification, within constraints of cost and time, so as to achieve beneficial change.*[11]

> *A project is an endeavour to accomplish a specific objective ... [it] has a well-defined objective – an expected result or product. The objective of a project is usually defined in terms of scope, schedule and cost.*[12]

> *[A project is] a unique process, consisting of a set of coordinated and controlled activities with start and finish dates, undertaken to achieve an objective conforming to specific requirements, including the constraints of time, cost and resources.*[13]

All four definitions clearly embody the same basic concept of a 'project', namely that of a temporary endeavour to accomplish an objective relating to a particular end product, system or facility, which needs to be created, engineered or improved. The goal or objective may only be expressed in broad terms, but nonetheless this is known or given at the start. All four definitions also use the same three performance criteria of specification (quality), cost and time, against which all real-world projects should be measured. Similar definitions can be found elsewhere, all of which point to the same basic image in most of the mainstream literature on project management. So, how does this mainstream image relate to the *Images of Projects* framework?

In our view, the mainstream view of projects represents a particular *image* of projects rather than an all-encompassing model as many of the college textbooks and other publications seem to imply. In *Images* terminology, it represents a particular *way of seeing* projects, but also, a *way of not seeing*, in that it illuminates and obscures certain aspects of projects and not others. With its origins in engineering and construction projects, the image itself and all its associated techniques is essentially a *production* view of projects, which focuses on a particular end product to be created, engineered or improved. Of course, this does not mean it is the 'wrong' perspective to adopt, only that it represents a particular *image* of projects, rather than an all-encompassing theory. As Gareth Morgan points out in *Images of Organization,* no single theory can provide an all-purpose point of view, and there can be no one 'correct' theory or framework for structuring everything we do.

This leads to one other important point about the mainstream image of projects and indeed all the images in this book, and that is they represent ways of thinking about reality, rather than descriptions of reality itself. In cartography, it is well known that the map is never the territory, and yet within the project management literature, the mainstream view of projects is often presented as if it were the territory. Not only is it a *particular* view of projects, it is also just that, a *view* of projects, and not a map of the actual reality. In other words, because of the complexity of the social world, it is important to distinguish between the *intellectual world of ideas and images,* and the *actuality of events and actions;* and maintaining awareness of this distinction is very important in the complex world of projects – see Figure 2.4.

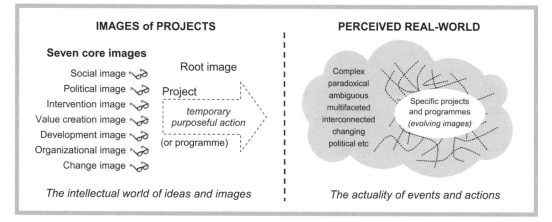

Figure 2.4   Intellectual world/real world distinction

Notice also on the left-hand side of Figure 2.4 the idea of *temporary purposeful action* as a more generic starting point for thinking about projects than the mainstream image of producing something to specification, cost and time. This subsumes the mainstream view as just one particular image of temporary purposeful action. As stated in the Overview, this more generic concept can be applied to any project or programme, including those not normally thought of as projects and programmes in the conventional sense, including university degree programmes.

There is no 'one best map' of a particular terrain. For any terrain there will be an indefinite number of useful maps, a function of the indefinite levels and kinds of description of the terrain itself.[14]

Brian Fay

Applying the Images in Practice

Now that we have introduced the *Images* concept and the seven images, we turn now to how they can be used in real situations, albeit briefly, since this is the main focus of Part 3. The first thing to say is that there is no 'right' way of using the images, for it all depends on the person's role in relation to a project or programme. For example, a programme sponsor might draw heavily on the social, political and value images, whereas a team leader might draw heavily on the development, organizational and change images. Different images will be more relevant to some roles than others, and it also depends of course on the person's interests and how they see their main role. Irrespective of these aspects, however, there are three quite distinct ways of using the images that are open to all practitioners.

Three types of use: selective, structured and shared use

Starting from the simple fact that people have to think and act in different situations, experience has shown that the *Images of Projects* framework can be usefully applied in at least three different ways, as shown in the following three independent examples:

"It seems to me the project is much more about developing the internal service operation than about implementing a new IT system, and if we were to adopt this view of the project, then the whole approach would be very different, including how the staff could be involved."

"Given the complexity of the situation, a structured review is needed to find an acceptable way forward for the project. And in carrying out this review, we need to look at the situation from various perspectives in order to reach an accommodation about the action needed."

[Person A] "From a development perspective, here are two possible concepts ..."
[Person B] "It seems to me, from a change angle, the first one is more achievable ..."
[Person C] "I agree, but politically, it might still be necessary to do the second ..."

Although these examples might seem similar, they illustrate three different types of use: the first illustrates the *selective use* of the images, by which we mean the use of certain images in particular situations; the second is an example of *structured use*, by which we mean a more systematic use of the images in a formal review for example; and the third is an illustration of *shared use*, where the images framework can be used as a sort of common language with which to think and talk about projects. (Note that by 'images' here, we mean either images or perspectives.) Moreover, the first one shows how the images can be used purely in the 'background' as it were, without the other people in the situation knowing that a framework is being used; in this case, the practitioner is simply using the development image to offer a different perspective on the project. And in other situations, like the third example, the images framework can be used much more openly as a way of prompting and steering discussions. For a summary of the three types, see Table 2.3.

Type of Use	Definition	Example Uses
1. SELECTIVE USE	The use of one or more images in a real situation for sensemaking purposes. *Individual use only.*	• Clarifying recent events • Reading the politics • Reflecting on power aspects • Conceptualizing outcomes • Suggesting actions
2. STRUCTURED USE	The use of multiple images and frameworks to get from a situation (S) to action (A). *Individual use.* *Group facilitation use.*	• Deciding what projects to do • Shaping a programme • Shaping a project concept • Reviewing a messy situation • Facilitating a stage review
3. SHARED USE	The use of the framework as a common language in group discussions. *Group use (2 or more people).*	• Preparing a proposal • Crafting a project plan • Tackling an issue • Talking about a next phase • Doing a post-project review

Table 2.3   Three Types of Use

Applicable across all phases of the lifecycle

Another aspect to mention is that all three types are applicable throughout the life of a project or programme, for the simple reason that practitioners have to deal with *situations* at all phases of the lifecycle, as shown in Figure 2.5. Also, the reason we use the three-phase model in Figure 2.5 is because it can be applied to any type of project or programme and also because it links directly to the images in Part 2. For example, depending on which images are being used and for what purpose, the three phases take on different meaning; for instance, if the *intervention* image is being used as a guide to action, then the

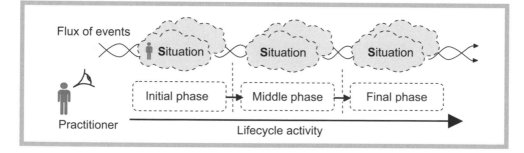

Figure 2.5   The occurence of situations at all phases of a project

three phases in Figure 2.5 could be a review phase, an execution phase and an evaluation phase; whereas if the *change* image is being used, the three phases could be seen as the upstream, midstream and downstream phases. In other words, the three generic phases in Figure 2.5 represent a *generic lifecycle model* that can be framed and reframed in different situations according to the type of project or programme being carried out and other relevant situational factors. Also, as any experienced practitioner knows, these situations arise and evolve through all phases of a project or programme, which is why the three types of use are applicable throughout the lifecycle, as shown by some further examples in Table 2.4.

Type of Use	Initial Phase	Middle Phase	Final Phase
SELECTIVE USE	*Example use* Conceptualizing the outcomes and outputs of a new project or programme. *Examples images* Value Development	*Example use* Rethinking the aims and objectives of an existing project or programme. *Example images* Intervention Change	*Example use* Clarifying the events leading up to a situation and reading the politics. *Example images* Social Political
STRUCTURED USE	*Example use* Initiating a project or programme. *Example images* Social Political Intervention Value Development Organizational Change	*Example use* Reviewing a project or programme. *Example images* Social Political Value Development Organizational Change Risk	*Example use* Resolving some contract issues. *Example images* Social Political Value Development Change
SHARED USE	*Example use* Producing an action plan for initiating a new project. *Example images* Social Political Value Change	*Example use* Working out what to do next in a project or programme. *Example images* Social Political Development Organizational	*Example use* Discussing the team's reflections on a project. *Example images* Social Political Intervention Value

Table 2.4   Example uses during the different phases of a project

Why complex situations in particular?

Whilst the images can be applied in any situation, they are particularly appropriate in complex situations, which we define as *those situations in which action is needed but what to do is unclear,* like those shown or implied in Table 2.4. The reason for this is that in these situations practitioners have to engage in *'a certain kind of work'* as the late Donald Schön describes it in the extract below:

> *in real-world practice, problems do not present themselves to the practitioner as givens. They must be constructed from the materials of problematic situations which are puzzling, troubling, and uncertain. In order to convert a problematic situation to a problem, a practitioner must do a certain kind of work. He [or she] must make sense of an uncertain situation that initially makes no sense. When professionals consider what road to build, for example, they deal usually with a complex and ill-defined situation in which geographic, topological, financial, economic and political issues are all mixed up … Once they have somehow decided what road to build and go on to consider how best to build it, they may have a problem they can solve by the application of available techniques; but when the road they have built leads unexpectedly to the destruction of a neighbourhood, they may find themselves again in a situation of uncertainty.*[15]

In writing about this in his seminal book *The Reflective Practitioner (1983)*, Schön calls this process *problem setting,* to distinguish it from the more familiar process of *problem solving,* and he describes this process more generally in the extract below:

> *it is this sort of situation [the road example] that professionals are coming increasingly to see as central to their practice. They are coming to recognize that although problem setting is a necessary condition for technical problem solving, it is not itself a technical problem. When we set the problem, we select what we will treat as the "things" of the situation, we set the boundaries of our attention to it, and we impose upon it a coherence which allows us to say what is wrong and in what directions the situation needs to be changed. Problem setting is a process in which, interactively, we name the things to which we will attend and frame the context in which we will attend to them.*[16]

Experience shows that most people do this subconsciously based on tacit knowledge and experience, which is generally sufficient in everyday situations. However, in messy situations, the process of problem setting becomes much more important and most people are often unaware of this, as Edward de Bono points out below:

> *[first-stage thinking] is taken for granted and often assumed not to be there at all. … [problem solving techniques] are never applied directly to a situation. They can only be applied when that situation has been divided into concepts, features, factors, effects, and other perceptual parcels. … These perceptual*

parcels are not themselves created by the application of any special techniques, but by the natural patterning processes of mind with all their limitations ... We assume that these starting concepts are correct ... In other words, we assume that thinking only starts at the second stage.[17]

To answer the question, then, the reason first-stage thinking is particularly important in complex situations is because the 'things' that are named and framed in a situation, or the 'perceptual parcels' as de Bono calls them, always reflect a particular *worldview*, and different worldviews always lead to different 'things' being seen and attended to. In other words, *experience* leads us to 'notice' certain things in situations and not others, and if one's 'outlook' is particularly narrow in seeing the situation, then no amount of subsequent effort will make up for this, as de Bono points out below:

no amount of excellence in [second-stage thinking] can ... make up for deficiencies in the first stage. ... Choice of attention area, choice of entry point, choice of factors, these are all part of the first stage of thinking. And such choices will predetermine the final result of the thinking process.[18]

This, then, is why the *Images* concept is so relevant to the world of projects, because the 'choices' made at this first 'stage' of thinking predetermine not only the final result of the thinking process, they also predetermine the final results of projects and programmes. As we showed in Chapter 1, if one's 'first-stage thinking' is deficient (for example, the project concept is flawed), then no amount of detailed planning or risk analysis can ever make up for this. So, what is the essential difference in using the images?

How is this different to what people already do?

Before moving on to Part 2, we end this chapter with an important question that is sometimes asked about the *Images* concept: *"How is this different to what I already do?"* Some readers, for instance, might say they already think about projects from different perspectives, based on experience and intuition, and no doubt this is true. But consider once again the three examples on page 37: the people in those situations are *consciously* thinking from multiple perspectives, rather than just relying on experience and intuition; in other words, as well as experience, they are deliberately using different images and frameworks to help think and talk about their particular projects. And it is *this* that can make an important difference in real situations: in short, the deliberate use of images and frameworks can direct attention to aspects of projects and programmes that might not otherwise be *thought* about, and hence can influence the *action* that follows, and the eventual *results* that might be achieved.

*In summary, the **Images** concept is simply an invitation to practitioners to do what they already do, but to do so more consciously, with the aid of some images and frameworks, as and when required.*

Part 2
Seven Core Images of Projects

Reality has a tendency to reveal itself in accordance with the perspectives through which it is engaged.

Gareth Morgan

Introduction to Part 2

Now that we have introduced the main ideas in Part 1, it is time to consider each core image in detail, and to do this we need to explain first the general format of the next seven chapters. This is important because each chapter follows the same basic format and understanding this will enable the reader to start with any particular image or aspect that might be of interest. As we stated in the Overview, the aim of this book is not to be prescriptive or all-encompassing, but rather to offer a set of images for the reader to think about in relation to their own ideas and perspectives. But before we introduce these images, we need to explain the chapter structure and how the images are structured so as to allow the reader to make comparisons with their own perspectives, and also comparisons between the images themselves.

Basic structure of chapters 3 to 9

Fundamentally, each chapter focuses on a single *perspective* and each one leads us to consider a selection of *aspects* that arise from taking that particular perspective. Of course, there might be other aspects to consider, and some of our chosen aspects for each perspective could also be considered from other perspectives, but that is not the point of each chapter; our aim is simply to illustrate the *kinds of aspects* that might be considered from each perspective, and for this we have chosen five that apply to most projects and programmes. Finally, at the end of each chapter, we then show how the five example aspects can be brought together to form an overall *image of projects* from that chapter's perspective. Of course, this is not the 'right' image to apply, as we stated in Chapter 2, and nor is it the only image that could be applied from that perspective; it is simply a framework for *making sense* of projects and programmes, as well as a starting point for thinking about the action that might be needed in real situations. And since all the images have strengths and limitations, we end each chapter with a brief summary of these for each core image.

Image structure: context/content/process

As well as using a common framework for Chapters 3 to 9, the images themselves are also structured using a common framework to emphasize the links between them and to help the reader make comparisons with their own mental models. Known as the *context/content/process* framework,[1] we use it here to model the six process images – *social, political, intervention, value, development and change* – simply because they are all processual images that can be modelled using the same structure of context/content/process. For the other image, the *organizational* image, we use a different model for this perspective because the temporary organization idea is an entity rather than a process. However, as we stated in Chapter 2, all seven images are not alternatives between which a choice has to be made and nor are they seen as all-encompassing; together, they form part of an overall framework that can be used in different ways in different situations. As we know, the real-world of projects is not divided up in the way this part might suggest, which is why the third part of the book is all about applying the images in practice. Before that, however, we need to cover the images themselves, and for this the reader is advised to study the guide below to understand how each image chapter is laid out and presented. Also, brief descriptions of all the projects and programmes used in Chapters 3 to 9 are provided on pages 49–55.

Specific format guide for chapters 3 to 9

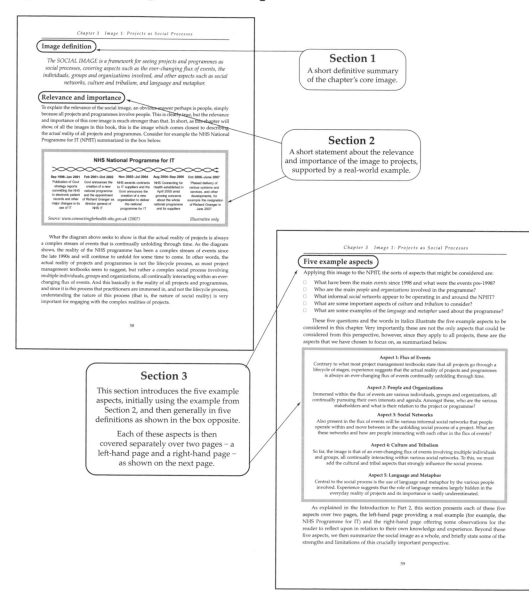

Format continued:

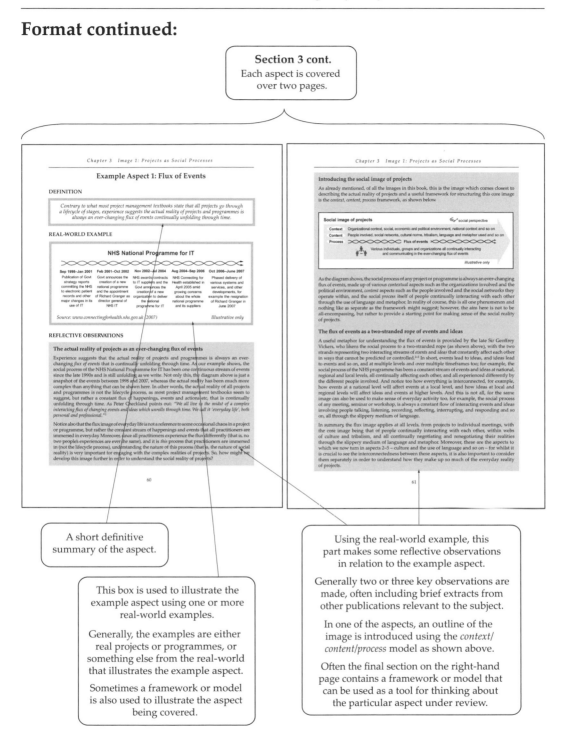

Section 3 cont.
Each aspect is covered
over two pages.

Chapter 3   Image 1: Projects as Social Processes

Example Aspect 1: Flux of Events

DEFINITION

Contrary to what most project management textbooks state that all projects go through a lifecycle of stages, experience suggests the actual reality of projects and programmes is always an ever-changing flux of events continually unfolding through time.

REAL-WORLD EXAMPLE

NHS National Programme for IT

Sep 1998–Jan 2001	Feb 2001–Oct 2002	Nov 2002–Jul 2004	Aug 2004–Sep 2006	Oct 2006–June 2007
Publication of Govt strategy reports committing the NHS to electronic patient records and other major changes in its use of IT	NHS announces the creation of a new national programme and the appointment of Richard Granger as director general of NHS IT	NHS awards contracts to IT suppliers and the Govt announces the creation of a new organization to deliver the national programme for IT	NHS Connecting for Health established in April 2005 amid growing concerns about the whole national programme and its suppliers	Phased delivery of various systems and services, and other developments, for example the resignation of Richard Granger in June 2007

Source: www.connectingforhealth.nhs.gov.uk (2007)   *Illustrative only*

REFLECTIVE OBSERVATIONS

The actual reality of projects as an ever-changing flux of events

Experience suggests that the actual reality of projects and programmes is always an ever-changing *flux of events* that is continually unfolding through time. As our example shows, the social process of the NHS National Programme for IT has been one continuous stream of events since the late 1990s and is still unfolding as we write. Not only this, the diagram above is just a snapshot of the events between 1998 and 2007, whereas the actual reality has been much more complex than anything that can be shown here. In other words, the actual reality of all projects and programmes is not the lifecycle process, as most project management textbooks seem to suggest, but rather a constant flux of happenings, events and actions etc, that is continually unfolding through time. As Peter Checkland points out: *"We all live in the midst of a complex interacting flux of changing events and ideas which unrolls through time. We call it 'everyday life', both personal and professional."*[5]

Notice also that the flux image of everyday life is not a reference to some occasional chaos in a project or programme, but rather the constant stream of happenings and events that all practitioners are immersed in everyday. Moreover, since all practitioners experience the flux differently (that is, no two peoples experiences are ever the same), and it is *this* process that practitioners are immersed in (not the lifecycle process), understanding the nature of this process (that is, the nature of social reality) is very important for engaging with the complex realities of projects. So, how might we develop this image further in order to understand the social reality of projects?

60

Chapter 3   Image 1: Projects as Social Processes

Introducing the social image of projects

As already mentioned, of all the images in this book, this is the image which comes closest to describing the actual reality of projects and a useful framework for structuring this core image is the *context, content, process* framework, as shown below.

Social image of projects   *social perspective*

Context	Organizational context, social, economic and political environment, national context and so on
Content	People involved, social networks, cultural norms, tribalism, language and metaphor used and so on
Process	Flux of events

Various individuals, groups and organizations all continually interacting and communicating in the ever-changing flux of events

Illustrative only

As the diagram shows, the social process of any project or programme is always an ever-changing flux of events, made up of various *contextual* aspects such as the organizations involved and the political environment, *content* aspects such as the people involved and the social networks they operate within, and the social *process* itself of people continually interacting with each other through the use of language and metaphor. In reality of course, this is all one phenomenon and nothing like as separate as the framework might suggest; however, the aim here is not to be all-encompassing, but rather to provide a starting point for making sense of the social reality of projects.

The flux of events as a two-stranded rope of events and ideas

A useful metaphor for understanding the flux of events is provided by the late Sir Geoffrey Vickers, who likens the social process to a two-stranded rope (as shown above), with the two strands representing two interacting streams of *events* and *ideas* that constantly affect each other in ways that cannot be predicted or controlled.[2–3] In short, events lead to ideas, and ideas lead to events and so on, at multiple levels and over multiple timeframes too; for example, the social process of the NHS programme has been a constant stream of events and ideas at national, regional and local levels, all continually affecting each other, and all experienced differently by the different people involved. And notice too how everything is interconnected, for example, how events at a national level will affect events at a local level, and how ideas at local and regional levels will affect ideas and events at higher levels. And this is not all, for the same image can also be used to make sense of everyday activity too, for example, the social process of any meeting, seminar or workshop, is always a constant flow of interacting events and ideas involving people talking, listening, recording, reflecting, interrupting, responding and so on, all through the slippery medium of language.

In summary, the flux image applies at all levels, from projects to individual meetings, with the core image being that of people continually interacting with each other, within webs of culture and tribalism, and all continually negotiating and renegotiating their realities through the slippery medium of language and metaphor. Moreover, these are the aspects to which we now turn in aspects 2–5 – culture and the use of language and so on – for whilst it is crucial to see the interconnectedness between these aspects, it is also important to consider them separately in order to understand how they make up so much of the everyday reality of projects.

61

A short definitive
summary of the aspect.

This box is used to illustrate the
example aspect using one or more
real-world examples.

Generally, the examples are either
real projects or programmes, or
something else from the real-world
that illustrates the example aspect.

Sometimes a framework or model
is also used to illustrate the aspect
being covered.

Using the real-world example, this
part makes some reflective observations
in relation to the example aspect.

Generally two or three key observations are
made, often including brief extracts from
other publications relevant to the subject.

In one of the aspects, an outline of the
image is introduced using the *context/
content/process* model as shown above.

Often the final section on the right-hand
page contains a framework or model that
can be used as a tool for thinking about
the particular aspect under review.

Format continued:

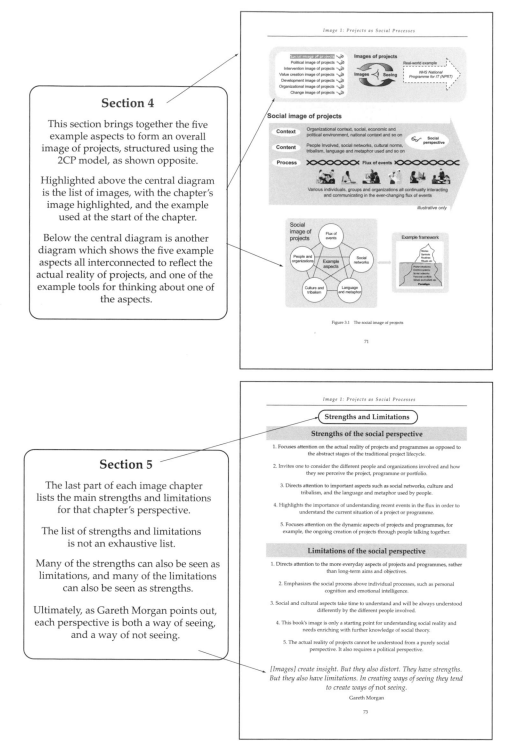

Section 4

This section brings together the five example aspects to form an overall image of projects, structured using the 2CP model, as shown opposite.

Highlighted above the central diagram is the list of images, with the chapter's image highlighted, and the example used at the start of the chapter.

Below the central diagram is another diagram which shows the five example aspects all interconnected to reflect the actual reality of projects, and one of the example tools for thinking about one of the aspects.

Section 5

The last part of each image chapter lists the main strengths and limitations for that chapter's perspective.

The list of strengths and limitations is not an exhaustive list.

Many of the strengths can also be seen as limitations, and many of the limitations can also be seen as strengths.

Ultimately, as Gareth Morgan points out, each perspective is both a way of seeing, and a way of not seeing.

List of projects and programmes used in chapters 3 to 9

Project or Programme	Chapter
The NHS National Programme for IT	Chapters 3 and 8
Introduction of Home Information Packs (HIPs)	Chapter 4
A New Deal for Braunstone	Chapter 5
ERP Project – Proform Business Services	Chapter 5
Prison Service Plus Project (PS Plus)	Chapter 5
London 2012 Olympic Games Project	Chapters 6 and 8
The Eden Project	Chapters 6 and 8
Big Food Group Strategic Programme	Chapters 6, 8 and 9
Project Allenby/Connaught	Chapters 6 and 8
B&Q Renewal Programme	Chapter 6
Equipment Direct Project	Chapter 6
Warburtons SAP Programme	Chapters 6 and 9
King's Cross Development Programme	Chapter 7
Coalfields Heritage Initiative Kent	Chapter 7
Rethinking Project Management Research Project	Chapter 7
Royal Liver Group Strategic Change Programme	Chapter 9

Brief descriptions of the projects and programmes

National Programme for IT   Chapters 3 and 8

The National Programme for IT (NPfIT) is a UK Government programme to create a national electronic patient record system for use by authorized health professionals in the National Health Service (NHS). Following a number of strategic reviews in the period 1998–2002, the programme was established in October 2002 *'to procure, develop and implement modern integrated IT infrastructure and systems for all NHS organisations in England.'*[2] Two years later, the Department of Health announced the creation of a new organization to deliver the programme and an agency called Connecting for Health was formed in April 2005. The programme has attracted major criticism from the start but according to NHS Connecting for Health *'many common misconceptions exist about NHS Connecting for Health and the programmes and services it delivers'.*[3] More information about this and current programme developments can be found on the agency's website and at http://en.wikipedia.org/wiki/National_Programme_for_IT.

Introduction of Home Information Packs (HIPs)   Chapter 4

Between August and December 2007, the UK Government made it a requirement that all properties put up for sale in England and Wales should have a Home Information Pack (HIP) which is *'a set of documents that provides the buyer with key information on the property and must be provided by the seller or the seller's agent'*.[4] Although not an official programme like NPfIT, the introduction of HIPS can be seen as a project dating back to 1997 when the UK Government initiated a strategic review of house buying and selling in England and Wales. Following various proposals, consultations and pilot studies, the Government stated in 2007 that HIPs were being introduced *'to improve the process of buying and selling a home. Currently this can be a stressful and costly experience which is prone to delay and failure'*.[5] But it should also be stated that this initiative has attracted strong opposition from various organizations, groups, and individuals, which is why we use this example in Chapter 4 to illustrate the differing interests and agenda that are present in all projects and programmes. More information about HIPS can be found at www. homeinformationpacks.gov.uk.

A New Deal for Braunstone   Chapter 5

A New Deal for Braunstone is the name of a £49.5m urban regeneration programme in a suburb of Leicester and is part of the UK Government's New Deal for Communities programme *'to tackle multiple deprivation in the most deprived neighbourhoods in the country, giving some of our poorest communities the resources to tackle their problems in an intensive and co-ordinated way'*.[6] In the Braunstone area of Leicester, an area identified in 1999 as one of the most deprived areas in the country, the aim is to improve the quality of life for local residents by carrying out various projects involving local people.[7] An organization called Braunstone Community Association (BCA) was formed in 2000 to manage the programme and more information about the association and the programme can be found at www. braunstone.com and http://en.www.wikipedia.org/wiki/Braunstone.

ERP Project – Proform Business Services   Chapter 5

Proform Business Services (PBS Ltd) is the anonymous name of a large office services company specializing in the recruitment of office personnel and the supply of office equipment to large and small organizations across all sectors. Based in the South of England, PBS has two main business units – Proform Recruitment Services (PRS) and Proform Office Supplies (POS) – and both businesses have offices in locations across South and South West England. In 2002, against a background of rising IT costs and the need to standardize some of the company's business processes, a project was initiated to implement a new IT system, known generally in the industry as an enterprise resource planning (ERP) system. It was stated in the project's business case that *'implementing the proposed ERP system will result in significant improvements to the business'* and yet not long after the project was initiated, it was found there were other more significant problems that needed to be dealt with.

Prison Service Plus Project (PS Plus)   Chapter 5

Prison Service Plus was a UK prison and community-based project to prepare ex-offenders both in prison and in the community for future employment. From 2002 the project delivered a range of services and interventions to help offenders become more employable and develop confidence, improved self-esteem, increased motivation and educational qualifications. Funded jointly by the European Social Fund (ESF) and the UK National Offender Management Service, PS Plus was the largest ESF-funded initiative of its type in Europe. The project itself involved several phases with the final phase focusing on achieving sustainability of outcomes to assist the ongoing objective of reducing reoffending. PS Plus is a good example of a social programme that illustrates this book's image of projects as interventions. Further information about PS Plus can be found at www.pslus.org.

London 2012 Olympic Games Project   Chapters 6 and 8

This project hardly needs an introduction for it is well known that London is the host of the next Olympic Games in 2012. The origins of the project date back to 2003 when a team led by Barbara Cassini was formed to begin work on the London bid. Two years later, on July 6th 2005 in Singapore, the President of the International Olympic Committee announced to the world that *'the Games of the XXXth Olympiad in 2012 are awarded to the city of ... London.'*[8] Four years on and a major programme of work is now underway to stage the Games that will start on July 27th 2012. More information about London 2012 can be found at www.london2012.com.

The Eden Project   Chapters 6 and 8

The Eden Project is another well-known project in the UK based on the site of an old china clay quarry in South West England. It was established as one of the Landmark Millennium Projects to mark the year 2000 and uses *'exhibits, events, workshops and educational programmes to remind people what nature gives to us and to help people to learn how to look after it in return.'*[9] In this book, we use the project to illustrate the idea of seeing projects and programmes as temporary organizations, for this is a much more applicable perspective as the example shows: *'The Eden Project is wholly owned by the Eden Trust, a UK Registered Charity. It is operated on behalf of the Trust by Eden Project Limited, a wholly owned subsidiary of the Eden Trust.'*[10] In other words, The Eden Project is essentially an organization just like conventional organizations such as Marks and Spencer and the University of Manchester, and hence why it provides a useful example of seeing projects as temporary organizations.

Big Food Group Strategic Programme   Chapters 6, 8 and 9

In August 2000 the Big Food Group Plc was a £5.3 billion organization created from the merger of Iceland Frozen Foods and Booker Cash & Carry. From the start, the merger met with problems: Booker and Iceland were very different businesses with different cultures and it was unclear as to how the new company would deliver the £50 million annualized synergy benefits promised at the time of the merger. Under the leadership of a new CEO, a strategic review was initiated to address a number of fundamental questions, including how the group should be structured and what the strategic direction should be for the various business units. To help achieve the new strategic vision, strategic plans were created for each of the business units and group functions, and these were broken down into clear quantifiable objectives, with each one consisting of various programmes and projects with detailed development plans and change management infrastructure to support their delivery. Overall, the whole programme consisted of over 350 initiatives carried out between 2001 and 2004.

Project Allenby/Connaught   Chapters 6 and 8

Project Allenby/Connaught is a major UK project to improve and service the living and working accommodation for approx 20 per cent of the British Army – 18 700 military and civilian personnel based in garrisons in the Salisbury Plain area and Aldershot. Led by a company called Aspire Defence Ltd, which was specifically formed in 2006 to deliver the project, Allenby/Connaught is a 35-year PFI project with a value of about £12bn through life, including £1.2bn for the construction cost. Geographically, the project is located in the South of England focusing on Aldershot to the east and garrisons in the west around the Army's main manoeuvre training area on Salisbury Plain. It is estimated that the construction work will take about 10 years to complete and will require 1100 construction workers and over 2000 people to provide services. On completion of the work, there will be over 2000 buildings to service, for which Aspire will receive about £240m annual revenue from the UK MOD.

B&Q Renewal Programme   Chapter 6

As part of the Kingfisher group, B&Q is the UK's largest DIY retailer with over 300 stores, and the third largest in the world with over 60 stores, including B&Q Beijing which is the largest B&Q store in the world. According to the CEO of Kingfisher, Ian Cheshire, the market focus is now on *'home improvement, rather than DIY'*[11] which is why B&Q is now engaged in a renewal programme as part of a longer-term strategy to capture more of the home improvement market. According to Kingfisher's 2007–08 annual report, B&Q's: *'retail profit was £131 million … after £29 million net revenue costs of the renewal programme … B&Q aims to grow its share of home improvement expenditure by strengthening its appeal to both the Do-it-Yourself (DIY) and Do-it-For-Me (DFM) customer. During 2007/08, B&Q underwent the biggest year of change in its history, which included updating product ranges, improving its store environments and introducing more services, to ensure B&Q is the first and only store for a greater proportion of customers' home improvement spend.'*[12] B&Q's current renewal programme provides a good example of how companies increasingly seek to create value through projects and programmes linked to corporate strategy.

Equipment Direct Project   Chapter 6

This is the project already described in Chapters 1 and 2 about providing disabled people with improved access to and greater choice in equipment services. Funded by a UK Government grant and led by a coalition of several organizations, the project has developed the country's first web-based equipment service called Equipment Direct. More details about the service can be found at www.equipmentdirect.org.uk.

Warburtons SAP Programme   Chapters 6 and 9

From its humble beginnings in northern England over 100 years ago, Warburtons is now the UK's largest independent baking business employing over 4000 people at 13 bakeries and 11 depots spread throughout the UK. Operating 24x7, the company produces over two million bakery products every day, mostly for the supermarkets rather than independent stores. Against this background in early 2000, the company embarked on a project to implement the SAP ERP system, and what makes this project a good example is the attention that was given to the final phase, which we view from both a value perspective and a change perspective. Very importantly, the project was organized and managed not as an IT project, but as a business project involving IT, with an expectation that the projected benefits of SAP would not just magically appear on day 1 of the system going live. Changes would be needed to reap the benefits of SAP through continuous process improvement, user involvement and changes to the SAP system. In short, far from being a weakness of the project, this was a major strength in that there was a clear expectation that further work was needed if the company was to realize the value of its investment in SAP.

King's Cross Development Programme   Chapter 7

King's Cross station is the southern terminus of the UK's East Coast Main Line, one of the major railway routes from London to Scotland. In the next 10 years, the number of people using King's Cross is expected to grow to 50 million and it will also be a major gateway for visitors to the London 2012 Olympics. The station is also in the centre of an urban regeneration area encompassing the new St Pancras International station, the new King's Cross/St Pancras Underground station and the King's Cross Central regeneration scheme. In 2005, a £400m redevelopment plan for King's Cross station was announced by Network Rail and this was approved in 2007. Network Rail, the organization responsible for maintaining and operating Britain's railway infrastructure, plans to redevelop the station with a modern transport hub that will meet the needs of passengers for many years to come. The programme is complex partly because of the need to integrate the works with neighbouring Underground and Channel Tunnel Rail Link developments, and also because the station needs to remain fully operational throughout the construction period. The key station works are due to be completed in late 2011, in time for the 2012 Olympics.

Coalfields Heritage Initiative Kent   Chapter 7

The focus of this initiative is on the Kent Coalfield area which has a rich and largely unrecorded history, and its aim has been to develop a virtual museum of life in the Kent coalfields, along with a travelling exhibition and some walking trails. To record East Kent's mining heritage, one of the main tasks has been to prepare a community archive comprising photographs, documents, text stories, oral memories and video clips. Another part of the project – the Miner's Way Trail – has used the information obtained to develop a walking trail focusing on the old sites and the surrounding countryside. According to the project's website: *'The trail is approximately 28 miles in length, exploring the picturesque countryside of East Kent, linking together pretty villages, small farmsteads, grand country estates and remains of this area's industrial and mining heritage.'*[13] As an example of a heritage project, this is an interesting project from a value creation perspective and a development perspective.

Rethinking Project Management Research Project   Chapter 7

As mentioned earlier in the book, *Rethinking Project Management* was the name given to a research project carried out between 2004 and 2006 to investigate the areas in which mainstream PM theory needs to develop to support practitioners working on today's projects and programmes. Funded by the UK Government, the rationale for the project centred on the developing practice of PM across different sectors, and the growing criticisms of mainstream PM theory, with the main argument being not that mainstream PM ideas should be abandoned, but rather they need to be extended and enriched beyond their current intellectual foundations. The reason for using it as an example in Part 2 is that from a development perspective the project illustrates the importance of the final phase of development, which for this project was the dissemination of the research findings to a number of different audiences.

Royal Liver Group Strategic Change Programme   Chapter 9

The Royal Liver Group consists of Royal Liver Assurance (a 164-year-old mutual life company with £3.5bn of assets) and a number of manufacturing and distribution businesses in the UK and Ireland. The life assurance business has traditionally been the cash generator but changes in both the market and regulatory environment have resulted in it no longer being possible to sell its traditional with-profits life policies, and hence is known internally as the 'sunset' business, in contrast to manufacturing and distribution, which are known as the 'sunrise' businesses. The resulting 'closed book' situation shows the number of policies under administration declining at an average of 10 per cent per annum directly impacting the company's revenue stream. The sunrise businesses cannot mitigate this revenue loss because of their different cost/margin ratios. The net effect is that by 2011 the Royal Liver Group will need to reduce its costs by 33 per cent and to achieve this it will need to make significant changes across the whole organization. Hence, in 2007 a strategic change programme was initiated to restructure the business in response to the current environment and future challenges.

All is flux, nothing stays still.

Heraclitus

Chapter Three

Image 1:
Projects as Social Processes

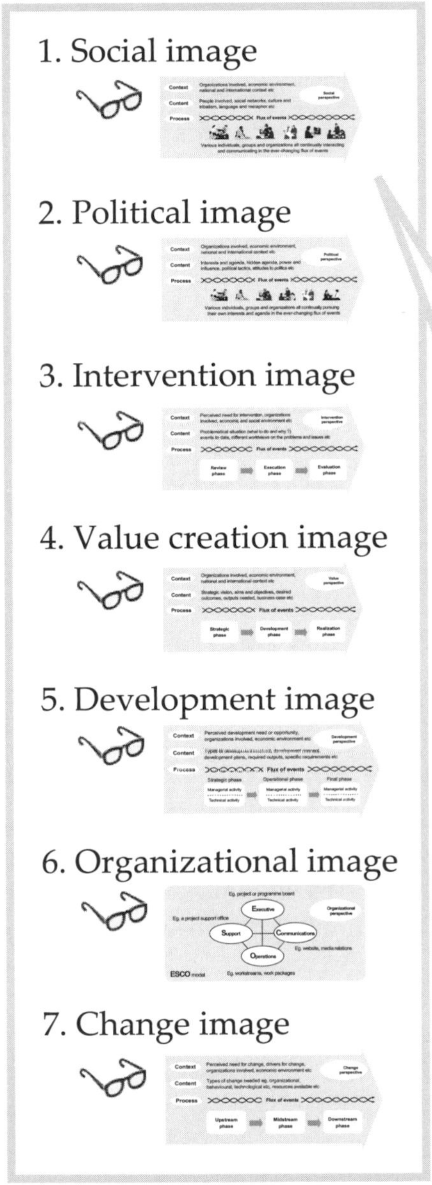
1. Social image
2. Political image
3. Intervention image
4. Value creation image
5. Development image
6. Organizational image
7. Change image

Social Perspective

Chapter Structure

Image Definition

Relevance and Importance

Five Example Aspects

Image Summary

Strengths and Limitations

Image Definition

The SOCIAL IMAGE is a framework for seeing projects as social processes, covering aspects such as the ever-changing flux of events, the individuals, groups and organizations involved, and other aspects such as social networks, culture and tribalism, and language and metaphor.

Relevance and Importance

To explain the relevance of the social image, an obvious answer perhaps is people, simply because all projects and programmes involve people. This is clearly true, but the relevance and importance of this core image is much stronger than that. In short, as this chapter will show, of all the images in this book, this is the image which comes closest to describing the *actual reality* of all projects and programmes. Consider for example the NHS National Programme for IT (NPfIT) summarized in the box below.

NHS National Programme for IT

Sep 1998–Jan 2001	Feb 2001–Oct 2002	Nov 2002–Jul 2004	Aug 2004–Sep 2006	Oct 2006–June 2007
Publication of Govt strategy reports committing the NHS to electronic patient records and other major changes in its use of IT	Govt announces the creation of a new national programme and the appointment of Richard Granger as director general of NHS IT	NHS awards contracts to IT suppliers and the Govt announces the creation of a new organization to deliver the national programme for IT	NHS Connecting for Health established in April 2005 amid growing concerns about the whole national programme and its suppliers	Phased delivery of various systems and services, and other developments, for example the resignation of Richard Granger in June 2007

Source: www.connectingforhealth.nhs.gov.uk (2007)   *Illustrative only*

What the diagram above seeks to show is that the actual reality of projects is always a complex stream of events that is continually unfolding through time. As the diagram shows, the reality of the NHS programme has been a complex stream of events since the late 1990s and will continue to unfold for some time to come. In other words, the actual reality of projects and programmes is not the lifecycle process, as most project management textbooks seem to suggest, but rather a complex social process involving multiple individuals, groups and organizations, all continually interacting within an ever-changing flux of events. And this basically is the reality of all projects and programmes, and since it is *this* process that practitioners are immersed in, and not the lifecycle process, understanding the nature of this process (that is, the nature of social reality) is very important for engaging with the complex realities of projects.

Five Example Aspects

Applying this image to the NPfIT, the sorts of aspects that might be considered are:

- What have been the main *events* since 1998 and what were the events pre-1998?
- Who are the main *people* and *organizations* involved in the programme?
- What informal *social networks* appear to be operating in and around the NPfIT?
- What are some important aspects of *culture* and *tribalism* to consider?
- What are some examples of the *language* and *metaphor* used about the programme?

These five questions and the words in italics illustrate the five example aspects to be considered in this chapter. Very importantly, these are not the only aspects that could be considered from this perspective; however, since they apply to all projects, these are the aspects that we have chosen to focus on, as summarized below.

Aspect 1: Flux of Events

Contrary to what most project management textbooks state that all projects go through a lifecycle of stages, experience suggests that the actual reality of projects is always an ever-changing flux of events continually unfolding through time.

Aspect 2: People and Organizations

Immersed within the flux of events are various individuals, groups and organizations, all continually pursuing their own interests and agenda. Amongst these, who are the various stakeholders and what is their relation to the project or programme?

Aspect 3: Social Networks

Also present in the flux of events will be various informal social networks that people operate within and move between in the unfolding social process of a project. What are these networks and how are people interacting with each other in the flux of events?

Aspect 4: Culture and Tribalism

So far, the image is that of an ever-changing flux of events involving multiple individuals and groups, all continually interacting within various social networks. To this, we must add the cultural and tribal aspects that strongly influence the social process.

Aspect 5: Language and Metaphor

Central to the social process of any project is the use of language and metaphor by the various people involved. Experience suggests that the role of language remains largely hidden in the everyday reality of projects and its importance is vastly underestimated.

As explained in the Introduction to Part 2, this section presents each of these five aspects over two pages, the left-hand page providing a real example (for example, the NHS Programme for IT) and the right-hand page offering some observations for the reader to reflect upon in relation to their own knowledge and experience. Beyond these five aspects, we then summarize the social image as a whole, and briefly state some of the strengths and limitations of this crucially important perspective.

Example Aspect 1: Flux of Events

DEFINITION

Contrary to what most project management textbooks state that all projects go through a lifecycle of stages, experience suggests the actual reality of projects is always an ever-changing flux of events continually unfolding through time.

REAL-WORLD EXAMPLE

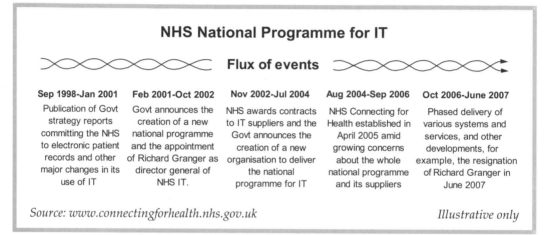

NHS National Programme for IT

Flux of events

Sep 1998-Jan 2001	Feb 2001-Oct 2002	Nov 2002-Jul 2004	Aug 2004-Sep 2006	Oct 2006-June 2007
Publication of Govt strategy reports committing the NHS to electronic patient records and other major changes in its use of IT	Govt announces the creation of a new national programme and the appointment of Richard Granger as director general of NHS IT.	NHS awards contracts to IT suppliers and the Govt announces the creation of a new organisation to deliver the national programme for IT	NHS Connecting for Health established in April 2005 amid growing concerns about the whole national programme and its suppliers	Phased delivery of various systems and services, and other developments, for example, the resignation of Richard Granger in June 2007

Source: www.connectingforhealth.nhs.gov.uk   *Illustrative only*

REFLECTIVE OBSERVATIONS

The actual reality of projects as an ever-changing flux of events

Experience suggests that the actual reality of projects is always an ever-changing *flux of events* that is continually unfolding through time. As our example shows, the social process of the NHS National Programme for IT has been one continuous stream of events since the late 1990s and is still unfolding as we write. Not only this, the diagram above is just a snapshot of the events between 1998 and 2007, whereas the actual reality has been much more complex than anything that can be shown here. In other words, the actual reality of all projects is not the lifecycle process, as most project management textbooks seem to suggest, but rather a constant flux of happenings, events and actions etc, that is continually unfolding through time. As Peter Checkland points out: *'We all live in the midst of a complex interacting flux of changing events and ideas which unrolls through time. We call it 'everyday life', both personal and professional.'*[1]

Notice also that the flux image of everyday life is not a reference to some occasional chaos in a project or programme, but rather the constant stream of happenings and events that all practitioners are immersed in everyday. Moreover, since all practitioners experience the flux differently (that is, no two people's experiences are ever the same), and it is *this* process that practitioners are immersed in (not the lifecycle process), understanding the nature of this process (that is, the nature of social reality) is very important for engaging with the complex realities of projects. So, how might we develop this image further in order to understand the social reality of projects?

Introducing the social image of projects

As already mentioned, of all the images in this book, this is the image which comes closest to describing the actual reality of projects and a useful framework for structuring this core image is the *context/content/process* framework, as shown below.

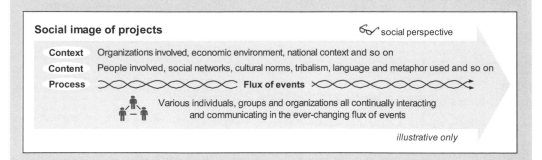

As the diagram shows, the social process of any project or programme is always an ever-changing flux of events, made up of various *contextual* aspects such as the organizations involved and the economic environment, *content* aspects such as the people involved and the social networks they operate within, and the social *process* itself of people continually interacting with each other through the use of language and metaphor. In reality of course, this is all one phenomenon and nothing like as separate as the framework might suggest; however, the aim here is not to be all-encompassing, but rather to provide a starting point for making sense of the social reality of projects.

The flux of events as a two-stranded rope of events and ideas

A useful metaphor for understanding the flux of events is provided by the late Sir Geoffrey Vickers, who likens the social process to a two-stranded rope (as shown above), with the two strands representing two interacting streams of *events* and *ideas* that constantly affect each other in ways that cannot be predicted or controlled.[2-3] In short, events lead to ideas, and ideas lead to events and so on, and at multiple levels and over multiple timeframes too; for example, the social process of the NHS programme has been a constant stream of events and ideas at national, regional and local levels, all continually affecting each other, and all experienced differently by the different people involved. And notice too how everything is interconnected, for example, how events at a national level will affect events at a local level, and how ideas and events at local and regional levels will affect ideas and events at higher levels. And this is not all, for the same image can also be used to make sense of everyday activity too, for example, the social process of any meeting, seminar or workshop, is always a constant flow of interacting events and ideas involving people talking, listening, recording, reflecting, interrupting, responding and so on, all through the slippery medium of language.

In summary, the flux image applies at all levels, from projects to individual meetings, with the core image being that of people continually interacting with each other, within webs of culture and tribalism, and all continually negotiating and renegotiating their realities through the slippery medium of language and metaphor. Moreover, these are the aspects to which we now turn in Example Aspects 2–5, for whilst it is crucial to see the interconnectedness between these aspects, it is also important to consider them separately in order to understand how they make up so much of the everyday reality of projects.

Example Aspect 2: People and Organizations

DEFINITION

> *Immersed within the flux of events are various individuals, groups, and organizations, all continually pursuing their own interests and agenda. Amongst these, who are the various stakeholders and what is their relation to the project or programme?*

REAL-WORLD EXAMPLE

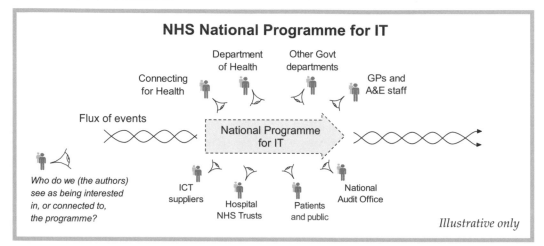

NHS National Programme for IT

Department of Health

Other Govt departments

Connecting for Health

GPs and A&E staff

Flux of events

National Programme for IT

Who do we (the authors) see as being interested in, or connected to, the programme?

ICT suppliers

Hospital NHS Trusts

Patients and public

National Audit Office

Illustrative only

REFLECTIVE OBSERVATIONS

Individuals, groups and organizations

Firstly, by *people and organizations* we mean the various individuals, groups and organizations that are seen to be interested in, or connected to, a particular project. The words 'seen to be' are important here, for the diagram above is a response to the question bottom left: in short, who do we (the authors) see as being interested in, or connected to, the NHS National Programme for IT? Being a 'stage 1' type question, this is a very important question, for it is here that we are starting to frame the programme.

Notice too that just as we (the authors) have a view of the programme, the same is also true of all the other people shown in the example above. In other words, the really important point here is that different people all have their own view of a project, just like the characters in the pig illustration opposite, who all have a different view of the

WHAT IS THE PIG?

Source: *Imaginization* by Gareth Morgan.
Sage Publications.[4]
Reproduced with kind permission.

pig. The analogy is no different: think of any project as the pig and the image is exactly the same. Moreover, the pig illustration raises other important questions as we now explain.

Who are the stakeholders?

For some projects and programmes, this might be an easy question to answer, however, for other projects and programmes such as the NHS National Programme for IT, the question is more problematical and depends on what we mean by 'stakeholder'. This might seem obvious perhaps, but singling out certain stakeholders in the flux of events presupposes some concept of what a 'stakeholder' is, and therefore it is important to know what that concept is when doing stakeholder analysis. Change the concept and the stakeholder list changes too. In other words, stakeholders do not exist 'out there' in the world just waiting to be named, it is *people* who exist out there, and it is the practitioner who names them as such according to what they take a stakeholder to be. Not only this, people in different roles will also identify different stakeholders depending on their organizational position.

Reflecting more on the people and organizations involved

Experience suggests that stakeholder analysis can be a useful exercise using frameworks like the one shown below. Such frameworks provide a useful prompt for understanding how different individuals, groups and organizations relate to a project and how they might be analyzed in terms of their perceived power and influence, and their general orientation towards the project. Moreover, some frameworks suggest particular action strategies according to the perceived stakeholder's position within the overall framework. Of course, such frameworks can only provide a general guide to action, and in real situations the actual judgements required will be much more complex. However, as explained in Chapter 2, when used as *prompts for thinking* rather than *prescriptions for action*, such frameworks can at least suggest things that might not otherwise be considered.

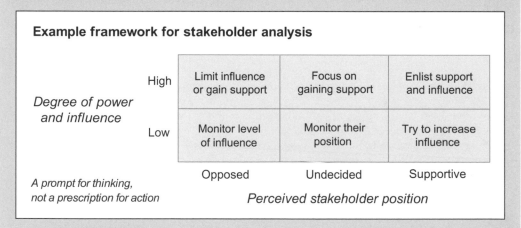

Example framework for stakeholder analysis

		Opposed	Undecided	Supportive
Degree of power and influence	High	Limit influence or gain support	Focus on gaining support	Enlist support and influence
	Low	Monitor level of influence	Monitor their position	Try to increase influence

A prompt for thinking, not a prescription for action

Perceived stakeholder position

Not only is it important to understand how individuals, groups and organizations relate to a project or programme, we also need to consider how they interact and communicate with each other, and what social networks they appear to operate within the field of action. For these important considerations, we turn now to Aspect 3.

Projects are human social endeavours, and are therefore always complex, ambiguous and uncertain: at the granular level of individuals and their personal actions and interactions, at the intermediate level of group and inter-group behaviours, and at the social-political level of organizations and their competing interests.[5]

Charles Smith

Example Aspect 3: Social Networks

DEFINITION

> *Also present in the flux of events will be various informal social networks that people operate within and move between in the unfolding social process of a project. What are these networks and how are people interacting with each other in the flux of events?*

REAL-WORLD EXAMPLE

The action is *IN* the interaction

Illustrative only

REFLECTIVE OBSERVATIONS

The action is *in* the interaction

Building on the previous two aspects, what the picture above seeks to show is how the social process of any project or programme follows the same basic pattern of activity, namely that of individuals and groups all continually interacting and communicating with each other in the ever-changing flux of events. As the diagram shows, people spend a considerable amount of time interacting in meetings and workshops, interacting on the phone, interacting electronically and interacting in other locations that are not shown such as corridors, the coffee room and the local pub. In other words, from a social process perspective, there are not separate processes operating 'out there', as most PM textbooks seem to imply, vis-à-vis the lifecycle process and all its sub-processes; rather, there is just *one* process in which the action of projects and programmes is *in* the interaction itself. And this is the process through which all projects and programmes are conducted.

Social interaction and all its facets is a large and complex subject area and much has been written about it which we cannot go into in this book. In essence, our purpose here is simply to highlight the importance of social interaction as one of the defining features of the social process, and to highlight another related aspect, namely that of the informal social networks in which much of this interaction takes place.

Social networks: how work really gets done in organizations and projects

Although concerned with organizations rather than projects, Rob Cross and Andrew Parker, authors of *The Hidden Power of Social Networks: Understanding How Work Really Gets*

Done in Organizations, make a really important point that is relevant to projects:

> *put an organizational chart in front of most employees from line workers to executives, and they will tell you that the boxes and lines do not really capture the way work gets done ... but most will be quick to acknowledge the critical influence that networks of informal relationships have on work.*[6]

There are obvious implications here for projects too, not least the importance of keeping track (as best one can) of the various conversations and discussions taking place within these social networks. As Rob Cross and Andrew Parker point out, the information within these networks is always changing:

> *information does not flow unchanged through a human network as it does through [routers]. People add context, interpretation, and meaning as they receive information and pass it along.*[7]

Hence why we use the analogy of trying to keep track (as best one can) of who is talking to who within these informal networks. To understand this further and how work really gets done in organizations, they recommend a useful technique called social network analysis, which results in a diagram like the one shown below.

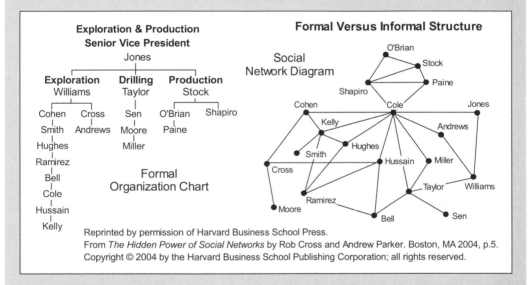

Reprinted by permission of Harvard Business School Press.
From *The Hidden Power of Social Networks* by Rob Cross and Andrew Parker. Boston, MA 2004, p.5.
Copyright © 2004 by the Harvard Business School Publishing Corporation; all rights reserved.

Firstly, notice Cole's position in the two diagrams: what a powerful position he occupies in the social network! In short, such a diagram can help to illuminate aspects and issues that might be central to why particular things are happening in a project and why other things are not. However, such diagrams on their own are not enough to make sense of why things happen the way they do, and for this we need to consider other aspects such as culture and tribalism which is what we turn to next.

Every company has two organizational structures: the formal one is written on the charts; the other is the everyday relationship of the men and women in the organization.[8]
Harold S Geneen

Example Aspect 4: Culture and Tribalism

DEFINITION

So far, the image is that of an ever-changing flux of events involving multiple individuals and groups, all continually interacting within various social networks. To this, we must add the cultural and tribal aspects that strongly influence this process.

REAL-WORLD EXAMPLE

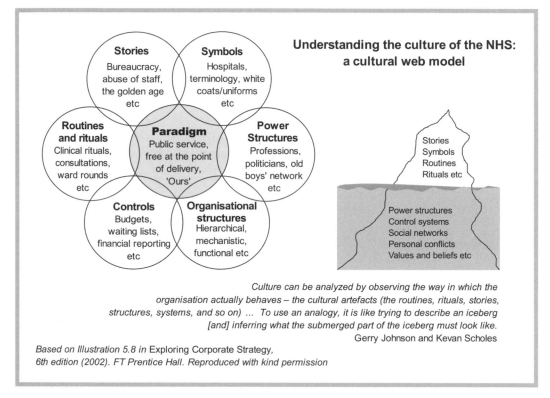

Understanding the culture of the NHS: a cultural web model

Culture can be analyzed by observing the way in which the organisation actually behaves – the cultural artefacts (the routines, rituals, stories, structures, systems, and so on) ... To use an analogy, it is like trying to describe an iceberg [and] inferring what the submerged part of the iceberg must look like.

Gerry Johnson and Kevan Scholes

Based on Illustration 5.8 in Exploring Corporate Strategy, *6th edition (2002). FT Prentice Hall. Reproduced with kind permission*

REFLECTIVE OBSERVATIONS

Culture as another important aspect to consider

Just as Rob Cross and Andrew Parker highlight the aspect of informal social networks, it is also important to understand other social and cultural aspects such as roles, routines, rituals and symbols and so on. Consider for example the model above which illustrates the culture and tribalism of the NHS as perceived by some of its managers in the 1990s. Basically, what the model seeks to show are some of the cultural and tribal aspects of the NHS, which many analysts believe have not been sufficiently understood in the Government's management of the National Programme for IT. Whether one agrees with this or not, the implication for all projects is clear: understanding the social, cultural and political context is hugely important at all levels, and models such as the cultural web model[9] above provide useful tools for doing this.

The iceberg analogy

As well as the cultural web model, another useful metaphor for understanding culture is to imagine the organization or the field of action as an evolving iceberg – see the diagram opposite. As the diagram shows, there are certain aspects that are visible 'above' the water line, such as routines and rituals, and others which are hidden 'below' the water line such as the informal social networks already discussed, and the beliefs and values of the people involved. Notice also that the submerged part in the diagram is much larger than the visible part, reflecting how so much of organizational life is driven by what is 'below' the line. Also, the iceberg analogy works well with respect to dealing with these aspects in real situations, as Barbara Senior points out in *Organisational Change:*

> as with an iceberg, they may not become apparent until one collides with them unwittingly.[10]

Linking this now to the NHS IT Programme, some analysts and academics have argued that the whole initiative in its early stages should have focused less on the technology (the visible element) and much more on the social and cultural aspects of the NHS. This being so, then the really crucial aspects are those 'below' the water line, including the political aspects relating to the differing interests and agenda of the various individuals and groups involved. Hence, understanding these is very important, both at the start of a project by reflecting on what these might be, and throughout the project by paying close attention to anything appearing 'above' the line (for example, stories, reports and press releases) which may provide further 'clues' as to the real interests and agenda 'below' the line.

Recognising tribalism

So far this discussion has centred on making sense of the cultural context at a macro level, and whilst this provides a helpful starting point, it is also important to understand the differing subcultures or 'tribes' that coexist within the overall field of action. As Charles Smith, author of *Making Sense of Project Realities*, points out:

> in most organizations there are a number of classic groups, well recognized and easily identified, such as accountants, lawyers, engineers … However, this is only a limited subset of the groups we can identify. There may be others, perhaps less clearly labelled, who are also highly influential in the running of the organization. These are the tribes of the organizational world, each tribe having its identification marks and its set of artefacts and rituals – the ideas and behaviours that set its members apart from the other tribes. To understand social interactions in projects … we must be able to identify these practice groups – the tribes – in any project situation.[11]

In reality of course, there might be many practice groups to identify (as there are in the NHS) and understanding their differing interests and agenda is very important. Also, understanding how they relate to each other is very important, bearing in mind that each one is largely concerned with their own interests. And once again, the iceberg analogy is useful in that each tribe or practice group can be likened to an evolving iceberg with a 'visible' part (for example, artefacts and rituals) and a 'submerged' part (for example, values and interests); and just as there are multiple icebergs in the natural world all continually evolving with some colliding, the same is also true of the social world with multiple tribes all continually interacting and jockeying for position within the ever-changing flux of events. Not only this, there is also another aspect of the social process which is fundamental to all this social interaction, namely the role of language. This is the final aspect that we now consider.

Example Aspect 5: Language and Metaphor

DEFINITION

Central to the social process of any project is the use of language and metaphor by the various people involved. Experience suggests that the role of language remains largely hidden in the everyday reality of projects and its importance is vastly underestimated.

REAL-WORLD EXAMPLE

April 17th 2007

The sickening £12 billion NHS fiasco

As civil servants prepare for a new government after the departure of Tony Blair, they could do worse than put signs above the door of every minister's office: "Beware the grand project!" Never would this advice have been more apt than for the most expensive health technology project in history, the national programme for IT in the NHS. In this case, hyperbole is appropriate. The project is costing more than £12 billion, enough to pay for 60 000 nurses for 10 years, or for Britain's participation in Iraq and Afghanistan twice over. Run by an agency called Connecting for Health, the vision (are you nervous yet?) is to link up the entire NHS for the electronic age.

June 16th 2006

NHS IT costs 'not disproportionate'

The cost is high, £12.4 billion, made up of £6.8 billion for procurement and the rest for implementation, training costs, and local costs. But this is a 10-year programme in an organization that spends £70 billion a year, so it is not disproportionate – £1.2 billion a year.

June 19th 2007

Ailing project at heart of NHS

FINANCIAL TIMES

September 29th 2006

NHS patient records project 'not holed below the water line'

REFLECTIVE OBSERVATIONS

The ongoing creation of projects through language and metaphor

The words above are just some of the many thousands of words written about the National Programme for IT in the last few years. Very importantly, although such words seem to suggest the project exists 'out there' in the world, there is in fact no such thing as the 'National Programme for IT' from this perspective; rather, all that exists of the 'National Programme for IT' (as opposed to the computer hardware and so on) are the many millions of words spoken and written about 'it' since the late 1990s. In short, since projects and programmes are what people perceive them to be, and no two people ever see them in *exactly* the same way, it is hard to see how programmes such as the NHS IT Programme exist *separately* from the people involved. Whether one agrees with this or not, there is no doubting the importance of language in the ongoing creation of projects. As Robert Eccles and Nitin Nohria point out in *Beyond the Hype: Rediscovering the Essence of Management,* language plays a much more significant role in management than many people realize:

> *management has a lot to do with the use of language ... Unfortunately, the use of language is such an everyday activity that it tends to be almost invisible. ... In a nutshell, managers live in a rhetorical universe – a universe where language is constantly used not only to communicate but also to **persuade**, and even to **create**.*[12]

Other writers offer a similar perspective on this, notably Iain Mangham in his book *Power and Performance in Organizations*:

> *organizations are created, sustained and changed through **talk**. There is nothing good or bad in this world or any other but talking makes it so. Organizations ... are constituted by willful individuals **talking** to each other.*[13] *(emphasis added)*

We believe this applies to all projects as well: in essence, they are created, sustained and changed through people continually *talking* to each other in the ever-changing flux of events; in other words, as the diagram in Aspect 3 shows, much of the action of projects is actually *in* the social interaction itself.

Hence, words matter!

As an example of why words are so important, consider the following extract from John Humphrys' book *Lost for Words*:

Tony Blair listens to Gordon Brown's advice.

now add the word 'only'. There are several places it could sensibly fit. In each case the new sentence would produce a radically different meaning. It could mean Blair listens to Brown and does nothing or that he listens to nobody but Brown or that no one but Blair listens to Brown. One little word in the wrong place and you rewrite [until recently] the most important relationship in British politics.[14]

In other words, change the language and social reality changes with it.

The invisible use of metaphor

Not only is the use of language such an everyday activity that it tends to be invisible, so too is people's frequent use of metaphor. For example, how often do you hear people say: *"We're on track to deliver"* or *"We need to get things back on track"* or *"We need to get person x on board"*? Such phrases illustrate the frequent use of metaphor in the ongoing social process which leads us to our main point: in short, people's use of metaphor is clearly a useful tool of language, evidenced by the fact that so many people use it, but metaphors also distort, as well as illuminate. For instance, consider the image of 'rolling out' changes through a business change project: the metaphor of 'rolling out' changes, as in rolling out a carpet, could be wholly inappropriate if the changes are perceived to be problematical. Moreover, if the activities of the project actually reflect this image too, then the project is likely to be firmly resisted by those affected. As Gareth Morgan points out in *Images of Organization*:

> *any given metaphor can be incredibly persuasive ... [however] in creating ways of seeing and acting, metaphors tend to create ways of not seeing and acting.*[15]

This completes our discussion of the five example aspects and we return now to summarize the social image as a whole and its main strengths and limitations.

Image Summary

Having introduced five example aspects to consider from a social perspective, we turn now to this book's social image of projects which encapsulates these five related aspects. As stated previously, our aim is not to be prescriptive or all-encompassing, but rather to offer a practical image of projects that the practitioner can use in a variety of different situations. Indeed, like all the images in this book, this particular image can be applied in many different ways, ranging from the occasional use of the whole image or just selected aspects, through to using it in a structured process, or as part of a common language with which to see and talk about the complex realities of a project. These example uses are covered in Part 3 *Applying the Images* but for now it is important to briefly summarize the social image of projects.

Projects as social processes

In essence, the core image here is that of *projects as social processes*, by which we mean an ever-changing flux of events involving individuals, groups and organizations, all continually interacting and communicating, within webs of culture and tribalism, and all continually negotiating and renegotiating their realities through the slippery medium of language. As explained at the start of this chapter, of all the images covered in this book, this is the image which comes closest to describing the actual reality of any project. Moreover, all projects can be made sense of using this core image, at all levels and over all time periods, including the events of a 10-year project for example, or just the events of a 2-hour meeting. The main diagram opposite shows this core image with the lower diagram showing the five example aspects all interconnected to reflect the social reality of projects. Moreover, to show how this book's social image contrasts with the mainstream image of projects, the rest of this section briefly discusses an important question which relates to all projects.

Do projects actually exist?

In essence, the question here is about whether from a social perspective, projects actually exist 'out there' in the world, in the same way that plants and trees exist. Most people, if asked, would probably accept that observable phenomena such as plants and trees do exist separately from the observer, that is, they exist independently of human beings and do not depend on people for their actual existence. In the case of projects, however, the reality is very different, in that what is *observed* is much more strongly linked to the *observer*. In essence, projects are always what people *perceive* them to be, and no two people's perceptions are ever *exactly* the same. And nor are two people's experiences ever *exactly* the same either, simply because the experienced phenomena of projects is not like plants and trees, but more like a flowing river which is continually

Images of projects

Images ⟷ Seeing

Real-world example

NHS National Programme for IT (NPfIT)

Social image of projects

Context   Organizations involved, economic environment, national and international context and so on

Content   People involved, social networks, culture and tribalism, language and metaphor and so on

Social perspective

Process   ✕✕✕✕✕✕✕ Flux of events ✕✕✕✕✕✕✕→

Various individuals, groups and organizations all continually interacting and communicating in the ever-changing flux of events

illustrative only

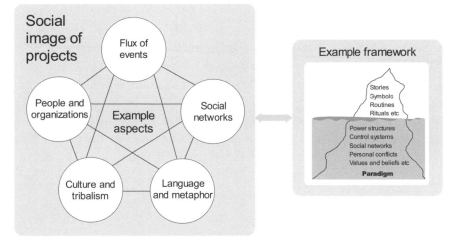

Figure 3.1   A social image of projects

changing and evolving through time. Indeed, for some practitioners, the image is more akin to the rapids, as Peter Vaill points out in his book *Managing as a Performing Art*:

> *a manager who attended a seminar I was conducting … supplied me with the metaphor of … "permanent white water". "Most managers are taught to think of themselves as paddling their canoes on calm, still lakes," he said. "They're led to believe that they should be pretty much able to go where they want, when they want, using means that are under their control. Sure there will be temporary disruptions during changes of various sorts – periods when they'll have to shoot the rapids in their canoes – but the disruptions will be temporary, and when things settle back down, they'll be back in the calm, still lake mode. But it has been my experience," he concluded, "that you never get out of the rapids! No sooner do you begin to digest one change than another one comes along to keep things unstuck. In fact, there are usually lots of changes going on at once. The feeling is one of continuous upset and chaos." … this manager suggested that we live in a world of* **permanent white water**[16] *(emphasis added).*

The image of permanent white water might seem rather extreme (or maybe not?), but the core image remains the same, namely that of a reality that is continually evolving through time and constantly changing. In the social world of people continually interacting, there is no single and separate reality 'out there', but rather everyone's own realities which are continually evolving and changing through time. As Peter Checkland elegantly points out in *Systems Thinking, Systems Practice*, social reality is:

> *the ever-changing outcome of the social process in which human beings, the product of their genetic inheritance and previous experiences, continually negotiate and re-negotiate with others their perceptions and interpretations of the world outside themselves.*[17]

From this standpoint then, experience suggests the actual reality of projects is always a complex social process in which people are continually negotiating and renegotiating their realities within an ever-changing flux of events. So, from this standpoint, the reality of projects is intrinsically processual like a flowing river and it is *this* reality that practitioners have to engage with in the complex world of projects. And of course the actual reality of projects is not just a social process, it is also a political process, which is why we turn next to the political image of projects. In summary, all of this suggests that the social reality of projects, and social reality in general, is fundamentally different to the physical reality of the natural world, something which Heraclitus, the Greek philosopher, pointed out over 2000 years ago, namely that *'you can't step into the same river twice'.*[18]

Strengths and Limitations

Strengths of the social perspective

1. Focuses attention on the actual reality of projects and programmes as opposed to the abstract stages of the traditional project lifecycle.

2. Invites one to consider the different people and organizations involved and how they perceive the project, programme or portfolio.

3. Directs attention to important aspects such as social networks, culture and tribalism, and the language and metaphor used by the people involved.

4. Highlights the importance of understanding recent events in the flux in order to understand the current situation of a project or programme.

5. Focuses attention on the dynamic aspects of projects and programmes, for example, the ongoing creation of projects through people talking together.

Limitations of the social perspective

1. Directs attention to the more everyday aspects of projects and programmes, rather than long-term aims and objectives.

2. Emphasizes the social process above individual processes, such as personal cognition and emotional intelligence.

3. Social and cultural aspects take time to understand and will always be understood differently by the different people involved.

4. This book's image is only a starting point for understanding social reality and could be enriched with further knowledge of social theory.

5. The actual reality of projects cannot be understood from a purely social perspective. It also requires a political perspective.

*[Images] create insight. But they also distort. They have strengths. But they also have limitations. In creating ways of seeing they tend to create ways of **not** seeing.*

Gareth Morgan

Man is by nature a political animal.

Aristotle

Chapter Four

Image 2:
Projects as Political Processes

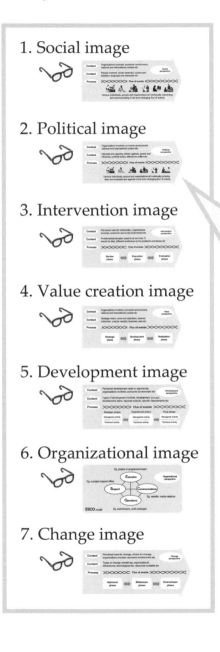

1. Social image

2. Political image

3. Intervention image

4. Value creation image

5. Development image

6. Organizational image

7. Change image

Political Perspective

Chapter Structure

Image Definition

Relevance and Importance

Five Example Aspects

Image Summary

Strengths and Limitations

Image Definition

The POLITICAL IMAGE is a framework for seeing projects as political processes, covering aspects such as the differing interests of the individuals, groups and organizations involved, hidden agenda, power and influence, political tactics and people's attitudes to politics.

Relevance and Importance

Just as all projects are inherently social because they involve people, they are also inherently political because of people's differing *interests and agenda*. As any experienced practitioner knows, all individuals, groups and organizations have their own interests in relation to projects, and it is this aspect more than any other which makes the political image so important. Indeed, the relevance of this image is easy to state, for in contrast to some of the other images in this book, which are less relevant to some projects, the political image is applicable to all projects. A good illustration of this is the UK Government's introduction of Home Information Packs (HIPs) in 2007, which was a highly political project involving many competing interests and agenda, as shown briefly below.

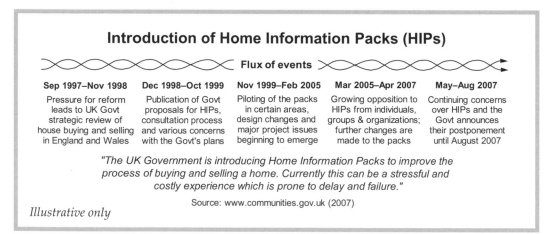

Notice above that we see the political aspects as being an integral part of the social process, simply because in reality the social and political aspects of projects are so inextricably linked. So, why two separate images you might say? Basically, although they are inextricably linked, the social and political aspects are sufficiently different to warrant their own consideration for analytical purposes, and hence separating them into two separate images is useful, as this chapter will show. However, when it comes to applying them in practice, both images are usually applied together to help make sense of any project or programme in a real situation.

Five Example Aspects

Applying this chapter's political image to the UK Government's HIPs project, the sorts of aspects that might be considered are:

- What are the differing *interests and agenda* of those involved in the initiative?
- What might be the *hidden agenda* of certain individuals, groups and organizations?
- Where does *power and influence* lie in relation to the Government's HIPs project?
- What *political tactics* have been used by those involved or interested in the project?
- What are the differing *attitudes to politics* displayed by the people involved?

These five questions and the words in italics illustrate the five example aspects to be considered in this chapter, which of course are not the only aspects that could be considered from a political perspective. However, since they apply to all projects, these are the aspects that we have chosen to focus on, as summarized below.

Aspect 1: Interests and Agenda

All projects and programmes involve multiple individuals, groups and organizations with differing interests and agenda, and it is this aspect more than any other, which creates the social and political context in which all practitioners have to operate.

Aspect 2: Hidden Agenda

Amongst the differing interests and agenda of the individuals, groups and organizations, will be hidden agenda perhaps, which are the real objectives and motivations for some of those involved, that are rarely, if ever, made explicit in real situations.

Aspect 3: Power and Influence

This aspect refers to the different sources of power and influence that are present in all situations. Example considerations could be: Who has the power and influence to make strategic decisions about the project? Who has power and influence to disrupt the project?

Aspect 4: Political Tactics

So far the image is that of multiple individuals and organizations all continually pursuing their own interests and agenda, with varying levels of power and influence. This aspect refers to the tactical behaviours and actions that people use to pursue their own interests.

Aspect 5: Attitudes to Politics

This final aspect refers to the differing attitudes to politics amongst the people involved. For example, what is their general stance to politics and how do they deal with politics? Do they see it as an unnecessary distraction or just a necessary feature of the flux?

As explained in the Introduction to Part 2, this section presents each of these five aspects over two pages, the left-hand page providing a real example (for example, the HIPs project) and the right-hand page offering some observations for the reader to reflect upon in relation to their own knowledge and experience. Beyond these five aspects, we then summarize the political image as a whole, and then briefly state some of the strengths and limitations of this second important perspective.

Example Aspect 1: Interests and Agenda

DEFINITION

> *All projects and programmes involve multiple individuals, groups and organizations with differing interests and agenda, and it is this aspect more than any other, which creates the social and political context in which all practitioners have to operate.*

REAL-WORLD EXAMPLE

What is the Home Information Pack?

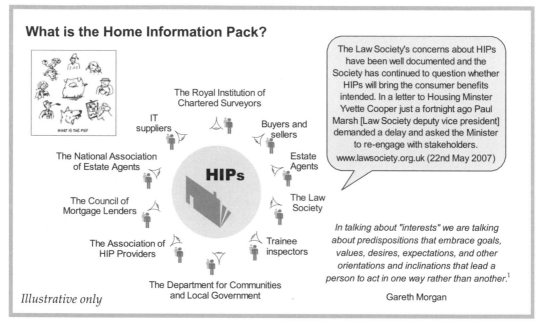

The Royal Institution of Chartered Surveyors

IT suppliers

Buyers and sellers

The National Association of Estate Agents

Estate Agents

HIPs

The Council of Mortgage Lenders

The Law Society

The Association of HIP Providers

Trainee inspectors

The Department for Communities and Local Government

Illustrative only

The Law Society's concerns about HIPs have been well documented and the Society has continued to question whether HIPs will bring the consumer benefits intended. In a letter to Housing Minster Yvette Cooper just a fortnight ago Paul Marsh [Law Society deputy vice president] demanded a delay and asked the Minister to re-engage with stakeholders.
www.lawsociety.org.uk (22nd May 2007)

In talking about "interests" we are talking about predispositions that embrace goals, values, desires, expectations, and other orientations and inclinations that lead a person to act in one way rather than another.[1]

Gareth Morgan

REFLECTIVE OBSERVATIONS

Differing interests and agenda

Just as all projects and programmes are inherently social because they involve people, they are also inherently political because of people's differing *interests and agenda*. In other words, all individuals, groups and organizations have their own interests in relation to projects and programmes, and it is this aspect more than any other which leads people to adopt certain views in situations and to act in particular ways – see the Law Society example above. In the case of the HIPs initiative, the interests are wide-ranging and all are entirely legitimate for the different people involved. Of course, one might not agree with the position of an individual, group or organization, but it is important to *recognize their entitlement to that position* and to understand why they adopt that position. For the Law Society, one of the purposes of a professional body is to serve the interests of its members and recognizing the legitimacy of this position is very important, but this does not mean trying to satisfy everyone in equal measure. As Jeff Pinto points out in his book *Power and Politics in Project Management*, a successful project manager is not someone who seeks to satisfy all the different parties, but rather one who negotiates with these different parties to try and maintain a balance between their needs and the overall needs of the project.[2]

Introducing the political image of projects

Although in reality the social and political aspects of projects are inextricably linked, it is useful for analytical purposes to focus separately on the political aspects, in the same way that we approached the social aspects in Chapter 3. And to do this, the same conceptual framework of *context/content/process* is used for the image here, but with the focus on the political aspects, as shown in the model below.

Political image of projects   political perspective

Context	Organizational context, social, economic and political environment, national context and so on
Content	Interests and agenda, hidden agenda, power and influence, political tactics, attitudes to politics
Process	Flux of events

Various individuals, groups and organizations all continually pursuing their own interests and agenda in the ever-changing flux of events

illustrative only

As the diagram shows, this book's political image is essentially that of individuals, groups and organizations all continually pursuing their own interests and agenda in the ever-changing flux of events. In more analytical terms, the *context* part refers to the general context of projects (for example, the organizational context), the *content* part refers to all the differing interests and agenda, and the tactics being used to pursue these, and finally, the *process* refers to the social process in which all the various interests are continually being pursued. Like the social image, this core image is not meant to be all-encompassing, but simply a starting point for making sense of the political reality of any project or programme.

Analyzing the differing interests

For the differing interests and agenda, two example models that might be used to help analyze these interests in real situations are shown below.

Tribal interests *(for example, property development)*   **Personal interests**

Principal interest	Cost	Quality	Value
Senior management	—	—	↑
Project management	↓	—	—
Client organization	—	↑	—

"The diagram illustrates the relationship and tension that often exist between one's job (task), career aspirations, and personal values and lifestyle (extramural interests)."

Task   Career

Extramural

Source: Images of Organization
by Gareth Morgan (2nd Edition), p.162.
Sage Publications. Reproduced with kind permission

The first model illustrates the possible *tribal interests* of several different practice groups in a property development project, and the right-hand model illustrates a way of thinking about the *personal interests* of those involved.[3] In short, no matter how much individuals, groups and organizations might collaborate and cooperate with each other, it is important to remain mindful of the differing interests and agenda that will always be present in real situations. Moreover, some of these interests are not always declared, as we now show.

Example Aspect 2: Hidden Agenda

DEFINITION

> *Amongst the differing interests and agenda of the individuals, groups and organizations, will be hidden agenda perhaps, which are the real objectives and motivations for some of those involved, that are rarely, if ever, made explicit in real situations.*

REAL-WORLD EXAMPLE

Bidding for Construction Contracts

The Guardian Newspaper, April 18th 2008

"More than a hundred British construction companies are facing the threat of heavy fines after the Office for Fair Trading accused them of rigging bids. In one of the competition watchdog's biggest investigations, the OFT probed thousands of tenders for construction work worth some £3bn covering schools, hospitals and private-sector developments ... The OFT said it had received 37 applications for leniency and another 40 companies had subsequently admitted some bid-rigging in exchange for a reduced fine. .... The OFT said much of the bid-rigging resulted from the practice known as cover-pricing, in which companies colluded with competitors to ensure their bids were too high to win the work." Mark Milner, Industrial Editor

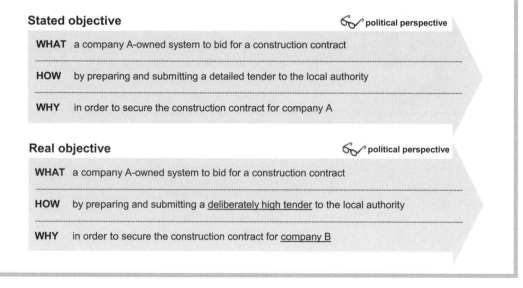

Stated objective   👓 **political perspective**

WHAT   a company A-owned system to bid for a construction contract

HOW   by preparing and submitting a detailed tender to the local authority

WHY   in order to secure the construction contract for company A

Real objective   👓 **political perspective**

WHAT   a company A-owned system to bid for a construction contract

HOW   by preparing and submitting a <u>deliberately high tender</u> to the local authority

WHY   in order to secure the construction contract for <u>company B</u>

REFLECTIVE OBSERVATIONS

Fraud and collusion in the world of projects

For many experienced practitioners, the example above will be of no surprise since fraud and collusion is not unusual in the world of projects. Indeed, recent research shows that it is more widespread than many people think and an example of this is given on the next page. Before we cover this, notice the difference between the two models in the example: the first one shows the *apparent* objective of company A in bidding for the contract, and the second one shows the *real* objective in bidding for the contract; the core purpose was not to secure the work for company A but to secure the work for company B, with both companies A and B forming a cartel of firms engaged in anti-competitive activity. Notice too, of course, the hidden agenda of company A would not be so obvious in a real situation, which is why 'reading' the politics of any situation is so important, especially the aspect of hidden agenda. Also, even if there is no collusion in a situation, there is still the possibility of a project or programme being a fraudulent activity. For example, a university research project funded by one of the research councils to achieve some approved objectives could find itself unable to achieve its objectives because its industry partners are no longer able to participate; and yet the project might continue because it serves the interests of the academics involved. In this situation, there is no collusion, but there is now a serious question about the *legitimacy* of this project, since the funding body is now, in effect, funding a research project that has not been formally approved. As Charles Smith points out in *Making Sense of Project Realities*:

> *a fraud has occurred when something is not what it purports to be.... frauds can arise and do so without the prelude of collusion. Experience shows that well-meaning honest and competent groups of people will, between them, create projects that are fraudulent.*[4]

More serious examples of fraudulent projects

We said earlier that recent research shows the widespread presence of hidden agenda, and a good example of this is Bent Flyvbjerg's book *Megaprojects and Risk*. According to the publisher, this book:

> *provides the first detailed examination of the phenomenon of megaprojects. It is a fascinating account of how the promoters of multibillion-dollar megaprojects systematically and self-servingly misinform parliaments, the public and the media in order to get projects approved and built. It shows, in unusual depth, that the Machiavellian formula for approval is:*

> ***underestimated costs + overestimated revenues + undervalued environmental impacts + overvalued economic development effects = PROJECT APPROVAL***[5]

Whether one sees this as a cynical conclusion or not, Flyvbjerg's book provides an important insight into the social and political realities of so-called megaprojects.

Looking for hidden agenda

A useful analogy when looking for hidden agenda is the iceberg metaphor introduced in Chapter 3. As explained in Aspect 4 of Chapter 3, just as certain things 'above' the line provide clues to aspects 'below' the line, the same analogy applies here; in short, people's words and actions 'above' the line usually provide clues as to their real objectives and motivations 'below' the line. The analogy helps because it shows that we can never know with absolute certainty what is in people's heads, but we can *surmise* what their real intentions and motivations might be, from what they *say* and *do* in real situations.

In addition to probing the overt goals and concerns of various stakeholders, project managers must look for hidden agendas.[6]

Jeffrey Pinto

Example Aspect 3: Power and Influence

DEFINITION

This aspect refers to the different sources of power and influence that are present in all situations. Example considerations could be: Who has the power and influence to make strategic decisions about the project? Who has power and influence to disrupt the project?

REAL-WORLD EXAMPLE

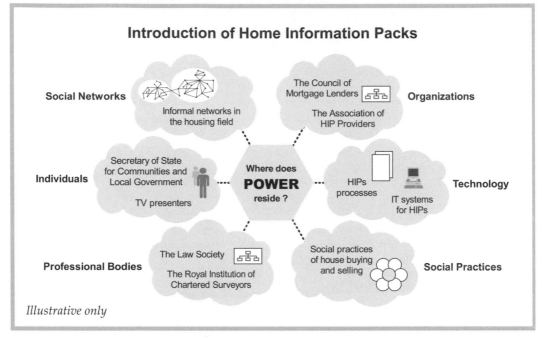

REFLECTIVE OBSERVATIONS

Power resides not just in individuals and organizations

As well as looking for hidden agenda, another important aspect to focus on from a political perspective is *power and influence:* for example, who has the power and influence to make strategic decisions about a project? Or alternatively, who has the power and influence to stop things from happening? Or if not to stop things, who has the power and influence to disrupt the project? And it's not just individuals who have power and influence either, as our HIPs example above shows; power also resides in organizations, the professional bodies, the informal social networks that operate within the housing field, and the less visible social practices of house buying and selling that have evolved over time. Interestingly, such practices are not 'owned' by anyone or any organization, and yet they exert considerable influence over the affairs of house buying and selling. Another example is the idea of an IT project which still exerts considerable influence over many IT-related projects. In summary, the principal message here is that power resides not just in individuals and organizations, but also in less visible elements such as social networks and social practices that continually evolve through time.

No easy way of defining power and influence

Whilst it might be easy to identify the different sources of power and influence in real situations, it is much less easy to define what the actual power and influence really is. As Gareth Morgan points out in *Images of Organization:*

> *in recent years, organizational and management theories have become increasingly aware of the need to recognise the importance of power in explaining organizational affairs. However, no really clear and consistent definition of power has emerged. While some view power as a resource (i.e., as something one possesses), others view it as a social relation characterised by some kind of dependency (i.e., as an influence over something or someone).*[7]

In short, different authors define power and influence in different ways, and therefore the actual reality can always be understood in different ways, depending on the constructs people use and the people using them. That said, however, there are some useful concepts and models available to the practitioner and some examples of these are given below.

Power and influence: example concepts

Starting first with Jeff Pinto's book *Power and Politics in Project Management*, he suggests that 'power' transcends situations and relationships, whereas 'influence' is more situation-specific and usually face-to-face. Also, as Pinto suggests, whereas power can be seen as the *authority* to get others to do things, influence can be seen as the *ability* to get others to do things when there is no significant power difference between them. This is a helpful distinction in a sense, but as Pinto points out, power and influence are also inextricably linked in different ways, and a useful framework which shows this is the one below from Barbara Senior's book *Organisational Change.*[8]

Power and Influence

Power as a source of influence

The possible sources of individual power which give one the ability to influence others are:

- *Physical power:* the power of superior force.

- *Resource power:* the possession of valued resources; the control of rewards.

- *Position power:* legitimate power; comes as a result of the role of or position held in the organization.

- *Expert power:* vested in someone because of their acknowledged expertise.

- *Personal power:* charisma, popularity; resides in the person and in their personality.

- *Negative power:* illegitimate power; the ability to disrupt or stop things happening.

Methods of influence

Different types of power are used in different kinds of ways. ... Some methods of influence draw on two or more sources of power:

- *Force:* derived from having physical power; physical bullying, hold-ups, loss of temper.

- *Rules and procedures:* derived from having position power, backed by resource power; devising rules and procedures to result in particular outcomes.

- *Exchange:* derived from having resource power; bargaining, negotiating, bribing.

- *Persuasion:* derived from having personal power; use of logic, the power of argument, evidence of facts.

- Magnetism: derives from personal and sometimes expert power; inspiring trust, respect, using charm, infectious enthusiasm.

Based on C.Handy (1993) Understanding Organizations
Source: Organisational Change *by Barbara Senior, 2nd Ed. (2002). FT Prentice Hall. Reproduced with kind permission*

In summary, frameworks such as the one above provide useful prompts for thinking about the power and influence aspects in real situations, and not only this, they also highlight the importance of political tactics, which is the next aspect we now consider.

Example Aspect 4: Political Tactics

DEFINITION

So far the image is that of multiple individuals and organizations all continually pursuing their own interests and agenda, with varying levels of power and influence. This aspect refers to the tactical behaviours and actions that people use to pursue their interests.

REAL-WORLD EXAMPLE

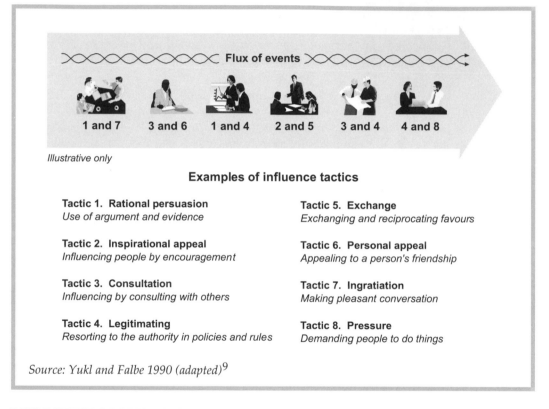

Flux of events

| 1 and 7 | 3 and 6 | 1 and 4 | 2 and 5 | 3 and 4 | 4 and 8 |

Illustrative only

Examples of influence tactics

Tactic 1. Rational persuasion
Use of argument and evidence

Tactic 2. Inspirational appeal
Influencing people by encouragement

Tactic 3. Consultation
Influencing by consulting with others

Tactic 4. Legitimating
Resorting to the authority in policies and rules

Tactic 5. Exchange
Exchanging and reciprocating favours

Tactic 6. Personal appeal
Appealing to a person's friendship

Tactic 7. Ingratiation
Making pleasant conversation

Tactic 8. Pressure
Demanding people to do things

Source: Yukl and Falbe 1990 (adapted)[9]

REFLECTIVE OBSERVATIONS

The use of political tactics

As the example above shows, by political tactics we mean the behaviours and actions that people continually use to further their own interests in the ever-changing flux of events. And this aspect, more than any other, is why projects and programmes need to be seen as political processes unfolding through time. Moreover, although we present these tactics as another example aspect, such tactics can only really be understood in relation to the differing interests and agenda of the people involved, their differing amounts of power and influence, and another aspect not yet considered, namely people's differing attitudes to politics. For example, as the next aspect will show, a person's attitude to politics can have a significant influence on how they behave in real situations and what tactics they use to pursue or protect their own interests.

Influence tactics

One set of tactics that people use in all situations is *influence tactics,* which as the examples opposite show, can range from rational persuasion at one end (for example, the use of argument and evidence) to blatant pressure at the other (for example, people demanding or threatening others to do things). In most project environments, research suggests that rational persuasion, inspirational appeal and consultation have the most positive effect on task commitment, whilst pressure, coalition and legitimating are usually less effective. Even so, how does one decide which tactics to use in different situations? According to Jeff Pinto in his book *Power and Politics in Project Management,* good influencers are situation-specific, in that they always tailor their approach and do not rely on just one particular method. He also points out that good influencers do not misuse or over use their abilities, and constantly remain sensitive to the needs and views of others.

Other examples of political tactics

As well as influence tactics, it is useful to be aware of other political tactics used by individuals, groups and organizations. As Jeff Pinto points out 'forewarned is forearmed', meaning that practitioners need to be aware of these tactics in order to become skilled in 'reading' the political tactics being used by individuals, groups and organizations in the pursuit of their own interests. And a useful framework for this is the one shown below, provided by Frederick Harrison in his book *Advanced Project Management.*[10]

Political Tactics

1. Gaining support from higher power sources
Examples: sponsorship, lobbying, co-optation

2. Alliance or coalition-building (close peers)
Examples: exchange of favours (IOU), bargains, bribery, establishing a common cause

3. Controlling a critical resource
Examples: money, people, expertise, reporting, centrality or gatekeeping, information

4. Controlling the decision process
Examples: control of decision criteria, control of the alternatives, control of information

5. Controlling the committee process
Examples: agenda content, agenda sequence, membership, minutes, chairmanship, calling of meetings, pre-agenda work

6. Use of positional authority
Examples: rewards, coercion

7. Use of the scientific element
Examples: planning, control

8. Deceit and deception
Examples: secrecy, surprise, hidden objectives, hidden agendas, two faces, all things to all people

9. Information
Examples: censoring or withholding, distorting

10. Miscellaneous games
Examples: divide and rule, whistle-blowing, in the same life boat, red herring game

Source: Advanced Project Management, *4th Ed, F.Harrison and D.Lock, Gower Publishing. (slightly adapted)*
Reproduced with kind permission

Whilst this is not the only framework available to practitioners, it is doubly useful because it provides not only a prompt for 'reading' the political tactics of individuals, groups, and organizations, but also a prompt for thinking about one's own political tactics. However, this does not mean that we are recommending all of the tactics shown!

Example Aspect 5: Attitudes to Politics

DEFINITION

This final aspect refers to the differing attitudes to politics amongst the people involved. For example, what is their general stance to politics and how do they deal with politics? Do they see it as an unnecessary distraction or just a necessary feature of the flux?

REAL-WORLD EXAMPLE

THE PROBLEM

"How can I be more political and still be myself?"

"I've been in the workplace for 20 years and my annual appraisals suggest that I am ambitious, hard-working and a team player. However, I have recently missed out on two promotions and been told I am not "politically astute" enough. I don't think of myself as political, and would like to know how to become so in a way that allows me to sit comfortably in my own skin."

Manager, male, 42

LUCY KELLAWAY: THE ANSWER

"Of course you can: political skills aren't bad; they are essential to getting anything done. Everything that happens in [organizations] is political. Being good at it doesn't mean you have to become a back-stabbing snake. It means being effective: reading which way things are going, and good at getting what you want. In some companies back-stabbing is helpful, but then the fault isn't political but cultural. I expect you are good at some "political" things or else you wouldn't have held down a job at all."

Source: *Financial Times*, 27th September 2006

REFLECTIVE OBSERVATIONS

Worldview 1: Politics as an unnecessary distraction

Focusing on the manager's words above, what they suggest is an attitude towards politics as something of an unnecessary distraction. Indeed, practitioners often remark how much more could be achieved if it weren't for the frequent distractions of organizational politics. For example, a survey carried out in 1997 by David Buchanan and Richard Badham found that people's attitude to politics was that it was a distracting side-issue compared with the issue of organizational performance. And not only this, many of the survey respondents also thought that organizational politics was actually damaging to the organization and should be eradicated wherever possible. In writing about this in her book *Organizational Change*, Barbara Senior suggests that:

> *most managers would like to manage without the need to resort to political behaviour yet acknowledge the reality of it particularly in the context of organizational change.*[11]

Indeed, for some people, the word 'politics' is a dirty word, as Gareth Morgan points out:

> *most people working in an organization readily admit in private that they are surrounded by forms of "wheeling and dealing" through which different people attempt to advance specific interests. However, this kind of activity is rarely discussed in public…. Politics, in short, is seen as a dirty word.*[12]

So this is it: politics is an unnecessary distraction which gets in the way of the real work within organizations? Or is it? Another perspective is to think of politics as being an integral part of the social process, and far from being a distraction, it is the process through which *all* work is accomplished in organizations.

Worldview 2: Politics as a necessary part of the social process

To explain this further, since no two people see the world exactly the same way and never have exactly the same interests, there will always be situations in which differences and tensions arise. As Gareth Morgan points out: *'Organizational politics arise when people think differently and want to act differently when confronted with alternative paths of action. This diversity creates a tension that must be resolved through political means.'*[13] In short, **politics** is all about how this tension is resolved, and as Morgan points out, there are many different approaches to this:

- an autocratic approach, for example, *"we'll do it this way"*
- a bureaucratic approach, for example, *"we're supposed to do it this way"*
- a technocratic approach, for example, *"it's best to do it this way"*
- a democratic approach, for example, *"how shall we do it?"*

In each case, the chosen path will depend on people's differing interests and agenda, and the power relations between people in different situations. And whether the practitioner likes it or not, this is the reality in *all* organizations, and how they deal with the politics of situations depends on their attitude to politics, as we now explain.

Differing attitudes to politics

In making sense of the example opposite, we turn again to Jeff Pinto's book *Power and Politics in Project Management* which provides a helpful framework for reflecting on people's differing attitude to politics, as shown in the table below.

Attitude	Naive	Sensible	Shark
"Politics is …"	Unpleasant	Necessary	An opportunity
Intent	Avoid at all costs	Pursuit of legitimate ends	Self-serving and predatory
Techniques	Tell it like it is	Networking	Manipulation
Tactics	Truth will win out	Negotiation	Bullying, use of friends

Adapted from Pinto 1996 (reference 2)

The implication of this table is clear and might have helped the manager opposite in his own reflections about the political realities of working in organizations. As Pinto suggests, the implication is simply this:

use politics or risk being used by politics.[14]

Image Summary

Having introduced five example aspects to consider from a political perspective, we turn now to this book's political image which encapsulates these five related aspects. As stated previously, our aim is not to be prescriptive or all-encompassing, but rather to offer a practical image of projects that the practitioner can use in a variety of different situations. Indeed, like all the images in this book, this particular image can be applied in many different ways, ranging from the occasional use of the whole image or just selected aspects, through to using it in a structured process, or as part of a common language with which to see and talk about the complex realities of a project or programme. These example uses are covered in Part 3 *Applying the Images* but for now it is important to briefly summarize the political image of projects.

Projects as political processes

In essence, the image here is that of *projects as political processes,* by which we mean individuals, groups and organizations all continually pursuing their own interests and agenda in the ever-changing flux of events. This aspect, more than any other, is what makes all projects political, and what makes them even more political is the existence of hidden agenda as explained in Aspect 2. Another important aspect of this book's political image is the complex phenomenon of power and influence, which is not limited to the power of individuals, groups and organizations. As explained in Aspect 3, less visible phenomena such as concepts and practices can also exert strong power and influence over projects, for example, the concept of IT projects as explained in Chapter 1. Finally, two other important aspects to consider are the political tactics used by individuals, groups and organizations in pursuit of their own objectives, and people's differing attitudes to politics, as shown in Aspects 4 and 5. Taken together, these five aspects constitute this book's political image of projects as shown in the diagram opposite.

Now contrast this political image with the mainstream image of projects, which as Charles Smith points out in *Making Sense of Project Realities,* is typically presented as '*a collective endeavour to achieve a specific objective, through a set of well-defined tasks, by a specified date and within a specified budget.'* He also goes on to state that '*the absurdity of this definition is that no such entity ever existed. Humans do not behave like this. If endeavours are collective, then they involve several parties whose objectives will be diverse and not specific'.*[15] Although the mainstream image is clearly deficient in the way Charles Smith points out, the central problem with the textbook image is not so much that it is apolitical, but the fact that so many textbooks continue to present it as if it were a description of the actual reality. As this book shows, the actual reality of projects is much more complex than any one particular image, which is why we advocate the use of multiple images, rather than approaching everything from the standpoint of one particular perspective.

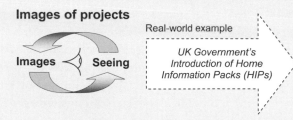

Social image of projects 👓
Political image of projects 👓
Intervention image of projects 👓
Value creation image of projects 👓
Development image of projects 👓
Organizational image of projects 👓
Change image of projects 👓

Images of projects

Images ⟨ ⟩ Seeing

Real-world example

UK Government's Introduction of Home Information Packs (HIPs)

Political image of projects

Context   Organizations involved, economic environment, national and international context etc

Content   Interests and agenda, hidden agenda, power and influence, political tactics, attitudes to politics etc

👓 **Political perspective**

Process   ✕✕✕✕✕✕ Flux of events ✕✕✕✕✕✕✕✕→

Various individuals, groups and organizations all continually pursuing their own interests and agenda in the ever-changing flux of events

illustrative only

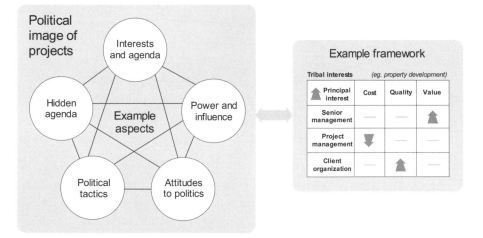

Political image of projects

Interests and agenda

Hidden agenda

Power and influence

Example aspects

Political tactics

Attitudes to politics

Example framework

Tribal interests	*(eg. property development)*		
▲ Principal interest	Cost	Quality	Value
Senior management	—	—	▲
Project management	▼	—	—
Client organization	—	▲	—

Figure 4.1   A political image of projects

Returning then to the political image shown in Figure 4.1, other ideas can of course be used, including the practitioner's own ideas and imagery from real experience. In a sense, it matters less what image or model is used and more the craft of continually 'reading' the political aspects in real situations. That said, however, it is impossible to 'read' these aspects without some kind of interpretive frame, which is why we offer a practical image of five generic aspects that can be applied to any project or programme. Notice also these five generic aspects are inextricably linked as shown by the five linked circles in Figure 4.1; for example, the political tactics of an individual or group cannot be 'read' without also considering their interests and underlying attitude to politics. Not only this, they are also inextricably linked to the social aspects in Chapter 2, which is why there is no method or technique here, in that all the social aspects can be analyzed first, and then all the political aspects; if only working on projects were that simple! In summary, the challenge for the practitioner is to try and understand the relationships between the various aspects, as much as the aspects themselves, since in reality they are all inextricably linked in different ways in different situations.

'Reading' the politics of situations

To end this chapter, it is important to say a few words about 'reading' the politics of situations, because this is a subject rarely covered in the mainstream literature on project management. Imagine finding out that someone you know has moved to another position within an organization and you are curious to know why this has happened; in short, it is impossible to know with *absolute certainty* why that person has moved. Of course, one could ask the person concerned, or perhaps some other people in the organization, but the reality is that we can never get inside people's heads. In other words, the actions of individuals are never fully transparent in organizational situations, which is why 'reading' the politics of situations is a very important craft skill. As Peter Checkland points out in one of his books:

> *politics is ultimately concerned with power and its disposition, issues not usually faced overtly in human dialogue. There is a natural reluctance to be blunt about the oddities of power, and there is a sense in which the real politics of a situation, not publicly acknowledged, will always retreat to a tacit level beyond whatever is the explicit level of analysis.*[16]

So what is it that guides practitioners in 'reading' the politics of situations? The short answer of course is knowledge and experience gained from previous projects and other life experience. However, relying solely on experience is not always the best guide, which is why we offer the political image shown in Figure 4.1 for use with the practitioner's own knowledge and experience. And of all the images in this book, this particular image is often the most important one of all.

Strengths and Limitations

Strengths of the political perspective

1. Encourages one to see how *all* project activity is interest based and to accept that organizational politics is an inevitable feature of projects.

2. Highlights the apolitical nature of the traditional textbook image of projects and debunks the myth of project rationality.

3. Emphasizes that project objectives may be rational but they are always linked to particular interests. Rationality is always political.

4. Directs attention to the power and influence aspects which continually influence the ever-changing flux of events in all projects and programmes.

5. Focuses attention on one's own attitude to politics and how one deals with the politics of situations in project environments.

Limitations of the political perspective

1. Can sometimes lead to over politicization of projects encouraging people to see politics everywhere in project environments.

2. Can sometimes lead people to look for hidden agenda even where there are none, which in turn can generate cynicism and mistrust.

3. Can sometimes cause people to 'misread' other people's intentions and motivations, thereby generating further mistrust and cynicism.

4. Excessive use of the political image can also generate further political behaviours and actions which can be very counter productive.

5. The political aspects of projects cannot be understood solely from a political perspective. They also require a social perspective.

*[Images] create insight. But they also distort. They have strengths. But they also have limitations. In creating ways of seeing they tend to create ways of **not** seeing.*

Gareth Morgan

Think 'problem situation' not 'problem'.
Peter Checkland

Chapter Five

Image 3:
Projects as Intervention Processes

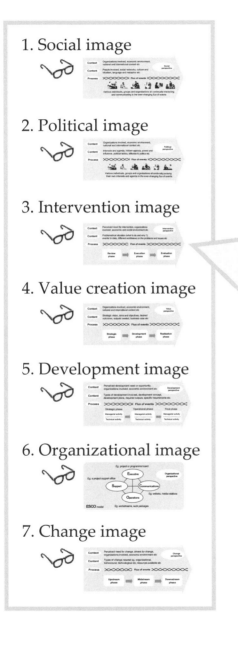

1. Social image

2. Political image

3. Intervention image

4. Value creation image

5. Development image

6. Organizational image

7. Change image

Intervention
Perspective

Chapter Structure

Image Definition

Relevance and Importance

Five Example Aspects

Image Summary

Strengths and Limitations

Image Definition

The INTERVENTION IMAGE is a framework for seeing projects as intervention processes, covering aspects such as the perceived situation to be improved, the type of intervention and the different phases of an intervention from an initial review phase through to an evaluation phase.

Relevance and Importance

Experience shows that whilst a project might deliver something to specification, cost and time, it can actually fail to deliver any significant improvement to the situation in which the project was carried out. And herein lies the root of another way of seeing projects which is essentially this: instead of seeing a project as delivering something to specification cost and time, the image here is essentially about seeing a project as *an intervention to improve a problematical situation.* Consider the example below.

A New Deal for Braunstone

A New Deal for Braunstone is a £49.5 million Government scheme to regenerate the Braunstone area in Leicester. The scheme is being managed by Braunstone Community Association and aims to improve the quality of life for local residents through many different kinds of projects with direct and active involvement of local people.

Source: www.braunstone.com

As the example shows, the primary task is not about construction or renovation, but rather that of improving the quality of life for local residents; in other words, the whole scheme is essentially an *intervention* aimed at community improvement. And not only is this a broader image than that of constructing or producing something, the intervention image is highly applicable in many situations. For example, imagine a situation in which action is needed, but what to do is unclear: from an intervention perspective, a useful approach could be to review the situation first to identify *what* improvements are needed and *why*, before then deciding on *how* the improvements should be implemented, for example, through one project or a programme of projects; in other words, think 'intervention' first, before 'project'. In summary, whatever approach is taken, the primary task is about improving a perceived problematical situation, rather than producing something to specification, cost and time.

Five Example Aspects

Applying the intervention image to the Braunstone example, the sorts of aspects that might be considered are:

- What are the local residents' views on the *problematical situation* in Braunstone?
- What *type of intervention* is the Braunstone scheme? E.g., will it change the situation?
- What has been the approach so far to the *review phase* of the intervention?
- How should the *execution phase* be organized? E.g., what projects need to be done?
- What plans are there for the *evaluation phase?* E.g., how will this part be done?

These five questions and the words in italics illustrate the five example aspects to be considered in this chapter, which of course are not the only aspects that could be considered from an intervention perspective. However, since they apply to most interventions, these are the aspects that we have chosen to focus on as shown below.

Aspect 1: Problematical Situation

A problematical situation is a perceived real-world situation in which there are differing views about what the problems and issues are, and little or no agreement amongst the people involved about the action needed to improve the situation.

Aspect 2: Type of Intervention

Interventions differ according to their complexity and scope. Examples are review-only type interventions which usually result in a set of proposals or recommendations, or complete interventions which actually change the problematical situation.

Aspect 3: Review Phase

The review phase of an intervention refers to the front-end of an intervention covering activities such as situation analysis, problem structuring, objectives setting and designing an appropriate intellectual framework to guide the intervention.

Aspect 4: Execution Phase

The execution phase of an intervention is the main phase of activity and depends on the type of intervention being carried out. Example activities could be service development, process improvement, organizational development and professional development.

Aspect 5: Evaluation Phase

The evaluation phase of an intervention is about assessing the effectiveness of an intervention. For example, how effective was the project or programme in relation to the original objectives? Has the original situation been improved?

As explained in the Introduction to Part 2, this section presents each of these five aspects over two pages, the left-hand page providing a real example (for example, the Braunstone scheme) and the right-hand page offering some observations for the reader to reflect upon in relation to their own knowledge and experience. Beyond these five aspects, we then summarize the intervention image as a whole, and briefly state some of the strengths and limitations of this important perspective.

Example Aspect 1: Problematical Situation

DEFINITION

> *A problematical situation is a perceived real-world situation in which there are differing views about what the problems and issues are, and little or no agreement amongst the people involved about the action needed to improve the situation.*

REAL-WORLD EXAMPLE (see page 50 for the background to this situation)

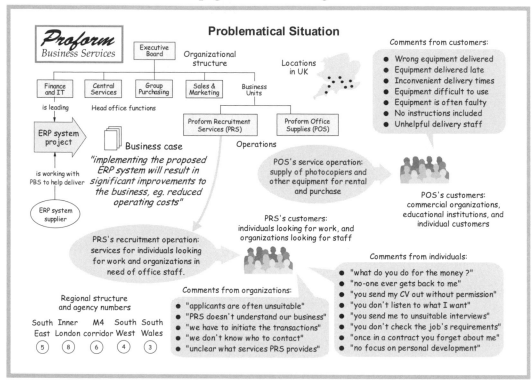

REFLECTIVE OBSERVATIONS

A problematical situation: is the ERP project the right project to be doing?

Imagine a situation in which someone has just been appointed to manage the ERP system project shown in the picture above. In short, the company is just about to embark on a major implementation of a new ERP system aimed at integrating the different parts of the business. As the picture shows, the project's business case claims the system will deliver major improvements to the business, notably reduced operating costs. Now imagine that the newly-appointed project manager soon finds the situation is not as straightforward as first presented. After meeting various people from the business and hearing about the problems in both PRS and POS, the project manager's impression is now of a much more complex situation. As the picture shows, the problems extend far beyond IT, and the project manager is now seriously concerned about whether the project should go ahead: in short, is it the right project to be doing in this situation?

Experienced practitioners will recognize this kind of situation which is not uncommon in projects and programmes involving IT, particularly at the front-end where there are often differing views about what the issues and priorities are, and what the way forward should be. Basically, what the example highlights is a serious mismatch between a project that is about to go ahead and the situation in which the project is being carried out; of course, it might still be desirable for an intervention to take place, but not in the way the project is currently framed. Looking at the situation opposite, there is clearly a need for action, but from this perspective, whether this involves one project or a programme of projects for example, is not something that is immediately knowable at the start, or even important for that matter. In summary, it is not the need to intervene that is in question here, but the current framing of the project, and hence in this kind of situation the intervention perspective becomes highly appropriate.

In messy front-end situations, think 'intervention' before 'project'

In many situations, it is often the case that insufficient thought is given to projects and programmes at the start, and hence people often find themselves in situations not unlike our example opposite. Usually, there are signs as to why certain projects and programmes are messy at the start, including the politics of the situation, and the fact that people often inherit ideas and plans that have already been approved. In other words, situations at the front-end can be messy in a number of respects, and it is in *these* situations that it is useful to think 'intervention' first, before 'project' or 'programme'.

In *Images* terms, this means seeing the work as an *intervention to improve a situation*, rather than a *project to achieve an objective*, which in the case of the example opposite, would mean an intervention to improve the company's situation, rather than a project to implement a new IT system. For a visual summary of these two images, see below.

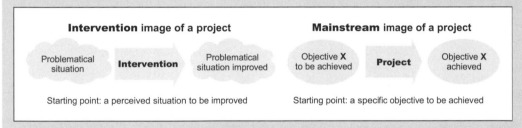

Applying the intervention image in problematical situations

In the case of the example opposite, it may be desirable for the ERP project to go ahead, but the message from an intervention perspective, based on the image above, is that the company really needs to review the situation first, before launching into what could be a very costly project. In other words, simply implementing a new IT system, no matter how sophisticated its functionality might be, will not address many of the company's current problems, as shown in the picture opposite. Indeed, in other situations, an IT-related project might not be the right project at all, where instead a completely different kind of intervention could be needed to improve the situation.

In summary, problematical situations at the start of projects call for a different approach to the standard textbook approach to projects, and in this chapter we approach them through the lens of an intervention, rather than through the mainstream image of projects. Also, experience shows that when the intervention image is applied in practice, it can often lead to the question: Is project X or programme Y the right thing to be doing?

Example Aspect 2: Type of Intervention

DEFINITION

Interventions differ according to their complexity and scope. Examples are review-only type interventions which usually result in a set of proposals or recommendations, or complete interventions which actually change the problematical situation.

REAL-WORLD EXAMPLES

Example 1 A New Deal for Braunstone   *Source: www.branstone.com*

'A New Deal for Braunstone' is a £49.5 million Government scheme to regenerate the Braunstone area in Leicester. The scheme is being managed by Braunstone Community Association and aims to improve the quality of life for local residents through many different kinds of projects with direct and active involvement of local people.

Example 2 What future for childhood?   *Source: The Guardian Newspaper, October 2006*

In 2006 the first comprehensive review of primary education in 40 years was launched. Led by Professor Robin Alexander of Cambridge University, the review is looking at childhood and child development, education's role in society and the education system itself. In short, it is asking the fundamental question: What is primary education for?

Example 3 Major IT-related project

A major IT-related project was started in 1997 to implement a new ERP system. The first phase was seen as a failure by the business with only 10 per cent of the work being completed in the first 18 months, and a substantial proportion of the budget had been used up. Action was clearly needed but what to do was unclear.

Example 4 Six sigma project

In 2004 a manufacturing company was experiencing problems with product quality and service delivery. In response to this, a business improvement project was carried out to review and improve the situation aided by the six sigma process of define, measure, analyze, improve and control. As a result, significant improvements have been made.

REFLECTIVE OBSERVATIONS

Seeing projects, programmes and other initiatives as interventions

As these examples show, there are many projects, programmes and other initiatives to which the intervention image can be applied. Although the people involved might not see them as interventions, all four examples are essentially concerned with improving a problematical situation through some kind of intervention. In other words, from an intervention perspective, the primary task is not about *constructing or producing something*, but rather that of *trying to improve a messy problematical situation*. That said, these two perspectives are complementary of course in that the concept of improving a situation is just a broader concept than that of constructing or producing something, which is why the intervention perspective is highly applicable in many situations. For example, imagine a situation in which action is needed but what to do is unclear: from an intervention perspective, a useful approach could be to review the situation first to identify *what* improvements are needed and *why*, before deciding on *how* the improvements should be implemented, for example, whether the intervention should involve one project, or a programme of projects for example. Furthermore, such a review could also be organized as a project in itself, or as the first stage perhaps in a whole programme of activity aimed at improving the situation being reviewed. In summary, whatever approach is taken, the mindset in applying the intervention image is always that of trying to improve a messy problematical situation, rather than producing or constructing something.

Different types of intervention

Looking at the examples opposite, it is useful to distinguish between two key elements: firstly, the *complexity* of the situation to be improved (for example, large-scale vs small-scale), and secondly, the *scope* of the work involved, by which we mean whether the intervention will actually change the situation, or whether it will only contribute towards improving it. With regard to the complexity aspect, there is not the space here to discuss this topic in any detail, suffice to say that the situation facing the independent review of primary education is far more complex than the two situations in examples 3 and 4. And similarly with the scope aspect, examples 1 and 4 are clearly different to examples 2 and 3, in how far they will actually change the situation. As the model opposite shows, there are *partial* interventions which tend to be review-only type interventions, as in examples 2 and 3, and there are *complete* interventions which seek to actually change the situation itself, as in examples 1 and 4.

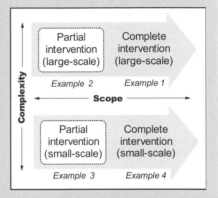

The lifecycle of an intervention compared to the lifecycle of a project

To understand the four types of intervention shown above, consider the diagram below.

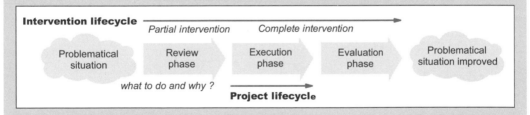

As the diagram shows, the lifecycle of an intervention is much broader than the traditional project lifecycle: firstly, it starts much earlier with a messy problematical situation, rather than an objective or goal to be achieved; and secondly, it ends much later at the point when (hopefully) the situation has been improved and evaluated, as opposed to when something has been produced and delivered, which is the traditional end-point of projects.

In summary, whilst the actual reality of intervening in situations is much more complex than the model above, the key point to note here is that this is a different way of seeing projects to the standard textbook view of projects. And not only this, the implications for action are different as the next three example aspects seek to show.

Example Aspect 3: Review Phase

DEFINITION

The review phase of an intervention refers to the front-end of an intervention covering activities such as situation analysis, problem structuring, objectives setting and designing an appropriate intellectual framework to guide the intervention.

REAL-WORLD EXAMPLE

Business Consultancy Project

In 2001 the lead author was asked to supervise a postgraduate consultancy project in a manufacturing company that produces specialist plastics products for the car industry. The objective of this apparently straightforward project was to determine a new system for improving communication between two of the company's manufacturing sites. Upon visiting the first site, it was found that no one knew anything about the project and nor was communication between the two sites seen to be an issue. Similarly at the second site, communication was not seen to be an issue either and it also transpired that the MD was unaware of the project's administrative fee that was coming out of his budget. Only a week in and there was already a complex situation to deal with.[1]

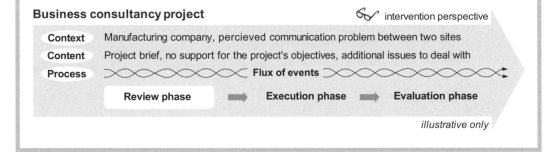

REFLECTIVE OBSERVATIONS

Framing the consultancy project as an intervention

The first point to make about the example above is that even though there was a well-defined brief at the start, the reality of the situation was that after just two meetings the whole project was seriously in question and a different way forward needed to be found. From an intervention perspective, although it seemed that some kind of intervention might still be helpful, there was now an urgent need to redefine the whole project in the light of what had transpired. A different project was required which was less *solution-focused* and more concerned with helping the company understand what improvements were needed to improve the relationship between the two sites. In other words, the mainstream image of developing a new system to some specification of requirements was completely inappropriate in this situation, and hence a different image was used to help guide the work of this particular project. As the example shows, the image adopted was the intervention image which we introduce more generally on the next page.

Introducing the intervention image of projects

In seeing projects as interventions, this book's image of an intervention is essentially that of a three-phase process, which does not purport to be a model of the actual reality, but rather a *framework for thinking* about projects from this particular perspective. Structured using the C2P framework, the three-phase process is shown below.

As the diagram shows, our intervention model consists of three main phases: a review phase, an execution phase and an evaluation phase. In essence, the review phase is about reviewing a problematical situation to determine the action needed; the execution phase is about implementing the agreed action to improve the situation; and the evaluation phase is about assessing the extent to which the situation has been improved. Taken together, these three phases constitute an intervention model which can be applied to many different types of project and programme, for example, the four examples in Aspect 2. Moreover, the image is highly applicable in many other situations where action is needed but no project or programme has yet been identified. And notice too that any real-world intervention is always a social and political process, which is why the flux of events is also shown in the model. And like the other images, this particular image is simply a *starting point* for approaching situations and projects from this particular perspective.

Approaching the review phase: an example of a structured approach

To initiate any review, two important questions to ask are: firstly, what is the situation? and secondly, what might be the core purpose of the intervention? These were the questions asked in the project situation opposite and to help answer these, a particular approach was used that is well-suited to the review phase of interventions. Known as Soft Systems Methodology (SSM), the assumed starting point of SSM is always a problematical situation in which action is needed, but *what* to do and *why* are unclear. Basically, when confronted with a problematical situation, the user of SSM generally enacts a four-stage process: the first stage is to understand the *situation* as best one can, including the social and political aspects; secondly, in the light of this, the aim then is to create some relevant *concepts* of purposeful activity, in the form of models for discussion; next, these models are then used to help structure *discussion* about the situation (for example, the aspects of *why, what* and *how*), leading finally to an accommodation about the *action* to be taken.[2]

Relating this to the example opposite, once the situation was known to be problematical and a different kind of intervention was needed, a totally new *concept* for the project was formulated using the techniques of SSM. This new concept, together with a suggested approach, was then discussed with the company and it was agreed that this should be the way forward for the project. In summary a new intervention had been agreed and it was clear to the people involved *what* the intervention was, *why* it was being carried out, and *how* it should be approached from this point on.

Example Aspect 4: Execution Phase

DEFINITION

The execution phase of an intervention is the main phase of activity and depends on the type of intervention being carried out. Example activities could be service development, process improvement, organizational development and professional development.

REAL-WORLD EXAMPLE

Improving Children's Services in the NHS

In 1997 one of Manchester's Health Authorities published two consultation documents which set out a vision for a more integrated approach to children's services in Greater Manchester. Achieving this vision would involve various NHS Trusts and agencies, and it was agreed that one of these Trusts would act as the coordinating organization for the whole initiative. In 1998 this particular Trust proposed to establish:

a joint project in Salford to consider further the shape of the Salford service ... The remit of the project would be to produce a service specification which operationalizes the proposals made by the Health Authority in its two consultation documents.[3]

In 1999 the lead author was invited to help plan the service specification project with a specific request for help in *'drawing up the project specification, scoping out the tasks required and facilitating the setting up of the project management framework'*. In summary, this was a project (amongst many others) that formed part of an overall intervention to improve children's services in Greater Manchester[4] – see diagram below.

Improving children's services in the NHS 👓 intervention perspective

- **Context** — Need to improve children's services, NHS health authorities, trusts and agencies
- **Content** — Children's services, problem of how to develop the service specification
- **Process** — ⋙⋘ **Flux of events** ⋙⋘

Strategic review ➡ **Service specification project** ➡ Implementation and service evaluation

illustrative only

REFLECTIVE OBSERVATIONS

Another example of a messy, problematical situation

The point of this example is to demonstrate that problematical situations do not just occur at the start of projects and programmes, but at all stages in the lifecycle. Consider for example the process model above: even though there was a strategic vision for improving children's services, the next phase was particularly problematical with regard to the service specification project: in short, this was not a project that could be planned using the traditional techniques of critical path analysis, estimating and work breakdown structures.

Firstly, there was no agreed definition of what was meant by a service specification and nor was there any agreement about which services were to be included within the scope of the project. Secondly, a number of different agencies were to be involved and many of the representatives from these agencies were known to have different views about the future of children's services. Moreover, the project would also need to incorporate a public consultation process that was expected to last for 3 months. And against all of this, the project was expected to provide a clear specification of the nature and provision of each element of care, that is, what, how, where for example, together with an acceptable model of how each element of care would be delivered. In summary, this was a project that did not fit the mainstream image of projects, and hence a different conceptual image was needed to guide this particular project.

In essence, it was agreed to organize the project as a *learning process*, the idea being that the people involved would *learn* their way to a new model of children's services through an organized programme of activity. The underlying technical approach was the learning system of SSM which was used to create an intellectual framework to help guide the work of the project. Furthermore, it was also agreed that the whole intervention to improve children's services should be organized as an integrated programme of projects, rather than a series of discrete projects and activities.

Reflection on the action that followed

In 2001 the author involved contacted the client to enquire about the action that followed and it was found that significant progress had been achieved in redefining the future of children's services. According to the client:

> *comments were made at the time in the way [the project's intellectual framework] speeded the whole process up and saved so much time. ... most projects [in our field] wobble after 6 months when everyone starts to ask "why are we doing this?" or even "what are we supposed to be doing?" whereas in this one it was very clear at all stages.*[4]

This was because the framework created was specific to this project and was deliberately created through an organized process involving many of the people involved. Moreover, what the example also shows is that problematical situations can be messy just in respect of *how:* as this example shows, in this situation, *what* was needed and *why* were both reasonably clear, namely a service specification for improving children's services, and the central problem in this situation was *how* to create the specification.

A guiding framework of activity rather than a detailed project plan

In seeing projects and programmes as interventions, another important difference is the idea of working with a guiding framework rather than following a detailed project plan. In the case of the NHS example, the team were guided by the intellectual framework referred to above, which was a unique framework created for this particular project. Moreover, actually creating this framework was not a trivial task either, for it was not just the service specification project that was organized as a *learning process*, so too was the process of creating the framework; in other words, the author and another consultant deliberately *learnt* their way to this intellectual framework, through a similar process of organized activity. And this too was approached using SSM, simply because of its wide applicability in these sorts of situations. As Peter Checkland points out:

> *SSM provides a set of principles which can be both adopted and adapted for use in any real situation in which people are intent on taking action to improve it.*[5]

Example Aspect 5: Evaluation Phase

DEFINITION

The evaluation phase of an intervention is about assessing the effectiveness of an intervention. For example, how effective was the project or programme in relation to the original objectives? Has the original situation been improved?

REAL-WORLD EXAMPLE

Prison Service Plus Project

Prison Service Plus (PS Plus) was a prison and community-based project to prepare ex-offenders both in prison and in the community for future employment. From 2002 the project delivered a range of services and interventions to help offenders become more employable and develop confidence, improved self-esteem, increased motivation and education qualifications. Funded jointly by the European Social Fund (ESF) and the UK National Offender Management Service, PS Plus was the largest ESF-funded initiative of its type in Europe. In its third phase of activity, PS Plus expanded its activities across various probabation areas by focusing increasingly on achieving sustainability of outcomes to assist the ongoing objective of reducing re-offending. Moreover, with funding due to expire in June 2008, many of the project managers involved in the programme were tasked in early 2008 with evaluating the effectiveness of the intervention in their respective probation areas.[6]

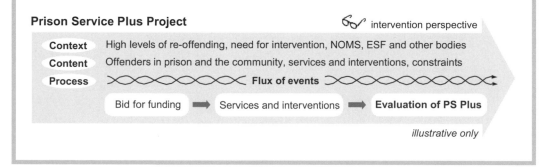

Prison Service Plus Project   👓 intervention perspective

Context	High levels of re-offending, need for intervention, NOMS, ESF and other bodies
Content	Offenders in prison and the community, services and interventions, constraints
Process	Flux of events

Bid for funding ➡ Services and interventions ➡ **Evaluation of PS Plus**

illustrative only

REFLECTIVE OBSERVATIONS

The largest offender resettlement programme in Europe

Of all the examples used in this chapter, the PS Plus Project is by far the most complex and challenging of the interventions considered. Consider for a moment what this project has been trying to do: in short, assisting 'hard to help' offenders to become more employable and to reduce re-offending in the longer term. And in doing this, the project has delivered a range of services and interventions aimed at developing offenders' self-confidence, self-esteem, motivation and so on, all of which makes for a highly challenging intervention. Being a social improvement project, the mainstream image of design and build is also inappropriate and hence the image of an intervention becomes highly applicable. Not only this, many of the other images in this book are applicable to this project too, notably the image of value creation which could prompt questions such as what value do the offenders seek and how might they be helped to create this?

A guiding framework for evaluating the work of PS Plus

Focusing now on the evaluation theme of this phase, one of the main tasks in early 2008, as the example states, was that of evaluating the effectiveness of PS Plus in the different areas in which the project had been carried out. Moreover, the lead author helped to shape this final phase by providing the various project managers with a guiding framework to help evaluate the project; in short, this was not a project plan, but an *intellectual framework* to help guide the group in their evaluation of PS Plus – see below.

Project manager's review of PS Plus: suggested process and perspectives

1. What was the background and the original brief?
   How did the project start and what were the original objectives and targets and so on?
   example perspectives: social, political, value, organizational

2. What has actually taken place over the life of the project?
   What is a factual summary of the key events and activities to date?   *This is a general framework*
   example perspectives: social, political, organizational, operational   *which can be adapted and*
   tailored as necessary.

3. What has actually been achieved through the project?
   What is your evaluation of the work so far in relation to the original objectives?
   example perspectives: value, for example outputs delivered, outcomes achieved and impact

4. What problems and issues has the project experienced?
   What problems and issues have you and your staff experienced with the project?
   example perspectives: social, political, organizational, operational, change, technology

5. What developments and ideas for improvement should be taken forward?
   What are some things that have worked well and what are some ideas for improvement?
   example perspectives: social, value, organizational, operational, change, technology

Source: Briefing Guide for Evaluation of PS Plus (2007)
Reference 6

Basically, the main aim of this evaluation framework was to help those involved address one central question: What is the situation *now* having run this project since 2002? For example, what difference has the project made and what have been the problems and issues experienced along the way? Or, more generally from this perspective, how effective has the intervention been in relation to the original objectives?

Experienced practitioners will notice a link here with post-project reviews, which many organizations carry out at the end of projects and programmes, not unlike the one being described here perhaps. The value of these reviews, however, is often questioned, which is why an intellectual framework was created to help guide the review. And not only this, if a project or programme is to be *really* understood rather than just superficially reviewed, then various perspectives need to be taken, including those which might not always be welcomed, notably the social and political perspectives.

Image Summary

Having introduced five aspects to consider from an intervention perspective, we turn now to this book's intervention image which encapsulates these five related aspects. As stated previously, our aim is not to be prescriptive or all-encompassing, but rather to offer a practical image of projects that the practitioner can use in a variety of different situations. Indeed, like all the images in this book, this particular image can be applied in many different ways, ranging from the occasional use of the whole image or just selected aspects, through to using it in a structured process, or as part of a common language with which to see and talk about the complex realities of a project or programme. These example uses are covered in Part 3 *Applying the Images* but for now it is important to briefly summarize the intervention image of projects.

Projects as intervention processes

In essence, the image here is that of *projects as intervention processes,* by which we mean an organized process to improve a messy, problematical situation, as opposed to the traditional image of producing something to specification, cost and time. Moreover, as explained in Aspect 2, two important elements to consider from this perspective are the complexity and scope of the intervention, by which we mean the perceived complexity of the problematical situation and the expected scope of the work involved. As explained in Aspect 2, in some situations the intervention may only be a partial intervention to review the situation, whilst in others it could be a full intervention to actually change the situation. Whatever the scope, it is useful to think of the intervention process in three main phases: a review phase, an execution phase and an evaluation phase. Taken together, these three phases constitute the intervention process shown in Figure 5.1, with the lower diagram showing the interconnectedness of the five example aspects.

Notice the flux of events is also shown in the diagram opposite to emphasize that in reality any intervention is always a social and political process; in other words, the three-phase process is not to be mistaken for the actual work itself which also needs to be understood through the images presented in Chapters 3 and 4. Although not as widely applicable as the social and political images, the intervention image is still a highly applicable image in many situations, either as a guide to action, or as framework for asking questions about existing projects or programmes in real situations. As explained in Aspect 1, front-end situations usually require a different perspective to the standard textbook view of projects, and this core image is highly applicable in these situations. That said, the politics of situations often make it difficult to challenge a particular project or programme, for instance, asking is this the right project to be doing? As the political image shows, all projects and programmes are inherently political in that they involve people with differing interests and differing amounts of power and influence. Hence, although it might be desirable to challenge a particular project or programme, it might not always be feasible in a real-world situation.

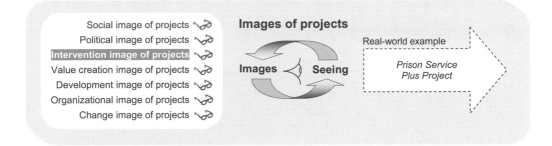

Intervention image of projects

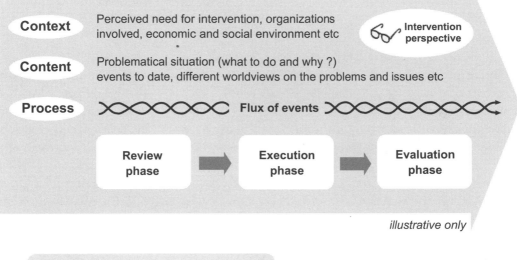

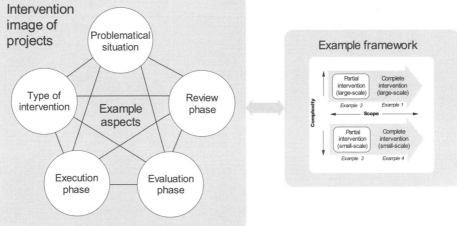

Figure 5.1   An intervention image of projects

What other perspectives are there on intervention?

Not surprisingly, there are other perspectives on intervention which are different to the image presented here. Consider for example the three definitions below:

> *to intervene is to enter into an ongoing system of relationship, to come between or among persons, groups or objects for the purpose of helping them;*[7]

> *the intervention process in organizational development can be seen as commencing with a diagnosis of problems, identifying changes required to address these problems and then putting the changes required into practice;*[8]

> *change begins with the intervention of the consultant in the system to be changed. Intervention refers to the entrance into the client system.*[9]

In *Images* terms, none of these definitions are intrinsically right or wrong, they are just different perspectives on the concept of 'intervention' and each one could be expanded further to create a more detailed image like the one shown in Figure 5.1. However, what is particularly important here is that each perspective has different implications for action, which means if used by the practitioner as a guide to action, the practitioner should be aware of the assumptions upon which each perspective is based. Consider for example the third definition in relation to this chapter's image of an intervention: in this chapter, the focus of the intervention process is on *a situation to be improved*, rather than *a system to be changed*; and this implies a different intellectual approach to the review phase for example.

What are some important principles from this perspective?

1. Think 'problematical situation' not 'problem'.
2. All problematical situations are unique.
3. Think 'action to improve' not 'solution'.
4. There is no 'right' approach to problematical situations.
5. Think: what is my role in this intervention?
6. Treat the design of an intervention very seriously.
7. Adopt an organized approach to the design process.
8. Look to create a situation-specific framework of activity.
9. Seek accommodations rather than consensus.
10. Think cycles of activity: situation-action, situation-action and so on.

Strengths and Limitations

Strengths of the intervention perspective

1. Directs the practitioner to think 'intervention' before 'project' or 'programme', which might be more helpful in certain situations.

2. Focuses attention on *what* to do and *why* before deciding *how* the work should be organized, that is, the image emphasizes process before structure.

3. Particularly relevant to the front-end of projects and programmes where *what* to do and *why* are often unclear or problematical.

4. Encourages the practitioner to think more flexibly about projects and programmes beyond the traditional engineering view of projects.

5. Highlights the importance of 'process' in carrying out interventions through projects, for example, how to involve people in the process.

Limitations of the intervention perspective

1. Not as widely applicable as some of the other images, for example, less relevant to projects such as engineering projects.

2. Can lead to difficulties in defining the scope of an intervention, for example, where to set the boundary of a problematical situation.

3. The notion of 'intervention' means different things to different people which might present difficulties in applying this perspective.

4. The evaluation of interventions to determine their effectiveness is a major intellectual and practical challenge, for example, who, when and how?

5. By itself, this perspective is not enough to understand any real-world intervention; most of the other images in this book will be needed.

*[Images] create insight. But they also distort. They have strengths. But they also have limitations. In creating ways of seeing they tend to create ways of **not** seeing.*

Gareth Morgan

Technology can deliver almost any value we design,
but we are lagging far behind in the design of value.

Edward de Bono

Chapter Six

Image 4:
Projects as Value Creation Processes

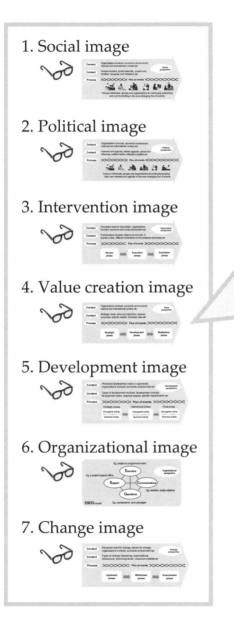

1. Social image

2. Political image

3. Intervention image

4. Value creation image

5. Development image

6. Organizational image

7. Change image

Value Perspective

Chapter Structure

Image Definition

Relevance and Importance

Five Example Aspects

Image Summary

Strengths and Limitations

Image Definition

The VALUE IMAGE is a framework for seeing projects as value creation processes, covering aspects such as the desired value and benefit, core purpose, outcomes and outputs, and the different phases of value creation from the strategic phase through to the value realization phase.

Relevance and Importance

Like the other images, the relevance and importance of the value image hardly needs stating, particularly now that the *primary concern* of projects and programmes is about creating value and benefit, rather than producing things to specification, cost and time. In other words, whilst the traditional production view still applies, the main concern now is essentially that of *value creation* rather than *product creation,* and it is this important shift that makes the value creation image very relevant to today's world of projects. Also, value here doesn't just mean financial value, it also covers other types of value and benefit such as social improvements, contributions towards economic regeneration, and contributions towards protecting the environment. Consider for example the strategic vision of the London 2012 Olympic Games below.

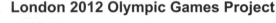

London 2012 Olympic Games Project

The Olympic Games and Paralympic Games will provide the catalyst for a huge programme of urban and environmental regeneration. The Olympic Park in east London will transform one of the city's most underdeveloped areas into a model for sustainable urban development, building inner city communities linked to sport, the environment and health.

Source: www.london2012.org

As the example shows, the concept of London 2012 is essentially about value creation, namely the regeneration of East London, rather than the development of new sports facilities and physical infrastructure. Clearly, the infrastructure development work is a major part, as will be the staging of the Games itself, but ultimately the whole project is about creating lasting value and benefit for the communities of East London. Also, this has major implications for the whole project too. Indeed, various implications flow from taking this perspective and the aim of this chapter is to explore a selection of these through a structured image of five example aspects.

Five Example Aspects

Applying this chapter's value image to the London 2012 Olympic Games Project, the sorts of aspects that might be considered are:

- What are some examples of the *value and benefit* being sought through this project?
- What is the *core purpose* of the project, i.e., the overall strategic vision?
- What are the desired *outcomes* of the project and what are the *outputs* needed?
- How did the organizations involved approach the *strategic phase* of the project?
- What plans are there for the final *realization phase* when the Games have ended?

These five questions and the words in italics illustrate the five example aspects to be considered in this chapter, which of course are not the only aspects that could be considered from a value perspective. However, since they have wide applicability, these are the aspects that we have chosen to focus on, as summarized below.

Aspect 1: Value and Benefit

Projects and programmes can create, or help to create, different types of value and benefit. Examples are: improvements to public services, reduced carbon emissions, increased sales, improved community relations and reduced youth offending.

Aspect 2: Core Purpose

The core purpose of a project or programme is an explicit definition of *what* it will do and *why* it is being done. Such definitions of purpose are usually expressed in terms of aims, goals and objectives, as used in project initiation documents (PIDs) for example.

Aspect 3: Outcomes and Outputs

From a value perspective, the outcomes of a project or programme represent the value and benefit being sought, that is, WHY something is being done. And the outputs represent WHAT needs to be developed to help achieve these outcomes.

Aspect 4: Strategic Phase

The strategic phase is the first phase of the value creation process and covers activities such as strategic analysis, portfolio definition, programme definition, project selection and project definition (such activities depend on the particular context).

Aspect 5: Realization Phase

The realization phase is the final phase of the value creation process in which the expected value should begin to emerge, or be realized altogether, and covers activities such as monitoring and refinement (depending on the context).

Like the previous chapters, this section presents each of these aspects over two pages, the left-hand page providing a real example (for example, the London 2012 project) and the right-hand page offering some observations for the reader to reflect upon in relation to their own knowledge and experience. Beyond these five aspects, we then summarize the value creation image as a whole, and briefly state some of the strengths and limitations of this very important perspective.

Example Aspect 1: Value and Benefit

DEFINITION

> *Projects and programmes can create, or help to create, different types of value and benefit. Examples are: improvements to public services, reduced carbon emissions, increased sales, improved community relations and reduced youth offending.*

REAL-WORLD EXAMPLES

Project or Programme	Development Perspective	Value Creation Perspective
The Eden Project	Development of the Eden site including the 'Biome' conservatories	Awareness and understanding of major environmental issues
London 2012 Olympics	Development of major infrastructure and new sports facilities	A sustainable legacy of benefits in culture, sport, business for East London
Project Allenby/Connaught	Development of new army garrison facilities and FM services	Improvements to the quality of life for army and civilian personnel
B&Q Renewal Programme	Development and renewal of stores and services	Increased sales, profit and shareholder value
Equipment Direct Project	Development of a new internet-based service for disabled people	Improved access to and greater choice in equipment services

REFLECTIVE OBSERVATIONS

Value creation as the prime focus of projects

The first thing to notice about the five examples is how they illustrate a crucial trend now emerging in the management of projects across different sectors, namely the emphasis on *value creation* rather than *product creation* as the primary concern. For increasing numbers of organizations, the primary concern is no longer the temporary production of physical assets, systems and facilities, but increasingly the challenge of creating different kinds of value and benefit. As the examples show, the core purpose is not about developing conservatories and sports facilities and so on, but rather that of raising awareness of environmental issues, regenerating East London, improving quality of life, increasing company profit and improving service quality. Notice also that the value perspective and the development perspective are not alternatives between which a choice has to be made; they represent complementary ways of seeing the same project or programme, one rooted in the image of projects as *value creation processes,* and the other rooted in the image of projects as *development processes* which is covered in Chapter 7.

What is the image here: value creation or contributing to value creation?

With regard to this book's image of value creation, an important point to consider first is whether projects and programmes can create value *directly*, or whether they only *contribute* towards some value-creating activity. Consider the B&Q renewal programme: the development of stores and services needs to be combined with the retail store and service operation, which together over a period of time, is aimed at increasing sales; in this case, the value image of the renewal programme is about *contributing* towards value-creating activity. In another context, however, the image could be that of a project or programme to create value *directly* within some agreed timeframe. For example, if the image of the *Equipment Direct Project* was to improve the daily living experience of disabled people, then the project would be expected to deliver some tangible improvements within the lifetime of the project. In summary, the concept of value creation in this book covers both contributing towards value creation and creating value directly.

Different types of value and benefit (i.e., value as *not* just wealth creation)

Another important feature of this book's concept of value creation is that 'value' doesn't just mean financial value, as in increased value for B&Q's shareholders for example. In this book, the concept of 'value' covers not just wealth creation, but also other types of value and benefit like the examples shown opposite, such as greater awareness of environmental issues, the regeneration of local areas and communities, and improvements to public services. And not only this, the same project or programme can also create different types of value for different beneficiaries. Consider for example the *Equipment Direct Project:* from a value perspective, the core purpose of the project is about improving disabled people's access to equipment services; however, it might also be seen as an opportunity for reducing the service providers' operating costs, and also an opportunity for developing the ICT skills of those involved. And not only this, it might also be seen as a project to develop a blueprint for use elsewhere in the NHS.

This is all very well in principle one might say, but what about the commercial realities of projects and all the other practical constraints that have to be dealt with? Clearly, such realities exist and practitioners have no choice but to deal with these constraints, not least the twin constraints of time and budget. But the really key point is this: the image being presented here is not a prescription but a *perspective*, and this has important implications for the way in which projects and programmes can be seen and organized. Consider for example the implications that could arise for the *Equipment Direct Project*: (i) multiple *outcomes* aimed at different beneficiaries, (ii) multiple *outputs* required to deliver the outcomes and (iii) multiple *workstreams* to deliver the required outputs. Clearly, these could be identified without taking this perspective, but the reverse is also true as well; in not taking this perspective, the project might simply be seen as an IT development project.

Stakeholder value versus shareholder value

Building on the pig illustration opposite, a useful concept which aligns with this book's value creation image is the concept of *stakeholder value* as opposed to *shareholder value*.[1] In this sense, the image here is about creating, or helping to create, different kinds of value for different people and organizations, including future generations who are not always included in stakeholder analysis exercises. As some people say *'we do not inherit the Earth from our parents, but borrow it from our children'* which is a thought-provoking perspective for any major project to consider.

115

Example Aspect 2: Core Purpose

DEFINITION

The core purpose of a project or programme is an explicit definition of WHAT it will do and WHY it is being done. Such definitions of purpose are usually expressed in terms of aims, goals and objectives, as used in project initiation documents for example.

REAL-WORLD EXAMPLE

Equipment Direct Project

Imagine a scenario in which there are problems with equipment services for disabled people and there is a concern that the currently defined project (re: page 23) will have little impact on these services. Given this scenario, what should be the core purpose?

Core purpose 1		Output	Outcome
WHAT	To develop an Internet-based information service	An Internet-based information service	Disabled people with improved access to information about living equipment
WHY	To provide disabled people with improved access to information about daily living equipment		

Core purpose 2		Output	Outcome
WHAT	To provide disabled people with more choice and faster access to daily living equipment	Disabled people with more choice and faster access to living equipment	The daily living experience of disabled people improved
WHY	To improve the daily living experience of disabled people		

Core purpose 3		Output	Outcome
WHAT	To improve the equipment services provided to disabled people	Equipment services improved	Disabled people enabled to do more things of their choice
WHY	To enable disabled people to do more things they would like to do		

Illustrative only

REFLECTIVE OBSERVATIONS

Importance of considering different concepts

The first thing to notice about the example above is the deliberate formulation of three different statements of purpose and how each statement represents a different concept of *what* the project might do and *why* it's being carried out from a value creation perspective. And notice too how each concept is fundamentally different, implying different value and benefit, depending on how the core purpose of the project is framed. For example, the development of an information service is clearly a different concept to that of improving equipment services. It is also important to add that none of these concepts are intrinsically right or wrong, they are just different *concepts*, and each one represents a different view of the project's core purpose. In practice, it can often be useful to explicitly formulate such concepts to help shape or clarify a project's aims and objectives. For example, is the core purpose of the *Equipment Direct Project* to provide disabled people with *improved access to information* about daily living equipment, or is it to provide *more choice and faster access* to this equipment? Or if the issue is about the quality of the equipment services themselves, then concept 3 could be a more relevant concept than simply developing a new Internet-based information service. As Edward de Bono states:

> *whenever we do anything there is an implicit concept. ... Different people may see the concept differently. ... Why should we want to make the concept visible? There a number of reasons why it is useful to be able to extract and make visible a concept.*[2]

One of the most important reasons relates to business cases: for example, for the *Equipment Direct Project*, the business case for an information service would be a different business case for improving equipment services; in other words, the business case depends entirely on the core purpose of the project. In practice, such concepts of purposeful activity can be made visible using a variety of techniques, notably the conceptual modelling techniques of Soft Systems Methodology (SSM), which were used to formulate the three concepts in the example opposite.

Aims, goals and objectives

The core purpose of any project or programme is usually expressed through statements of aims, goals and objectives, and by this we mean the declared purposes, as opposed to the undeclared ones. However, a problem with such statements, which often goes unnoticed, is that one person's 'aim' can be another person's 'goal', and one person's 'goal' can be another person's 'objective'. This is important because when the objectives of a project represent the *why* to one group and the *what* to another, there is clearly scope for misunderstanding, which usually goes unnoticed until people start asking: "What are we trying to achieve and why?"

Experience also shows that it is important to work with 'local' terminology rather than a standard framework for all projects and programmes. For example, consider the following worked example used to promote a proprietary programme management framework:

* ❖   one of the programme's *objectives* is to reduce operational running costs;
* ❖   the *requirement* is to find ways of encouraging lower staff turnover;
* ❖   the *deliverable* is a training scheme that achieves a 2 per cent year on year reduction.

To apply this framework, one must first identify the *objectives*, then the *requirements* and then the *deliverables*. This might be helpful in certain situations, but as a framework for *all* programmes, it is simply impractical. Experience shows that words such as 'objective', 'requirement' and 'deliverable' mean different things to different people; for example, to somebody else, the word *objective* could mean the *requirement* to find ways of encouraging lower staff turnover, and similarly the word *requirement* could mean the *deliverables* of the training scheme. In short, there is no right or wrong answer here, only that such terms will always mean different things to different people, which is why we advocate using more generic terms such as *why, what* and *how,* and then translate these into local terminology. And the same point applies to the development concept aspect in Chapter 7, which is strongly linked to the core purpose aspect being discussed here – see Aspect 2 in Chapter 7.

Example Aspect 3: Outcomes and Outputs

DEFINITION

> *From a value creation perspective, the outcomes of a project, programme or portfolio represent the value and benefit being sought, that is, WHY something is being done. And the outputs represent WHAT needs to be developed to help achieve these outcomes.*

REAL-WORLD EXAMPLES

Project or Programme	Example Outputs	Example Outcomes
The Eden Project	'Biome' conservatories	More informed public
London 2012 Olympics	New sports facilities	Employment opportunities
Project Allenby/Connaught	New garrison facilities	More satisfied personnel
B&Q Renewal Programme	Revamped stores	Increased sales and profit
Equipment Direct Project	Internet system	Improved access to services

Equipment Direct Example

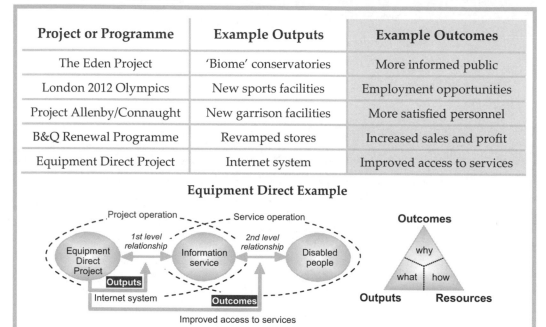

Based on reference 3.

REFLECTIVE OBSERVATIONS

Outcomes and outputs: a useful conceptual distinction

Another important aspect of this book's image of value creation is the distinction between *outcomes* and *outputs*, the concept here being that *outcomes* represent the value and benefit sought from a project or programme, and *outputs* represent what needs to be developed to help achieve these outcomes, as shown in the examples above. Some publications choose to make a further distinction between outcomes and benefits, but this is not a distinction we make here. Our concern is simply to distinguish between *why* a project or programme is being carried out, in terms of the outcomes sought, and *what* outputs need to be developed to help achieve these outcomes. How this conceptual distinction is applied in practice, including what language to use for outcomes and outputs, is best worked out in relation to the actual project or programme. In short, given the complexity of projects, the notion of trying to follow a prescriptive framework of detailed concepts and definitions for all projects and programmes is simply inappropriate.

Outcomes and outputs: first- and second-level relationships

A useful way of understanding the distinction between outcomes and outputs is to think of them in terms of two levels of customer relationship. Although about companies rather than projects, the following extract from a book called *Reframing Business* by the late Richard Normann is particularly relevant to projects:

> *a particularly fruitful way of reframing, in our experience, is to focus on the customer of the company as the major stakeholder, and to mentally frame oneself as **part of the customer's business**. .... A major conceptual implication of doing so is to move away from the traditional industrial view of the customer offering as an **output** of one's production system to a view in which the customer offering is seen as an **input** in the customer's value-creating process. This requires the company to understand the customer's business and value-creating process and use that as the basic framework within which one defines one's business. .... Therefore, true customer orientation means that one has to go beyond the direct relationship between oneself and one's customers to understand the relationship between the customers and the customers' customers – from the 'first' to the 'second-level customer relationship'.*[3]

Interestingly, although the focus here is on companies, the main thrust of Normann's value creation model offers a highly relevant perspective with which to think about the outcomes and outputs of projects. As the example opposite shows, the Internet system output relates to the first-level relationship and the outcome of improved access to services relates to the second-level relationship. In other words, from a value creation perspective, the core purpose of the *Equipment Direct Project* is essentially about improving the *second-level relationship* between the new Iinternet-based information service and disabled people. And notice too that the overall output is an information *service*, and not just a new *system*, which has important implications for achieving the desired outcome for disabled people. Also, the new service is not principally an output either, for as Normann's model shows, the new service is more usefully seen as an *input* to the disabled people's own value-creating processes, thus enabling them to create value in their own activities. As Normann states: *'The goal of a company is not to create value for customers but to mobilize customers to create their own value from the company's various offerings.'*[4] Being a value creation concept for companies, this is particularly insightful and the same concept can be applied to projects too, such as the Eden Project, the London 2012 Olympics and the other examples opposite: *The goal [of a project or programme] is not to create value for customers but to mobilize customers to create their own value from the [project or programme's] various offerings.*[5]

Reframing the traditional PM triangle from a value creation perspective

To summarize this aspect of outcomes and outputs, a useful model is the reframed model of the traditional PM triangle shown opposite. The traditional model of specification, cost and time is a very useful model that can be applied to any project; however, from a value perspective, the model is entirely *output-focused* and neglects the crucial dimension of *outcomes*. Hence, from a value creation perspective, it is necessary to incorporate this crucial dimension as shown in the triangle opposite. In summary, all three dimensions are now represented: *why* something is being done, *what* needs to be developed and *how* this will be achieved with the resources available.

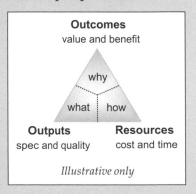

119

Example Aspect 4: Strategic Phase

DEFINITION

> *The strategic phase is the first phase of the value creation process and covers activities such as strategic analysis, portfolio definition, programme definition, project selection and project definition (such activities depend on the context).*

REAL-WORLD EXAMPLE

Big Food Group Strategic Programme

In August 2000 the Big Food Group Plc was a £5.3 billion organization created from the merger of Iceland Frozen Foods and Booker Cash & Carry. From the start, the merger met with problems: Booker and Iceland were very different businesses with different cultures and it was unclear as to how the new company would deliver the £50 million annualised synergy benefits promised at the time of the merger. Under the leadership of a new CEO, a strategic review was initiated to address a number of fundamental questions, including how the group should be structured and what the strategic direction should be for the various business units. To help achieve the new strategic vision, strategic plans were created for each of the business units and group functions, and these were broken down into clear quantifiable strategic objectives, each of which consisted of a portfolio of programmes and projects with detailed development plans and change management infrastructure to support their delivery. The whole strategic programme consisted of over 350 initiatives carried out between 2001 and 2004.[6]

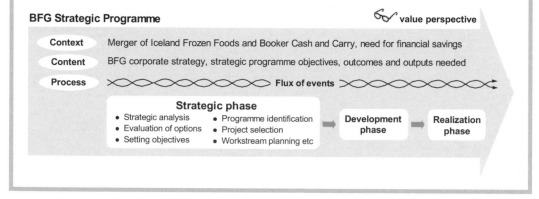

REFLECTIVE OBSERVATIONS

A portfolio of programmes and projects to recreate shareholder value

The example above is useful because it demonstrates three important aspects relating to value creation through projects: (1) firstly, it shows the increasing trend in organizations of linking projects and programmes to business strategy; (2) it demonstrates the different levels of management activity involved, namely portfolio, programme and project; and (3) it demonstrates that grand strategic visions and well-made plans are no guarantee to long-term success. In short, 3 years after the programme started, the Big Food Group was sold and broken up into separate businesses. The strategic programme clearly contributed to the partial recovery in BFG's share price, but whether it contributed to the events that followed is difficult to know. For this we would need to apply the social and political images to understand the actual events at the time, but this is beyond the scope of this book. Hence, we turn now to this book's value creation image of projects.

Introducing the value creation image of projects

In seeing projects as value creation processes, this book's image of value creation is essentially that of a three-phase process aimed at creating value and benefit for different individuals, groups and organizations. Structured using the framework of *context/content/process*, the three phase process is shown below.

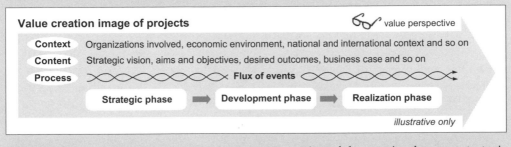

As the diagram shows, the value creation process consists of three main phases: a strategic phase, a development phase and a realization phase. Fundamentally, the strategic phase is concerned with the outcomes and outputs needed; the development phase is concerned with delivering the outputs; and the realization phase is concerned with using and refining these outputs to realize the desired outcomes. And being generic, this core image of value creation can be applied at all levels, from corporate portfolios, as in the example opposite, to individual projects and programmes, as in the five examples shown in Aspect 1. And notice too that this is a much broader image than the mainstream image of producing something to specification, cost and time; in effect, the product creation image is subsumed by the development phase. Also, like the other three-phase images of intervention, development and change, it is important not to see this particular image as a description of reality; it is simply a *starting point* for thinking about projects, programmes and portfolios from a value creation perspective.

Example activities that might be carried out in the strategic phase

From a value perspective, example activities that might be carried out in the strategic phase are shown below, and some references to these can be found in Appendix E. Also, notice the link here to the development image of projects in Chapter 7, which is why we skip the development phase to focus on the realization phase in the final aspect.

Value creation image of projects   👓 value perspective

Example activities   **Strategic phase**

- Strategic analysis (context)
- Analysis of strategic options (content)
- Implementation planning (process)
- Portfolio definition and project selection

- Benefits modelling and analysis
- Business case development
- Programme definition
- Concept definition (WHAT & WHY)

Development phase : **Realization phase**

Illustrative only

Example Aspect 5: Realization Phase

DEFINITION

> *The realization phase is the final phase of the value creation process in which the expected value should begin to emerge, or be realized altogether, and covers activities such as monitoring and refinement (dependent on the context).*

REAL-WORLD EXAMPLE

Warburtons SAP Programme

From its humble beginnings in northern England over 100 years ago, Warburtons is now the UK's largest independent baking business, employing over 4000 people at 13 bakeries and 11 depots spread throughout the UK. Operating 24x7, the company produces over two million bakery products every day, mostly for major supermarkets rather than independent stores. It was against this background in early 2000 that the company embarked on a business project to implement the SAP enterprise resource planning system (ERP), aimed at achieving a number of business objectives. To show how these were achieved, the image below illustrates the final realization phase.

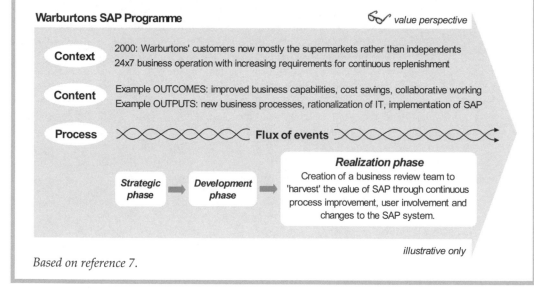

Based on reference 7.

REFLECTIVE OBSERVATIONS

A business project involving IT rather than an IT project

What makes the Warburtons project a good example of value creation is the attention that was given to the project's final phase, what we term the *realization phase* in which the expected value and benefit from a project or programme should begin to emerge or be realized altogether. Very importantly, the Warburtons project was organized and managed not as an IT project, but as a business project involving IT, with an expectation that the projected benefits of SAP would not just magically appear on day 1 of the system going live. As the model opposite shows, a cross-functional team was formed to 'harvest' the benefits of SAP through a process of continuous improvement, user involvement and changes to the SAP system. Far from being a weakness of the project, this was a major strength in that there was an acceptance that further work was needed if the company was going to realize the value of its significant investment in SAP.[8] Indeed, the example raises an interesting question about the end point of projects involving IT, for according to the traditional image of IT projects, a project generally ends once the new system has been installed and handed over. In *Images* terms, this reflects a *development view* rather than a *value creation view* and from this perspective, the development phase is only the middle phase of the process in which activities such as installation and handover are not the end point at all; in fact, they are not even part of the realization phase from this perspective, but rather the back end of the development phase. In summary, to realize the value from any project or programme, this final phase is very important, and planning for it in advance is an important activity for any project or programme.

Is it not programmes that deliver benefits rather than projects?

In a word, no. This might well be a useful distinction to apply in some situations, but as a prescription for all projects and programmes, it is simply impractical, not least because the words project and programme mean different things to different people. Also, from a value creation perspective, the important distinction is not between programme and project, but between outcome and output. So long as *this* conceptual distinction is made, it matters less whether the whole initiative is called a project, programme or something else. What really matters is knowing *why* a project or programme is being done, in terms of the outcomes sought, and *what* needs to be done to help achieve the outcomes.

Importance of monitoring and review at all stages

Whilst for many projects and programmes, the desired outcomes only emerge during the realization phase, this is not to suggest that the outcomes sought should only be reviewed in the final phase, which might be the impression given by the example opposite. In all three phases, continuous monitoring and review of projects and programmes is crucially important for maintaining continuity and relevance of purpose and a continuing focus on the desired outcomes. This can be done informally and formally at any time, informally for example by 'reading' the events to see if any corrective action is needed, and formally, by holding structured reviews (for example, stage-gate reviews) at regular stages throughout the life of a project or programme. An example of this is the Gateway™ review process developed by the Office for Government Commerce in the UK.[9]

Value and benefit can also emerge in the development phase

According to this book's image of value creation, the value being sought is normally not realized until the realization phase, however, there are cases where the value and benefit might emerge, or begin to emerge, in the development phase. Consider for example a construction project: if one of the desired outcomes was that of developing workforce skills in brick laying, then this could be achieved during the development phase. And this, in summary, is why this book's image of value creation is just that, an *image* for thinking about projects and programmes as value creation processes and *not* an all-encompassing model that tries to cover all eventualities.

Image Summary

Having introduced five aspects to consider from a value perspective, we turn now to this book's value creation image which encapsulates these five related aspects. As stated previously, our aim is not to be prescriptive or all-encompassing, but rather to offer a practical image of projects that the practitioner can use in a variety of different situations. Indeed, like all the images in this book, this particular image can be applied in many different ways, ranging from the occasional use of the whole image or just selected aspects, through to using it in a structured process, or as part of a common language with which to see and talk about the complex realities of a project or programme. These example uses are covered in Part 3 *Applying the Images* but for now it is important to briefly summarize the value creation image of projects.

Projects as value creation processes

In essence, the image here is that of *projects as value creation processes*, by which we mean an organized process to create value and benefit for different individuals, groups and organizations. Also, by value and benefit we do not just mean financial value, but other types of value and benefit such as improvements to services, quality of life improvements and contributions towards protecting the environment. In some instances, the image could be that of a project or programme to create value *directly*, within the lifetime of the project, or the image could be that of a project or programme to *contribute* to some wider value-creating activity, as in the B&Q renewal programme. Whatever the scope, however, there are some aspects to always consider from this perspective, namely the core purposes of a project or programme, the desired outcomes and the outputs needed to achieve these outcomes. Also, as this chapter has shown, it useful to frame the value creation process in terms of three core phases: a strategic phase concerned with the desired outcomes, a development phase concerned with delivering the required outputs and a realization phase concerned with using and refining these outputs to realize the desired outcomes. Together, these three phases constitute this book's value creation image as shown in Figure 6.1 opposite.

Notice the flux of events is also shown in the diagram opposite to emphasize that in reality the creation of value through projects and programmes is always a social and political process; in other words, the three phase process of value creation is not to be mistaken for the actuality of projects and programmes which can be more usefully understood through the images in Chapters 3 and 4. However, as a guide to action, the three-phase process is a pragmatic framework for approaching any project or programme from a value creation perspective, partly because it highlights the importance of thinking strategically at the start, and also because it highlights the importance of the final phase if the desired value and benefit is to be realized.

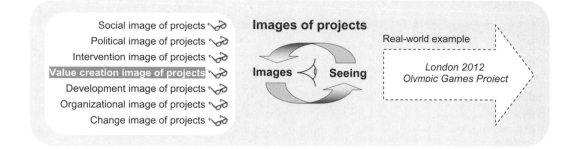

Value creation image of projects

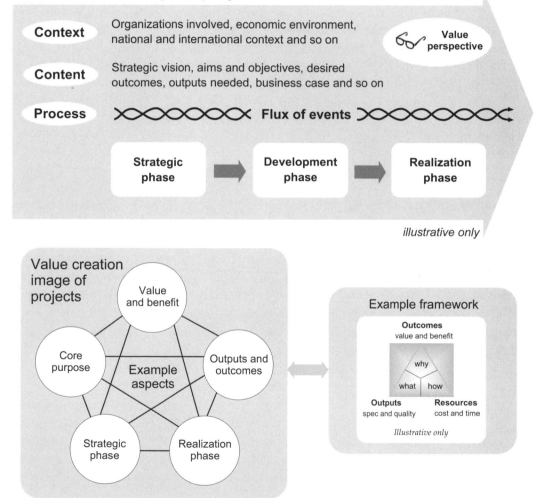

Figure 6.1   A value creation image of projects

The ultimate challenge of projects

As we stated at the start, the main concern now in the management of projects is no longer the production of physical assets, but increasingly the challenge of creating value for different stakeholder groups. Whilst industry reports continue to highlight the familiar problems of product quality, missed deadlines and cost overruns, the same reports also highlight the need for a more strategic approach towards the management of projects, and a greater focus on the value and benefits that projects can create, or help to create for different people and organizations. A useful perspective on this is provided by Dennis Cohen and Robert Graham in their book *The Project Manager's MBA* in which they argue that: *'The old success criteria of meeting outcome, cost and schedule constraints are no longer adequate,'* and that a fundamental shift is needed *'from meeting fixed specifications to satisfying customers ... from coming in on a fixed budget to managing cash flow ... from meeting a fixed deadline to selecting the best time to market ... [and] from just getting the project done to helping to implement organizational strategy.'*[10] In other words, value creation is now the main challenge and the ultimate challenge we believe is the creation of value for different individuals and groups involved in the same project; for example, a construction project is not just a commercial opportunity, it can also be viewed as an opportunity to develop people's knowledge and skills, which to use Normann's words, will then mobilize these people to create their own value in future activities.

Can value really be 'delivered' through projects?

Being the value chapter, a useful point to end on is the word 'delivery', which has become a popular buzzword in recent times, particularly in phrases such as 'project delivery' and 'benefits delivery' for example. But can projects and benefits really be 'delivered' in the same way that post can be delivered to doors and babies can be delivered by midwives? As the FT columnist Lucy Kellaway writes: *'If you think "delivery" is something that involves a truck, and which IKEA charges for, you are sadly out of date. Accenture [for example] delivers all manner of things, none of which requires a truck or even a bicycle. "Innovation Delivered", it says on the cover [of their 2002 Annual Report], which sounds splendid and is ambiguous enough to be unchallengeable.'*[11] So, what does delivering value and benefit really mean in the context of projects? A short pragmatic answer is that value and benefit are the perceived *results* that emerge over time from the combined activities and interactions of all those involved, as opposed to being physical 'things' that can be delivered. They are *emergent* phenomena and as the late Richard Normann points out, creating value has much to do with dialogue and learning, for as he states *'value creation is a community process'.*[12] And being an emergent community process, value creation can often take considerable time, as Richard Dowden of the Royal African Society argued for the Make Poverty History campaign: This *'should have carried the subtitle: a 50-year project'.*[13]

Strengths and Limitations

Strengths of the value perspective

1. Directs attention to *why* a project or programme is being carried out in terms of the value and benefit being sought. What is the core purpose?

2. Highlights an important distinction between outcomes and outputs: the outcomes being sought and the outputs needed to achieve these.

3. Directs attention to the link between projects, organizational strategy and long-term value creation. What is the current portfolio of projects?

4. Highlights the importance of the final phase of projects and programmes to help realize the desired value and benefit. How is this being done?

5. Focuses attention on the ultimate purpose of projects and programmes to create value and benefit, or to contribute towards value creation.

Limitations of the value perspective

1. Can sometimes lead people to see value creation as an extended production process when in reality it is much more social and emergent.

2. Can lead to the over objectification of projects and programmes if value is not seen as value for whom? Rationality is always political.

3. The words 'value' and 'benefit' mean different things to different people which can make it difficult to apply this perspective with consistency.

4. Evaluation of projects and programmes to determine their value and benefit is a major intellectual challenge, for example, whose evaluation?

5. The value creation aspects of projects and programmes cannot be understood without also considering the social and political aspects.

*[Images] create insight. But they also distort. They have strengths. But they also have limitations. In creating ways of seeing they tend to create ways of **not** seeing.*

Gareth Morgan

I keep six honest serving-men
(They taught me all I knew);
Their names are WHAT and WHY and WHEN
And HOW and WHERE and WHO

Rudyard Kipling

Chapter Seven

Image 5:
Projects as Development Processes

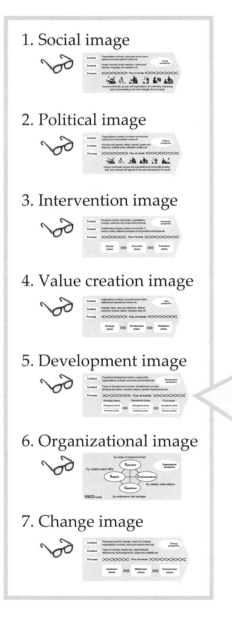

1. Social image

2. Political image

3. Intervention image

4. Value creation image

5. Development image

6. Organizational image

7. Change image

Development Perspective

Chapter Structure

Image Definition

Relevance and Importance

Five Example Aspects

Image Summary

Strengths and Limitations

Image Definition

The DEVELOPMENT IMAGE is a framework for seeing projects as development processes, covering aspects such as the type of development (for example, infrastructure development), the core development concept, and the different phases of development activity.

Relevance and Importance

The relevance and importance of the development image is easily understood by just considering some of the many different types of development now being carried out through projects and programmes: product development, service development, organizational development, infrastructure development, professional development, community development and so on. For a real example of infrastructure development, consider the King's Cross Development Programme below.

King's Cross Development Programme

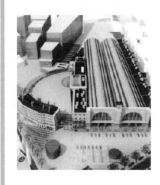

King's Cross station is getting more and more crowded and, over the next ten years, we expect the number of people passing through it to grow to 50 million. ... Network Rail plans to DEVELOP King's Cross into a modern transport hub that will meet the needs of passengers for many years to come. ... The construction work will be complex, involving full integration with neighbouring Underground and Channel Tunnel Rail Link developments. The key station works should be completed in late 2011, in time for the 2012 London Olympics. We plan to keep King's Cross station fully operational throughout the construction period. (capitals added)

Source: www.networkrail.co.uk

As an example of infrastructure development, this is just one of many different types of development now being carried out through projects and programmes. And notice too from the other examples above that this book's development image is not just concerned with engineering, construction and IT; as this chapter will show, this book's image of development is much broader than the traditional lifecycle view of producing something to specification, cost and time. Indeed, being more generic, it can be applied to any area of development, including areas not normally associated with mainstream project management, such as professional development and community development. Also, this has important implications for the way in which projects and programmes are approached, particularly at the front-end of projects.

Five Example Aspects

Applying this chapter's development image to the King's Cross Programme, the sorts of aspects that might be considered are:

- What *type of development* is the King's Cross Development Programme?
- What is the *development concept* of the whole programme? E.g., the strategic vision?
- What has been the approach to the *strategic phase* of the programme?
- What is the approach to the *operational phase*? E.g., how is the work organized?
- What plans are there for the *final phase* when all the major works are complete?

Like the previous chapters, these five questions and the words in italics illustrate the example aspects to be considered from a development perspective. Although not the only aspects that could be considered, these are the aspects that we have chosen to focus on because of their wide applicability to most projects and programmes.

Aspect 1: Type of Development
This aspect refers to what is essentially being developed or being proposed for development. Examples could be: a new product or service, new or existing infrastructure, people's knowledge and skills, organizational development, or community relations and so on.

Aspect 2: Development Concept
The development concept is the core concept of a proposed development project or some existing development activity. Sometimes expressed as the strategic vision or the mission, the development concept defines: WHAT is to be developed and WHY.

Aspect 3: Strategic Phase
The strategic phase of the development process refers to the front-end of projects and programmes covering activities such as strategic and commercial analysis, concept definition, the development plan, strategic procurement and contract negotiations.

Aspect 4: Operational Phase
The operational phase of the development process refers to the main part of a project or programme covering the technical activity of development (for example, construction or training) and the managerial activity of planning, organizing and control.

Aspect 5: Final Phase
The final phase of the development process refers to the back-end of projects and programmes, where the activity of this phase (like the other phases) depends on the type of development being carried out and the actual project or programme itself.

As explained in the Introduction to Part 2, this part of the chapter presents each of these five aspects over two pages, the left-hand page providing a real example (for example, the King's Cross Programme) and the right-hand page offering some observations for the reader to reflect upon in relation to their own knowledge and experience. Beyond these five aspects, we then summarize the development image as a whole, and briefly state some of the strengths and limitations of this particular perspective.

Example Aspect 1: Type of Development

DEFINITION

> *This aspect refers to what is essentially being developed or being proposed for development. Examples could be: a new product or service, new or existing infrastructure, people's knowledge and skills, organizational development, community relations and so on.*

REAL-WORLD EXAMPLE

King's Cross Development Programme

King's Cross station is getting more and more crowded and over the next ten years we expect the number of people passing through it to grow to 50 million. King's Cross is already a key entry point to the capital and from 2007 will be part of the new international interchange at St Pancras. It will also become a gateway for visitors to the 2012 London Olympics.

The station is at the heart of a massive urban regeneration area encompassing the new St Pancras International station, the new King's Cross/St Pancras Underground station and the King's Cross Central regeneration scheme. Network Rail plans to DEVELOP King's Cross into a modern transport hub that will meet the needs of passengers for many years to come. ... The construction work will be complex, involving full integration with neighbouring Underground and Channel Tunnel Rail Link developments. The key station works should be completed in late 2011, in time for the 2012 London Olympics. We plan to keep King's Cross station fully operational throughout the construction period. (capitals added)

Source: www.networkrail.co.uk (2005)

REFLECTIVE OBSERVATIONS

A major infrastructure development programme

In seeing projects as development processes, two important aspects to consider are the type of development and the wider development context. In the case of the example above, the type of development is infrastructure development, and moreover, the example usefully highlights some important contextual aspects: firstly, the immovable date of the London 2012 Olympics; secondly, the need for the King's Cross Programme to integrate with neighbouring Underground and Channel Tunnel Rail Link developments; and thirdly, the need for King's Cross station to remain fully operational throughout the construction period; quite a challenge by any standard. In short, all of these contextual aspects have major implications, not only for the redevelopment of the station, but for the organization and management of the programme. And notice that some developments such as King's Cross involve other types of development within the main programme, for example, information systems development (such as, electronic display systems), product development (for example, retail units) and service development (for example, station maintenance services).

Different types of development

Developing King's Cross station is just one of many types of development now being carried out through projects and programmes, as shown by the examples opposite. Looking at the list opposite, notice that the development perspective here is not just concerned with projects and programmes in engineering, construction and IT. This book's development image can be applied to any type of development, including those not normally associated with project management, for example, professional development. Notwithstanding the differences between them, all the examples opposite are basically about developing something, and moreover, much of the work in these areas is now being approached through projects and programmes. Starting then from this view of development, how might we start to think about projects and programmes from this perspective?

Types of development
- System development
- Product development
- Property development
- Infrastructure development
- Process development
- Service development
- Knowledge development
- People development
- Professional development
- Business development
- Organizational development
- Community development
- Nation state development
- International development

Introducing the development image of projects

Like the intervention, value and change images, this book's development image is a three-phase process model set against the social and political process, with the primary focus being on development as shown below.

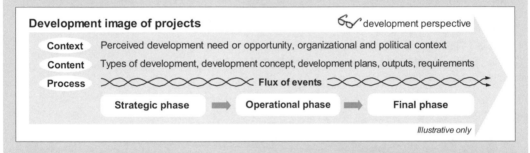

As the diagram shows, the development process is organized into three main phases: a strategic phase, an operational phase and a final phase. Fundamentally, the strategic phase is concerned with deciding *what* needs to be developed and *why*; the operational phase is concerned with developing the outputs needed; and a final phase which depends on the type of development being carried out. And notice too that this is a much broader image than the traditional lifecycle process of define, plan, execute, control and close. By 'development' we mean a complete end-to-end process covering strategic and commercial type activity at the front-end, followed by operational activity (for example, construction or training etc), and then a final phase that depends on the type of development being carried out; in other words, it is all of this activity together, that forms the development process above, and it is this core image that informs the development perspective within this book.

Notice also the overlap with the value creation image (for example, the strategic phase), which is quite deliberate and something we return to at the end of the chapter. Turning now to the other development aspects, the image above also identifies the next four aspects to be considered, starting with the development concept, followed by the three main phases in Aspects 3 to 5.

Example Aspect 2: Development Concept

DEFINITION

> *The development concept is the core concept of a proposed development project or some existing development activity. Sometimes expressed as the strategic vision or the mission, the development concept defines: WHAT is to be developed and WHY.*

REAL-WORLD EXAMPLE

King's Cross Development Programme

Network Rail plans to develop King's Cross into a modern transport hub that will meet the needs of passengers for many years to come. Our aims:

- *to reduce over-crowding on the concourse at busy peak times*
- *to create a modern, spacious passenger environment*
- *to allow for improved train services to carry more passengers*
- *to create more convenient connections with St Pancras station, the Underground ...*
- *to make a positive contribution to the development of the King's Cross area.*

What we are planning?

Network Rail intends to build a modern concourse to the west of the station as an integral part of a key transport hub. The new concourse will be three times the size of the existing area, creating a bright, open, semi-circular structure on two levels.

Ground floor
- *A new travel centre*
- *A large waiting and seating area*
- *Highly visible customer information screens*
- *Shops catering for customers' needs*
- *Integrated escalator, lift and stair links*
- *Left luggage, toilets and other facilities.*

Source: www.networkrail.co.uk (2005)

REFLECTIVE OBSERVATIONS

Importance of the development concept

From a development perspective, a very important aspect to consider is the development concept which defines *what* is to be developed and *why*. Basically, no matter what type of development it is, every project or programme should arguably be based on a clear and coherent concept of *what* the project or programme is, and *why* it is being carried out. As the King's Cross example shows, there is a clear concept of *why* the station is being developed (for example, to reduce over-crowding), and *what* Network Rail is planning to develop (for example, a new concourse). Of course, as with any large-scale development, this might take some time to establish before the work can proceed, and it might be seen or expressed in different ways, but without such a concept, it is difficult to see how any meaningful and value-creating development can be achieved. Indeed, for any project, large or small, it is important to know *what* is being envisaged, and *why*, as we now explain.

Clarifying the WHAT and the WHY

Although just two simple words, WHAT and WHY are immensely powerful for clarifying the overall concept of any project or programme, as the following example shows from Erling Andersen et al's book *Goal Directed Project Management*:

> *a car importer wanted to develop a computer-based customer service system, a common project task. Before taking on the task, discussions were held about what the organization wished to achieve. What emerged from these discussions was that it wished to treat customers in a way that would encourage them to remain customers for life. This insight lead to an analysis of which aspects of car ownership and maintenance gave rise to brand loyalty and what that implied for service and quality standards in all branches of the organization. Only after completing this process was the purpose of the project clarified. The project [concept] thus went from the development of a simple computer system to a composite project where staff also worked to improve service and quality in all customer contact areas. The project had acquired a purpose ('Our customers remain loyal to the organization for life') that genuinely supported something of importance for the organization.*[1]

As this extract shows, not only is it important to clarify WHAT needs to be developed, but also WHY the development is being undertaken. In other words, for any new or proposed development, it is usually important to clarify the wider aims first and then how the development ideas will help to achieve these aims. And in principle, only when WHY and WHAT are known, or at least signposted in some way, should the focus then shift to HOW the work should be organized, for example, whether the proposed development is one project, several projects or a programme of projects for example. Also, in clarifying the *core purpose* of a project, programme or any proposed scheme of development, we would also use the value perspective presented in Chapter 6. For example, applying it to the car importer example, the revised concept identifies a clear distinction between the main *outcome* sought (for example, long-term customer loyalty) and the *outputs* needed to help to achieve this, for example, service and quality improvements in all customer contact areas.

In summary, the importance of having a coherent development concept is clear to see, for it is this concept that drives the whole project or programme (excluding other agenda of course!) Also, getting to this concept is rarely straightforward, as the discussion shows in the example above, which is another reason why this aspect is very important. Consider once again the words of Edward de Bono about the importance of first stage thinking:

> *it is in the first stage of thinking that the **concepts** ... are put together. Choice of attention area, choice of entry point, choice of factors, these are all part of the first stage of thinking. And such choices will predetermine the final result of the thinking process.*[2] *(emphasis added)*

Experience also shows that such choices predetermine not only the result of the thinking process, but also the final result of the whole project or programme. In other words, if the project or programme concept is flawed or incoherent, then arguably the likelihood of anything useful emerging is greatly reduced. And as we mentioned in an earlier chapter, the other thing to note here is that no amount of planning or risk analysis etc can ever reverse this.

Example Aspect 3: Strategic Phase

DEFINITION

The strategic phase of the development process refers to the front-end of projects and programmes covering activities such as strategic and commercial analysis, concept definition, the development plan, strategic procurement and contract negotiations.

REAL-WORLD EXAMPLE

Coalfields Heritage Initiative Kent

The focus of this initiative is on the Kent Coalfield area which has a rich and largely unrecorded history, and its aim has been to develop a virtual museum of life in the Kent coalfields along with a travelling exhibition and some walking trails. To record the East Kent's mining heritage, one of the primary tasks has been to prepare a community archive comprising photographs, documents, text stories, oral memories and video clips. Another part of the project – the Miner's Way Trail – has utilized the information obtained to develop a coalfields trail focusing on the old sites and the surrounding countryside. The idea has been to have three linked trails not only suitable for walkers, but also cyclists and horse-riders. The trails feature signage, interpretation and artwork.

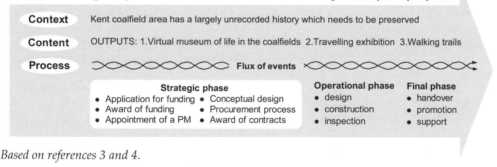

Based on references 3 and 4.

REFLECTIVE OBSERVATIONS

The all-important front-end of projects and programmes

Whatever the initial phase is called, the *front-end* of projects and programmes is arguably the most important phase of any project or programme, simply because the judgements made here are strategically important for the whole project or programme; remember, for example, the importance of the development concept in Aspect 2. Consider also the image above of the Coalfields Heritage Project: deciding who should manage the project, and which contractor should be awarded the construction contract for the walking trails are both strategically important judgements that will affect the whole project, which from a development perspective, is why we refer to the front-end as the *strategic phase*. Notice also that the model above is only illustrative of the sorts of activities that might form part of the strategic phase for this particular project, and is not a general representation of the strategic front-end of projects. Despite what certain PM publications seem to imply, there is no one 'best way' of approaching the front-end of projects and programmes, for it clearly depends on the type of development involved, and also things such as the organizational perspective from which the project or programme is being viewed; for example, a client's view of a procurement process will clearly be different to the contractor's view of that process. Moreover, the issues at the front-end of projects are always complex and cannot be understood from just one perspective; hence, whatever type of development it is, all of the perspectives in this book are likely to be needed during the initial phase of any project or programme, in order to make sense of the issues and to craft the action going forward.

Focus more on WHAT and WHY rather than HOW

From a development perspective, whatever activity might form part of the strategic phase, the important mindset at this stage is that of continuing to think WHAT and WHY, as in aspect 2, rather than thinking about questions of HOW. For example, some people might argue the Coalfields Heritage Project should be seen as a programme rather than a project, which could well be a more useful perspective; however, in our view, this is not a *strategic* consideration, when compared to say other considerations such as the expected *scope* of the project, and the top level *requirements* for each of the expected outputs. For example, WHAT is being envisaged with the virtual museum: is it mainly an *IT-related* development, or does it encompass *organizational development* as well? And similarly with the travelling exhibition, is the expected output a *product* essentially (for example, a mobile unit), or is it this plus the development of an education *service* for the local community? Clearly, the answers to these questions have a very significant bearing on the scope and activities of the project or programme, something which can be easily neglected at the start of any development. Other strategic considerations could be that in order to attract more visitors to the area – which might be another WHY – the trail needs to also form part of a broader scheme of infrastructure development that is being planned, in which case this part of the Coalfields project also becomes part of another programme. To conclude, whether we see things as a project or programme at this stage (that is, how to organize the work), is much less important (we believe) than the more strategic considerations of WHAT and WHY.

Example activities that might be carried out in the strategic phase

From a development perspective, example activities that might be carried out during this phase are listed below, and more information on these can be found in Appendix E.

Development image of projects   👓 **development perspective**

Example activities   **Strategic phase**

- Strategic and commercial analysis (context)
- Concept definition (WHAT and WHY)
- Strategic development planning
- Feasibility assessment (client organization)
- Strategic requirements definition (for example, outputs)
- Strategic procurement (for example, tendering activity)

- Tender submissions
- Contract negotiations and award
- Operational planning
- Risk and uncertainty analysis
- Financial planning, estimating
- Team development

Operational phase | **Final phase**

Note 1. Some of these activities overlap with the value creation model in Chapter 6.

Note 2. Some of these activities will be different for different organizations, for example, construction projects (client and contractor).

Illustrative only

Example Aspect 4: Operational Phase

DEFINITION

> *The operational phase of the development process refers to the main part of a project or programme covering the technical activity of development (for example, construction or training) and the managerial activity of planning, organizing and control.*

REAL-WORLD EXAMPLE

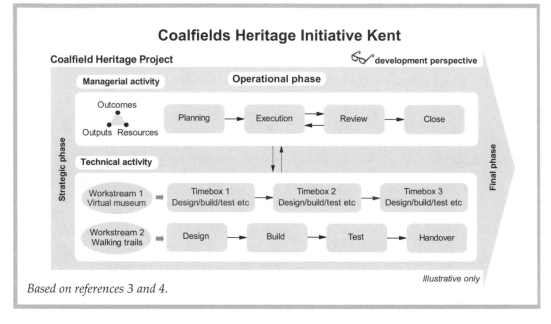

Coalfields Heritage Initiative Kent

Coalfield Heritage Project — development perspective

Illustrative only

Based on references 3 and 4.

REFLECTIVE OBSERVATIONS

No one 'best way' of approaching the operational phase of development

Just as there is no one 'best way' of approaching the front-end of projects and programmes, the same is true of the *operational phase*, which is where the main work of any project or programme is usually carried out. Like the strategic phase, this phase also depends on the type of development involved, and also for instance whether there is more than one type of development within the same project, as in the example above. As the model shows, workstream 1 is an *IT-related* development, which could be approached through a series of so-called 'timeboxes' (a term used in the IT industry for incremental development), and workstream 2 being *infrastructure* type development, could be approached through a more traditional lifecycle process of design, build, test and so on. Moreover, to help produce the outputs, the workstreams could be managed using any mainstream project management approach such as GDPM (Goal Directed Project Management), PRINCE2™ (Projects in Controlled Environments) or an in-house approach combining several approaches.

Another point to note is that traditionally, projects in construction, engineering, IT and so on have tended to focus on the development of a single output (for example, a new building, engine, or IT system), however, the focus in many areas now is on delivering multiple outputs from within the same project or programme. In aerospace engineering for example, new engine projects focus not just on developing the engines, but also the service infrastructure needed to support these engines in service. And similarly with IT-related developments, the focus now is not just on developing new IT systems, but also business processes and new working practices and so on; in other words, in the case of IT-related projects, the general concept is no longer that of *system development* but rather that of *business transformation* for example, which is a different concept. In summary, from a development perspective, the primary focus across most sectors now is no longer the production of physical assets and systems, but rather the development of new and improved products, service capabilities and so on, all aimed at creating different kinds of value and benefit for different individuals, groups and organizations, as discussed in Chapter 6.

Technical activity versus managerial activity

Although each type of development is different, with its own practices and activities, it is useful in planning the operational phase of any project to distinguish between two kinds of activity: the *technical activity* of the project (for example, the technical activity of developing new IT systems, aero engines, buildings, people, and organizations), and the *managerial activity* needed to plan, monitor and control this activity. For example, with the Coalfields Heritage Project, the model opposite shows two streams of technical activity, one concerned with the virtual museum and another concerned with the walking trails; and then above these, the managerial activity of planning, monitoring and controlling these two workstreams. In reality of course, all of the activities in any project or programme are heavily interconnected, which is one of the reasons why this distinction is useful in planning the operational phase. Before we explain why, note that by 'technical activity', we do not mean technical engineering type activity, but rather the technical activity of any project or programme, which may or may not be technology-related. For example, if the type of development was organizational development, then the technical activity would be the activity of organizational development, and similarly for professional development, the technical activity could be modules and workshops. In summary, such a distinction is useful because it means the operational phase of the project or programme can be more coherently designed and planned, both the technical part and the managerial part, which in turn means the actual work of the project or programme can then be more effectively monitored and reviewed.

Example activities that might be carried out in the operational phase

Although only illustrative, the diagram below shows some examples of technical activity and managerial activity that might form part of the operational phase of projects. For some references relevant to the managerial activity, please see Appendix E.

Development image of projects　　　　　　　　　　👓 development perspective

	Operational phase		
Managerial activity			
• Planning and scheduling	• Risk and uncertainty analysis	• Progress reporting	
• Estimating and budgeting	• Contract management	• Stage reviews	
Technical activity			
• Systems engineering	• Property development	• Professional development	
• Systems development	• New product development	• Organizational development	

(Strategic phase → Final phase)

Illustrative only

139

Example Aspect 5: Final Phase

DEFINITION

The final phase of the development process refers to the back-end of projects and programmes, where the activity of this phase (like the other phases) depends on the type of development being carried out and the actual project or programme itself.

REAL-WORLD EXAMPLE

Rethinking Project Management Research Project

Funded by the UK Government, *Rethinking Project Management* was the name given to a research project carried out between 2002 and 2007 to investigate the areas in which mainstream project management theory needs to develop to support practitioners working on today's projects and programmes.[5] From a development perspective, the important phase here is the *final phase* of the programme, which involved not only the publication of a special issue of an academic journal, but also the delivery of various presentations and seminars to different practitioner audiences – see below.

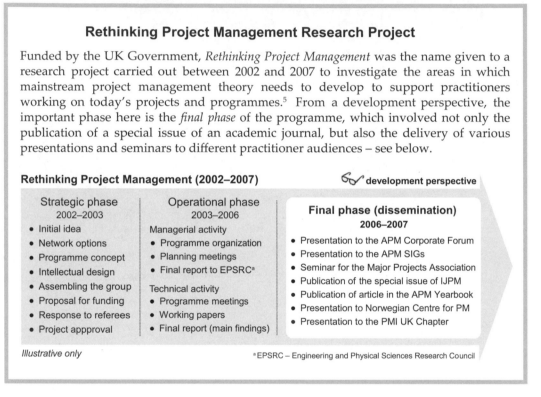

Rethinking Project Management (2002–2007)   development perspective

Strategic phase 2002–2003	Operational phase 2003–2006	Final phase (dissemination) 2006–2007
• Initial idea	Managerial activity	• Presentation to the APM Corporate Forum
• Network options	• Programme organization	• Presentation to the APM SIGs
• Programme concept	• Planning meetings	• Seminar for the Major Projects Association
• Intellectual design	• Final report to EPSRC[a]	• Publication of the special issue of IJPM
• Assembling the group		• Publication of article in the APM Yearbook
• Proposal for funding	Technical activity	• Presentation to Norwegian Centre for PM
• Response to referees	• Programme meetings	• Presentation to the PMI UK Chapter
• Project appproval	• Working papers	
	• Final report (main findings)	

Illustrative only   [a] EPSRC – Engineering and Physical Sciences Research Council

REFLECTIVE OBSERVATIONS

A project for both researchers and practitioners

Launched in March 2004, *Rethinking Project Management* was not just an academic research project to develop a research agenda for the PM research community, it was also a project to help develop the knowledge of practitioners, by distilling the key messages from the research findings and disseminating these through organizations such as the Association for Project Management and the Major Projects Association. In other words, the project continued *beyond* the publication of the main research findings into a third and final phase of disseminating the key messages to practitioners in different organizations. In essence, the concept from the start was always that of sharing the results with practitioners, as well as developing a research agenda for advancing the subject of project management. Not only this, but the model opposite also provides another illustration of the three core phases of development: as the diagram shows, the *strategic phase* involved various activities such as drafting some options, designing the programme, assembling the group, and the writing of a funding proposal to the research council. Next, the *operational phase* then involved the *technical activity* of the research itself (that is, the meetings and working papers and so on) and the *managerial activity* of directing the project, planning the meetings and so on.[6] And then to complete the whole project, a *final phase* of dissemination activity was carried out between 2006 and 2007. So, how does this final phase idea relate to other projects and programmes?

Development doesn't end at the point of installation or handover

In seeing projects as development processes, we would suggest the *final phase* of activity strongly depends on the type of development and also the actual project or programme itself. And like the other two phases, there is no prescriptive model for the back-end either, but what is hopefully clear from the example opposite is that this final phase extends well beyond the traditional end-point of production, as we illustrate below.

Example project or programme	Final phase of the process
University research project	Presentations and seminars
Commercial property development	Marketing and sales
Infrastructure programme	Transition into operation or service
Business change programme	Refinements to processes and systems
Organizational training programme	Reflective evaluation workshops

As these examples show, the final phase is clearly a separate phase of activity that extends well beyond the traditional lifecycle of projects, which typically ends at the point when a product, system or facility has been delivered. Consider for example the end-point of a commercial property development (example 2 above): at what point does this project end? A traditional lifecycle view would suggest the project ends when the properties have been built and handed over to sales; this, however, represents a *production* view, which is different to the *development* view being presented here. Seen from this book's development image, handing over the new properties would form part of the back-end of the *operational phase*, before the *final phase* of marketing and sales to realize the commercial value being sought from the property development.

Our last point about the *final phase* of this book's development's image is that it does not include the operations part of an organization, as in a PFI service operation for example: in this project, the final phase would be the *transition* from development to operations, and this would be the end of the development process. From an organizational perspective, however, the service part of a PFI project could be seen as the 'operations' part of the temporary project organization and this is what we turn to next. To conclude, what this shows again is that all projects and programmes are not just development processes, they can also be viewed as social and political processes, value creation processes, temporary organizations, change processes and so on, and hence why they need to be considered from other perspectives too. As Arthur Battram states:

To engage with complexity, we need perspectives which admit the
possibility that more than one thing can be true at once.

Arthur Battram

Image Summary

Having introduced five aspects to consider from a development perspective, we turn now to this book's development image which encapsulates these five related aspects. As stated previously, our aim is not to be prescriptive or all-encompassing, but rather to offer a practical image of projects that the practitioner can use in a variety of different situations. Indeed, like all the images in this book, this particular image can be applied in many different ways, ranging from the occasional use of the whole image or just selected aspects, through to using it in a structured process, or as part of a common language with which to see and talk about the complex realities of a project or programme. These example uses are covered in Part 3 *Applying the Images* but for now it is important to briefly summarize the development image of projects.

Projects as development processes

In essence, the image here is that of *projects as development processes*, by which we mean an organized process to develop things such as products, systems, services, civil infrastructure and people's knowledge and skills. As explained in Aspect 1, this core image can be applied to any type of development, including areas not normally associated with project management, such as professional development and community development. Moreover, it is important to see 'development' here as meaning either developing something new (for example, a new hotel) or improving something that already exists (for example, refurbishing an existing hotel). As explained in Aspect 2, this book's development image is strongly linked to the value creation image in Chapter 6, which means that links can be made to other ideas such as sustainable development and community development for example; further discussion about these, however, is beyond the scope of this book. Finally, a useful way of framing the development process is to think of it in three main phases as shown opposite, with the lower diagram showing the interconnectedness between the various aspects.

Notice in Figure 7.1 that the flux of events is shown to emphasize that the reality of any development work is always a social and political process; in other words, like the other process models of intervention, value creation and change, the three-phase development process is not to be mistaken for the actuality of projects, which is always more complex than any single image of purposeful activity. Notice also the development model is broader than the traditional model of delivering something to specification, cost and time; in short, deciding *what* to deliver and *why* is not covered by the traditional lifecycle, and similarly at the other end of the process, this book's development model extends the traditional lifecycle model with a final phase of activity linked to the type of development being carried out. A case in point here is the Heathrow Terminal 5 Project which was heavily criticized for underestimating the work involved in the final 'transition' phase of the project.

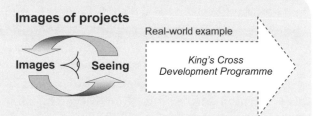

Social image of projects
Political image of projects
Intervention image of projects
Value creation image of projects
Development image of projects
Organizational image of projects
Change image of projects

Images of projects

Images ⟷ Seeing

Real-world example

*King's Cross
Development Programme*

Development image of projects

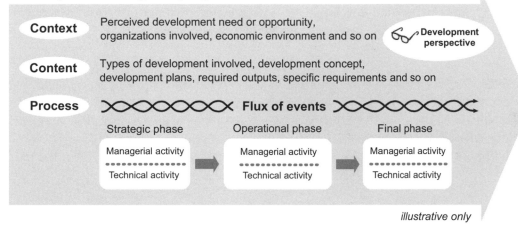

Context — Perceived development need or opportunity, organizations involved, economic environment and so on

Development perspective

Content — Types of development involved, development concept, development plans, required outputs, specific requirements and so on

Process — Flux of events

Strategic phase   Operational phase   Final phase

Managerial activity   Managerial activity   Managerial activity
....
Technical activity   Technical activity   Technical activity

illustrative only

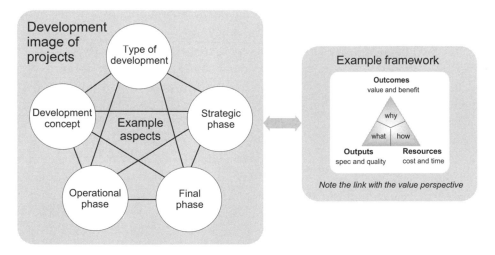

Development image of projects

Type of development

Development concept

Example aspects

Strategic phase

Operational phase

Final phase

Example framework

Outcomes
value and benefit

why

what   how

Outputs   **Resources**
spec and quality   cost and time

Note the link with the value perspective

Figure 7.1   A development image of projects

143

A guiding framework and not a prescription

It is important to state that whilst this image is applicable to all types of development, it doesn't prescribe or stipulate any particular approach to the development process. It simply provides a *starting point* for thinking about projects and programmes from a development perspective. For example, in the case of new developments, it doesn't stipulate whether the new development is one project, or a programme of projects, or something else perhaps; this is something to be worked out during the strategic phase. Also, in another context, the approach to all three phases could be a stage-gate approach or some other approach; it simply depends on the perceived context and the type of development being carried out. In other words, as a guiding framework, the model in Figure 7.1 can be used with other frameworks and approaches, including the UK Government approaches of PRINCE2™ and MSP™[7,8]. For IT-related developments, a useful concept to apply during the strategic phase could also be the PSO concept provided by Erling Andersen et al in their book *Goal Directed Project Management:*

> *PSO development is an abbreviation for the development of people, system and organization. … When introducing a new IT system, a frequent mistake is to overemphasize the technical work. The development of people and organization necessary to enable the system to function well is either totally neglected or paid insufficient attention. … Using the PSO concept requires a little thought and extra effort, but the reward is a broader view of what the project involves.*[9]

Is a different perspective needed?

Finally, whatever other concepts, frameworks and approaches are used, it is important to recognise the key assumption behind any model of development. Irrespective of the type of development, the key assumption is that some entity X (for example, a new building or a new weapon system) needs to be developed, in other words, there is an underlying *worldview* that developing X is a good thing to do. This generally is the worldview behind all projects and programmes that start with a perceived need or opportunity for development. But what if the starting point is more problematical than this? What if the starting point is a situation in which there are serious concerns about a proposed development (for example, is it the right thing to do?), or perhaps a situation in which there is no clear view at all about *what* needs to be developed and *why*. In these situations, the development image is far less appropriate, or initially to start off with at least, and a different perspective might be needed. For example, from an intervention perspective, a useful approach could be to review the situation first to decide what action is needed, which might conclude that something different is needed, or that the resources would be better used elsewhere.

Strengths and Limitations

Strengths of the development perspective

1. Directs attention to the primary activity of projects and programmes, for example, the development of a new building or professional development.

2. Highlights the different types of development that can be carried out through projects and programmes. Not just engineering and construction.

3. Provides a pragmatic framework that can be used with other frameworks, models and approaches, both technical and managerial.

4. Provides a broader image of development than the traditional image of delivering something to specification, cost and time.

5. Highlights the importance of the front-end of projects and programmes, notably, the strategic phase of the development process.

Limitations of the development perspective

1. A generic perspective that needs to be adapted to the particular type(s) of development involved. Requires other more detailed models too.

2. Can lead to a unitary view of development when in reality the process is different for different players, for example, client and contractor.

3. Can lead to difficulties in deciding the end point of a project or programme, for example, the duration of the final phase.

4. Assumes that development is needed, for example, that developing a new weapon system is preferable to some other course of action.

5. Neglects other important aspects of projects and programmes, such as the social and political aspects of development.

*[Images] create insight. But they also distort. They have strengths. But they also have limitations. In creating ways of seeing they tend to create ways of **not** seeing.*

Gareth Morgan

The achievements of an organization are the results of the combined effort of each individual.
Vince Lombardi

Chapter Eight

Image 6: Projects as Temporary Organizations

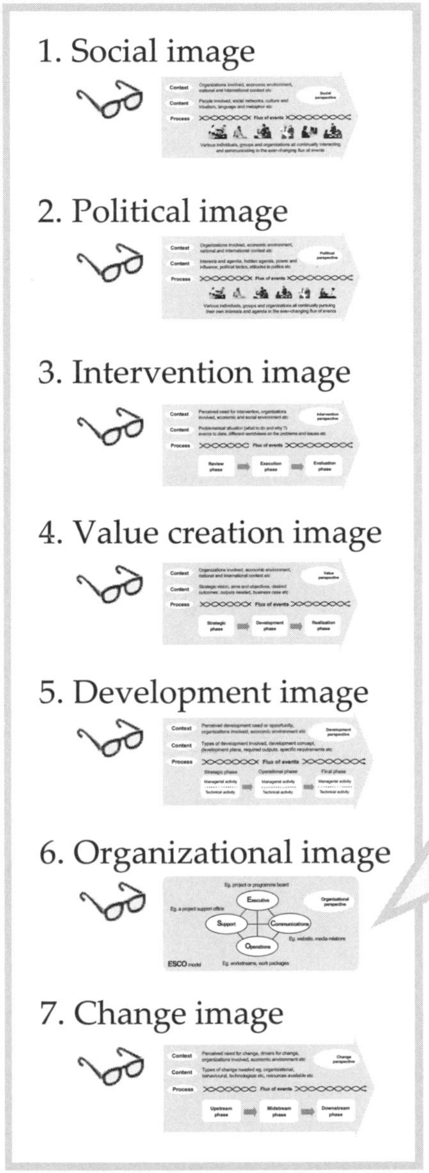
1. Social image
2. Political image
3. Intervention image
4. Value creation image
5. Development image
6. Organizational image
7. Change image

Organizational Perspective

Chapter Structure

Image Definition

Relevance and Importance

Five Example Aspects

Image Summary

Strengths and Limitations

Image Definition

> *The TEMPORARY ORGANIZATION IMAGE is a framework for seeing projects as being like conventional organizations, covering aspects such as the executive (for example, roles and responsibilities), support activity (for example, training), communications and marketing, and operations.*

Relevance and Importance

Since all projects and programmes involve aspects such as roles and responsibilities, the relevance and importance of this core image hardly needs stating either. For any project or programme, there are always organizational aspects to consider, and many of these need careful consideration as this chapter will show. Typical examples are roles and responsibilities, team structure, reporting structures, support functions, governance arrangements and so on. But this is not all, for in taking this perspective, the emphasis here is not just on the organizational aspects of projects, but actually a very different way of seeing projects to the other images presented so far. Consider, for example, the Eden Project below.

The Eden Project
The Eden Project is wholly owned by the Eden Trust, a UK Registered Charity. It is operated on behalf of the Trust by Eden Project Limited, a wholly owned subsidiary of the Eden Trust.

www.edenproject.com

The first thing to notice about the example above is that the Eden Project is essentially an organization just like Marks and Spencer and the University of Manchester. And herein lies another way of seeing projects that is very different to the mainstream image of projects: in contrast to the lifecycle image of projects, this perspective is about seeing projects as being like conventional organizations, such as Marks and Spencer and the University of Manchester. In other words, projects such as the Eden Project can be seen as *temporary organizations*,[1] the only difference being they are temporary rather than semi-permanent, which is the phrase we use for organizations such as Marks and Spencer. Another example is the UK Government agency, Connecting for Health, the organization set up in 2005 to manage the NHS National Programme for IT. Moreover, as this chapter will show, the image of projects as temporary organizations can also be applied to organizational change projects yielding useful insights and ideas that might not otherwise be considered.

Five Example Aspects

Applying this chapter's temporary organization image to the Eden Project, the sorts of aspects that might be considered are:

- What is the structure of the *organizational entity* known as the Eden Project?
- How is the *executive part* organized and what are its responsibilities?
- What are the activities of the *support part* and what are the main roles?
- How is the *communications part* organized and what are its main responsibilities?
- How is the *operations part* organized and what are the roles and responsibilities?

Like the other chapters, these five questions illustrate the five example aspects to be considered from this chapter's temporary organization perspective. Although not the only aspects that could be considered, these are the aspects that we have chosen to focus on because of their wide applicability to most projects and programmes.

Aspect 1: Organizational Entity

The organizational entity is the project, programme or portfolio that is analogous to a conventional organization and is seen to consist of four linked parts: an executive part, a support part, a communications part and an operations part.

Aspect 2: Executive Part

The executive part of projects, programmes and portfolios is analogous to the executive part of organizations, covering aspects such as the executive structure, senior management roles and responsibilities, governance arrangements and so on.

Aspect 3: Support Part

The support part of projects, programmes and portfolios is analogous to the support part of organizations, covering aspects such as administration, IT, PM training and development, and so on (re: PSOs, PMOs and so on).

Aspect 4: Communications Part

The communications part of projects, programmes and portfolios is analogous to the communications part of organizations, covering aspects such as external and internal communications, project and programme marketing, public relations and so on.

Aspect 5: Operations Part

The operations part of projects, programmes and portfolios is analogous to the operations part of organizations, covering aspects such as the organization of work (for example, workstreams), roles and responsibilities, and team structure.

As explained in the Introduction to Part 2, this next part of the chapter presents each of these five aspects over two pages, the left-hand page providing a real example (for example, the Eden Project) and the right-hand page offering some observations for the reader to reflect upon in relation to their own knowledge and experience. Beyond these five aspects, we then summarize the temporary organization image as a whole, and briefly state some of the strengths and limitations of this important perspective.

Example Aspect 1: Organizational Entity

DEFINITION

> *The organizational entity is the project, programme, or portfolio that is analogous to a conventional organization and is seen to consist of four linked parts: an executive part, a support part, a communications part and an operations part.*

REAL-WORLD EXAMPLE

The Eden Project

The Eden Project is wholly owned by The Eden Trust, a company limited by guarantee and a UK regsitered charity. The Eden Project is operated on behalf of the Trust by Eden Project Ltd (EPL). Eden Project Limited is managed by a board of executive and non-executive directors, who remain ultimately responsible to the Trustees of the Eden Trust.[2]

REFLECTIVE OBSERVATIONS

An organization just like other organizations

Notice the words in the box above: the Eden Project is wholly owned by a company called the Eden Trust and the project itself is operated by a company called Eden Project Ltd, on behalf of The Eden Trust. In other words, the important thing to notice here is that the Eden Project is essentially an *organization*, just like other organizations such as Marks and Spencer and the University of Manchester. And herein lies another important way of seeing projects which is very different to the traditional textbook image of projects.

Projects as temporary organizations

In contrast to seeing projects as lifecycle processes, the image here is about seeing projects as *temporary organizations,* in other words, whole organizations in themselves, except that they are temporary rather than semi-permanent. In fact the Eden Project might well evolve into a semi-permanent organization, but we use it here to illustrate the idea of seeing projects as temporary organizations. Moreover, it also illustrates the difference with the mainstream image of projects: in short, whereas the mainstream image starts with the lifecycle concept and *then* considers the organizational aspects, this perspective *starts* by seeing projects as whole organizations in themselves, and then considers the organizational aspects which flow from this. As the Eden example shows, such a perspective clearly applies to project organizations such as Eden Project Ltd, and the same perspective can also be applied to other large-scale projects and programmes. For example, seeing projects and programmes as businesses can generate useful insights and ideas which might not otherwise be considered. And similarly for internal projects and programmes, such as strategy implementation programmes and organizational change projects, it can be useful to see these initiatives as temporary organizations too, and to consider how they might be organized and managed in ways similar to the design and operation of conventional organizations.

Introducing the temporary organization image of projects

In order to start applying this perspective, we need a generic model of organizations that can be easily applied to projects. A particularly useful model is the ESCO model shown below.[3-4]

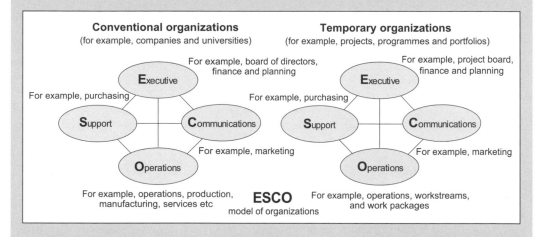

As the diagram shows, the ESCO model of conventional organizations can also be applied to projects and programmes such as the Eden Project opposite. Just like conventional organizations, Eden Project Ltd can be conceptualized as an organization consisting of four linked parts: it has an *executive* part in the form of a board of directors with various roles and responsibilities; a *support* part responsible for activity such as purchasing; a *communications* part responsible for activity such as media relations; and an *operations* part covering the whole Eden site operation with its biome conservatories. In effect, the only conceptual difference, from this perspective, is that Eden Project Ltd is just a less permanent organization than say Marks and Spencer or the University of Manchester. Another good example is the Connecting for Health organization responsible for the NHS National Programme for IT (re: Chapter 3), which could also be conceptualized using the ESCO model. Basically, the reason we use the ESCO model is that it can be applied at all levels – projects, programmes and portfolios – and it can also be used to conceptualize programmes within portfolios, and projects within programmes and so on, as this chapter will show.

In adopting this perspective, it is important to state that this is not the only way of thinking about the organizational aspects of projects, and nor are we suggesting that the challenges of temporary project organizations are necessarily the same as those of conventional organizations. However, as the Eden example demonstrates, seeing projects as temporary organizations is not just a different way of seeing, it is actually a more representative view of the organizational status of many of today's projects, for example, the Eden Project and the NHS National Programme for IT. Not only this, the ESCO model also provides a practical framework that can be applied to all projects and programmes, including non-legal entities such as business change programmes for example. To illustrate this further, each part of the ESCO model will now be considered in more detail.

Example Aspect 2: Executive Part

DEFINITION

The executive part of projects, programmes and portfolios is analogous to the executive part of organizations, covering aspects such as the executive structure, roles and responsibilities, governance arrangements and so on.

REAL-WORLD EXAMPLE

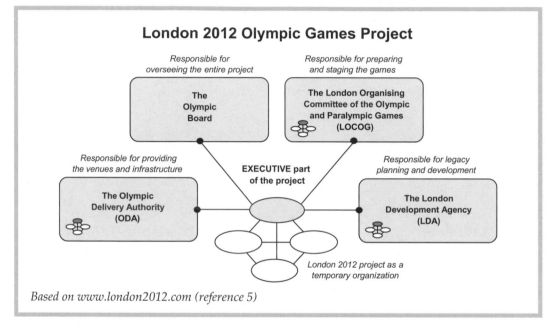

London 2012 Olympic Games Project

Responsible for overseeing the entire project

The Olympic Board

Responsible for preparing and staging the games

The London Organising Committee of the Olympic and Paralympic Games (LOCOG)

Responsible for providing the venues and infrastructure

The Olympic Delivery Authority (ODA)

EXECUTIVE part of the project

Responsible for legacy planning and development

The London Development Agency (LDA)

London 2012 project as a temporary organization

Based on www.london2012.com (reference 5)

REFLECTIVE OBSERVATIONS

A complex executive structure involving multiple organizations

Notice firstly that the *executive part* of the London 2012 Project is not a single organizational entity but rather a combination of the executive parts of four different organizations.

The Olympic Board is responsible for overseeing the entire project and for ensuring delivery of the commitments made to the International Olympic Committee when the Games were awarded in July 2005. The Board is currently made up of the Olympics Minister, the Mayor of London, the Chair of the British Olympic Association and the Chair of the London 2012 Organizing Committee.

The London Organizing Committee of the Olympic and Paralympic Games (LOCOG) is responsible for preparing and staging the 2012 Games. Led by a chair and a chief executive, LOCOG is a limited company whose funding comes mainly from the private sector. Current predictions at the time of writing are that £2 billion will be raised from sources including sponsorship, broadcasting rights and selling merchandise.

The Olympic Delivery Authority (ODA) is the public body responsible for providing the venues and infrastructure for the Games and their use post 2012. Led by a chairman and CEO, the ODA was established by the London Olympic Games and Paralympic Games Act in March 2006. As a public body, the ODA is accountable to the UK Government, the Greater London Authority and other stakeholders for its work.

The London Development Agency (LDA) is the organization currently responsible for legacy planning beyond 2012 and ensuring a lasting legacy for the area of East London.

It is important to recognize that what we are focusing on here is the executive part of the whole London 2012 Project and not just the Olympic Board, or the executive parts of LOCOG, ODA or the LDA. From a temporary organization perspective, the executive part of the whole London 2012 project is essentially a four-part structure comprising the Olympic Board working in partnership with the executive parts of LOCOG, the ODA and the LDA. Notice too we are only focusing on the executive parts of these organizations and not the other parts such as operations, which is what the little ESCO icon inside the LOCOG, ODA and LDA boxes opposite seeks to show. And this leads to another important point about the ESCO model: notice also how this temporary organization perspective using the ESCO model could be applied separately to any one of these organizations; for example, the model might be used to ask questions about how the governance arrangements of the ODA relate to the governance arrangements of LOCOG. Like all the examples in this book, however, the London 2012 project is simply an illustration of how this particular perspective, through the use of the ESCO model, can be applied to a particular project. Further discussion of the project itself is beyond the scope of this book.

Example structures, roles and responsibilities

Thinking more generally about the executive part of projects, it is important to state that there is no single or correct structure for all projects and programmes, and nor is there a standard framework of executive type roles, with job titles and responsibilities, to which all executive roles conform. For example, a senior project manager with executive responsibilities in company A, might be called a programme manager in company B; and similarly, a programme manager in company C might be called a projects director in company D. That said, it is clearly possible to identify various executive-type structures, roles and responsibilities in practice, and a selection of these appears in the table below. Further discussion of these, however, is beyond the scope of this book, and Appendix E contains some advice on where to find out more. The next aspect to be considered from a temporary organization perspective is the *support* part.

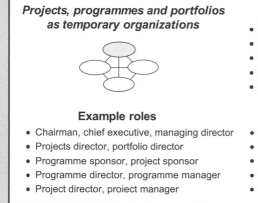

Projects, programmes and portfolios as temporary organizations	**Example structures**
	• Board of trustees (for example, the Eden Trust)
	• Board of directors (for example, Eden Project Ltd)
	• Steering group, steering committee
	• Programme board (for example, MSP)
	• Project board (for example, PRINCE2)
Example roles	**Example responsibilities**
• Chairman, chief executive, managing director	• Strategy, policy and governance
• Projects director, portfolio director	• Financial planning, investment appraisal
• Programme sponsor, project sponsor	• Programme selection, project selection
• Programme director, programme manager	• Contractor negotiations, awarding of contracts
• Project director, proiect manager	• Programme reviews, project reviews

Example Aspect 3: Support Part

DEFINITION

> *The support part of projects, programmes and portfolios is analogous to the support part of organizations, covering aspects such as administration, IT, PM training and development and so on, (re: PSOs, PMOs and so on).*

REAL-WORLD EXAMPLE

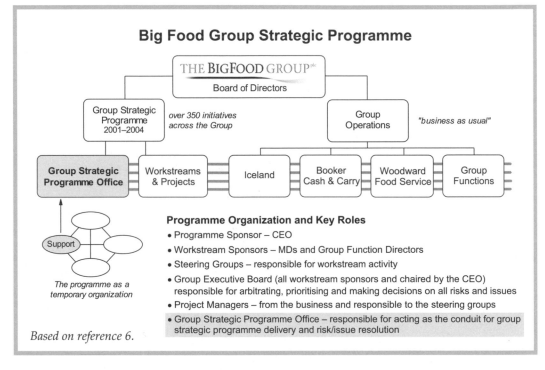

Big Food Group Strategic Programme

THE BIGFOOD GROUP plc
Board of Directors

Group Strategic Programme 2001–2004 — *over 350 initiatives across the Group*

Group Operations — *"business as usual"*

Group Strategic Programme Office | Workstreams & Projects | Iceland | Booker Cash & Carry | Woodward Food Service | Group Functions

Support — *The programme as a temporary organization*

Programme Organization and Key Roles

- Programme Sponsor – CEO
- Workstream Sponsors – MDs and Group Function Directors
- Steering Groups – responsible for workstream activity
- Group Executive Board (all workstream sponsors and chaired by the CEO) responsible for arbitrating, prioritising and making decisions on all risks and issues
- Project Managers – from the business and responsible to the steering groups
- Group Strategic Programme Office – responsible for acting as the conduit for group strategic programme delivery and risk/issue resolution

Based on reference 6.

REFLECTIVE OBSERVATIONS

A programme support office

As the diagram shows, the example here is that of a programme office that formed the support part of a Group Strategic Programme within the Big Food Group Plc between 2001 and 2004. In August 2000 the Big Food Group Plc was a £5.3 billion organization created from the merger of Iceland Frozen Foods and Booker Cash & Carry. At the time of the merger, Iceland owned 766 stores nationwide and Booker Cash & Carry was a long-established British company that had its origins in the sugar trade. Hailed as a major strategic development, the merger of the two businesses met with problems from the start: Booker and Iceland were very different businesses with very different cultures and it was unclear as to how the new company would deliver the £50 million annualized synergy benefits promised at the time of the merger. Under the leadership of a new CEO, a comprehensive strategic review was initiated to address a number of fundamental questions, including how the group should be structured and what the strategic direction should be for the various business units. To help achieve the new strategic vision, strategic plans were created for each of the business units and group functions, and these were broken down into clear quantifiable strategic objectives, each of which consisted of a portfolio of programmes and projects with development plans and change management infrastructure to support their delivery. As a temporary organization, the whole strategic programme consisted of over 350 initiatives and the primary task of the programme support office was to help track and facilitate the delivery of the programme and the rolling strategic planning process.

Notice how the temporary organization perspective and the ESCO model is being applied here: the programme being conceptualized as a temporary organization is the Group Strategic Programme and the *support* part of this programme is the Group Strategic Programme Office, both shown in the diagram opposite. In other words, not only is the perspective applicable to temporary project organizations with legal status (for example, Eden Project Ltd and the Olympic Delivery Authority), the same perspective can also be applied to internal projects and programmes concerned with strategy implementation, business development, and organizational change. As the example opposite shows, the *executive* part was implemented through an executive board chaired by the CEO, the *operations* part was implemented through various workstreams and projects, and the *communications* part was implemented mainly through the programme support office.

Example structures, roles and responsibilities

Thinking more generally about the support part, it is important to emphasize that the ESCO model prompts consideration of *what* support is needed, and *not* what the support activities should actually be, or *how* the support part should be organized. In other words, a project or programme support office is just one of the ways in which the support part might be implemented, and moreover the actual activities of such an office will always depend on the particular project. Other support-type activities could be, for example, procurement and contract administration, training and development, and process improvement; and some of these could even be organized as projects and programmes in their own right (to which the ESCO model could again be applied). In summary, like the executive part of the model, there is no single or correct approach to the support part, and there are many different examples as shown below. And like the executive part, the detail is beyond the scope of this book, and advice on where to find out more can be found in Appendix E. The next aspect to consider is the *communications* part.

Projects, programmes and portfolios as temporary organizations

Example roles

- Programme office manager
- Project or programme support director
- Project support consultant
- Project administration officer
- Business support consultant

Example structures

- Programme management office (PMO)
- Project or programme support office (PSO)
- Contracts and procurement office
- Business support group (internal consultancy)
- Training and development centre

Example responsibilities

- Project and programme planning
- Facilitation support (for example, workshop facilitation)
- Risk assessment and uncertainty analysis
- Progress administration and progress reporting
- Training and development

Example Aspect 4: Communications Part

DEFINITION

> *The communications part of projects, programmes and portfolios is analogous to the communications part of organizations, covering aspects such as external and internal communications, project and programme marketing, public relations and so on.*

REAL-WORLD EXAMPLE

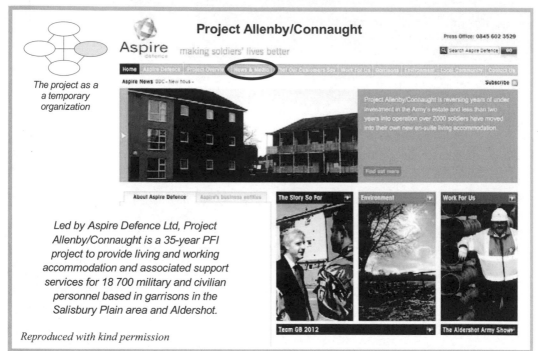

The project as a a temporary organization

Led by Aspire Defence Ltd, Project Allenby/Connaught is a 35-year PFI project to provide living and working accommodation and associated support services for 18 700 military and civilian personnel based in garrisons in the Salisbury Plain area and Aldershot.

Reproduced with kind permission

REFLECTIVE OBSERVATIONS

Project Allenby/Connaught as a temporary organization

To briefly explain the example above, Project Allenby/Connaught is a major project to improve and service the living and working accommodation for approx 20 per cent of the British Army – 18 700 military and civilian personnel based in garrisons in the Salisbury Plain area and Aldershot. Led by Aspire Defence Ltd, the company specifically set up to deliver the project in 2006, Allenby/Connaught is a 35-year PFI project with a value of about £12 billion through life, including £1.2 billion for the cost of construction. Geographically, the project is located in the South of England focusing on Aldershot to the east and separate garrisons in the west around the Army's main manoeuvre training area on Salisbury Plain. Being a large-scale project, it is estimated that the construction work will take about 10 years to complete and will require 1100 construction workers and over 2000 people to provide services. Finally, on completion of this work, there will be over 2000 buildings to service, for which Aspire will receive about £240m in annual revenue from the UK MOD. Before focusing on the communications part, notice firstly how the project can usefully be seen as a *temporary organization* to deliver improvements and services to the British Army over the next 35 years. Like conventional organizations, Aspire Defence Ltd has an *executive* board of directors with various executive roles and responsibilities; a *support* part responsible for contract administration, purchasing, IT and so on; a *communications* part responsible for media relations, keeping staff informed and so on; and an *operations* part covering all the major construction work and future services.

Turning to the *communications* part, one of the ways in which this project communicates with its various stakeholders, is through the 'News & Media' part of the website, as circled opposite, which contains links to various press releases about the project. And similarly for staff and other stakeholders, a magazine called *Aspirations* is published and distributed in hard copy form and through the company website – see example opposite. From an organizational perspective, these are just two examples of how a project or programme can communicate formally with its stakeholders, and there are many other ways in which this can be done. But most importantly, what this example highlights is the importance of regular and purposeful communication with the various people and organizations involved.

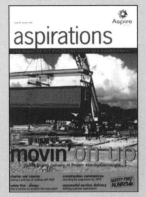

Example structures, roles and responsibilities

Thinking more generally about the communications part of any project or programme, it is important to see this part as encompassing not just communication-type activity, but also (potentially) other areas of conventional organizational activity, such as marketing, media relations and public relations. In other words, from a temporary organization perspective, disciplines such as marketing can be directly relevant to certain projects and programmes, and the aim of the ESCO model is simply to prompt consideration of what these might be for individual initiatives. And like the other parts of the model, there is no single or correct approach to this part either, and there are many examples used in practice as shown below. Moreover, like the other aspects, the more detailed elements of this are beyond the scope of this book, and suggested references can be found in Appendix E. Finally, the fourth part of the ESCO model to consider is the *operations* part.

Projects, programmes and portfolios as temporary organizations

Example structures

- Directorate of communications
- Marketing and communications unit
- Media centre or media relations unit
- Press office or press relations centre
- Project or programme support office (PSO)

Example roles

- Director of communications
- Director of marketing and communications
- Media relations manager
- Senior press officer
- Project communications officer

Example responsibilities

- Handling relations with the media and public
- Communicating development plans
- Reporting regularly on progress and results
- Preparing and staging external events
- Advising others on communication strategies

Example Aspect 5: Operations Part

DEFINITION

The operations part of projects, programmes and portfolios is analogous to the operations part of organizations, covering aspects such as the organization of work (for example, workstreams or work packages), roles and responsibilities, team structure and so on.

REAL-WORLD EXAMPLES

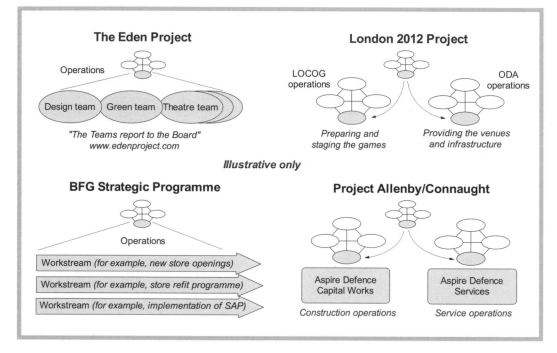

The Eden Project

Operations

Design team   Green team   Theatre team

"The Teams report to the Board"
www.edenproject.com

London 2012 Project

LOCOG operations

ODA operations

Preparing and staging the games

Providing the venues and infrastructure

Illustrative only

BFG Strategic Programme

Operations

Workstream *(for example, new store openings)*

Workstream *(for example, store refit programme)*

Workstream *(for example, implementation of SAP)*

Project Allenby/Connaught

Aspire Defence Capital Works

Aspire Defence Services

Construction operations

Service operations

REFLECTIVE OBSERVATIONS

No one 'best way' of structuring operations

As our four examples show, there is no single way of structuring the 'operations' part of projects and programmes, and like the other parts of the ESCO model, there is no one 'best way' of approaching this part either. Experience shows this part depends on the project or programme, and needs to take account of the particular circumstances in which the project or programme is being carried out. In other words, experience suggests that a pragmatic approach is generally more effective than following a prescriptive approach or method, with its own recommended structure. Such methods might provide useful guidance of course, but drawing on guidance is different to 'following' a prescriptive approach with little or no regard for the actual realties of the particular project. Even projects of the same type, such as two engineering projects, might need to be organized very differently because of the particular circumstances in which they are being carried out. In summary, what is appropriate for one project or programme might be totally inappropriate for another, and hence a pragmatic approach is likely to be the most effective.

Applying the ESCO model to the 'operations' of projects and programmes

❖   Notice firstly the concern here is *how* not *what,* in other words, not what the operations are, but *how* they should be organized in the context of a particular project or programme. As the diagram shows, the Eden operation is a *team-based* structure, whereas the operation of the Big Food Group Programme was organized into different *workstreams.*

❖   Secondly, notice how the operations part can be organized in many different ways; the ESCO model doesn't prescribe any particular approach, it merely provides a *starting point* for thinking about how the operations of a project or programme might be organized.

❖   Thirdly, notice how the model directs attention to certain aspects and not others. For example, if the model is applied to the whole London 2012 project, then the operations part encompasses the operations of every organization involved in the 2012 project, notably LOCOG and the ODA, as shown opposite. However, the model can also be applied to individual organizations such as LOCOG and the ODA, and here the focus would only be on the *operations* of these organizations, as opposed to the operations of the whole project. In short, change the focus and the scope of the model changes too.

❖   Finally, notice how the operations part of a project or programme can encompass not just development-type operations, but also service operations too. For example, if we see the whole of Project Allenby/Connaught as a temporary organization, as shown opposite, then the operations part consists of not just construction, but also the service delivery part too. And this increasingly is the pattern of operations for many large-scale PFI projects, where the development part covers not just the primary development activity, but also the development of the service operation too. And once this service operation is actually operating, the project is no different fundamentally to any other service organization, which is another reason why it is useful to see these kinds of projects and programmes as temporary organizations.

Example structures, roles and responsibilities

To complete the ESCO model, the box below lists some example structures, roles and responsibilities used in practice, and like the other three parts of the model, advice on where to find out more can be found in Appendix E. This also completes the five example aspects and we return now to the temporary organization image as a whole, and some of the strengths and limitations of this perspective.

Projects, programmes and portfolios as temporary organizations

Example structures
- Operations division (for example, a limited company)
- Operations directorate (for example, a public body)
- Teams, workgroups, IPTs
- Portfolios, programmes, projects
- Workstreams, milestone structures

Example roles
- Managing director, operations director
- Programme director, project director
- Programme manager, project manager
- Team leader, integrated project team (IPT) leader
- Workstream leader, work package owner

Example responsibilities
- Operations design and planning
- Contract negotiations
- Managing the supply chain
- Resolving development issues
- Service monitoring and control

Image Summary

Having introduced five aspects to consider from an organizational perspective, we turn now to this book's organizational image which encapsulates these five related aspects. As stated previously, our aim is not to be prescriptive or all-encompassing, but rather to offer a practical image of projects that the practitioner can use in a variety of different situations. Indeed, like all the images in this book, this particular image can be applied in many different ways, ranging from the occasional use of the whole image or just selected aspects, through to using it in a structured process, or as part of a common language with which to see and talk about the complex realities of a project or programme. These example uses are covered in Part 3 *Applying the Images* but for now it is important to briefly summarize the organizational image of projects.

Projects as temporary organizations

In essence, the image here is that of *projects as temporary organizations*, by which we mean the idea of seeing projects as whole organizations in themselves, except that they are temporary entities rather than semi-permanent. And the organizational model we use for this perspective is the ESCO model which sees an organization as consisting of four main parts – an executive part, a support part, a communications part and an operations part – all of which form a practical model that can be applied to any project, programme or portfolio. It is particularly applicable to legal project organizations such as the Eden Project and the Connecting for Health organization responsible for the NHS IT programme; and it can also be applied to organizations *within* projects and programmes, such as the Olympic Delivery Authority within the London 2012 Project.

Of course, this is not the only organizational model that can be applied to projects and there are many other models and images of organizations that could be used in practice. However, it is not the *make* of 'lens' that is important here, but the 'lens' itself, namely the 'lens' of a *temporary organization,* and the insights that can flow from this particular perspective. In summary, the aim of this chapter has not been to cover the detailed organizational aspects such as roles, responsibilities and team structures and so on, but to provide a *starting point* for thinking about these aspects through the lens of a temporary organization model – see Figure 8.1 opposite.

Another important point about the ESCO model is that it can be easily applied with project and programme management approaches such as PRINCE2™ and MSP™. The guidance they offer, for example, on project and programme boards could be used to help design the *executive part*, and similarly for the support part, the guidance they offer on project and programme support offices could be highly relevant. Further information, however, about these aspects is beyond the scope of this chapter.

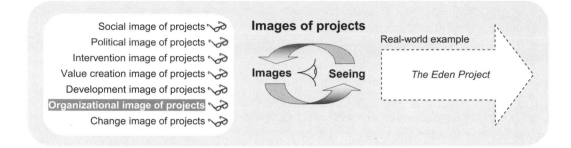

Organizational image of projects

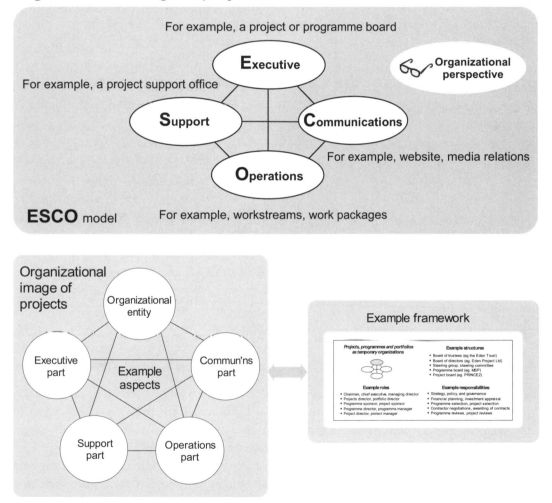

Figure 8.1   An organizational image of projects

Another feature of the ESCO model is its scalability: for example, at a *portfolio* level, the 'operations' could be a set of programmes and projects to achieve some corporate aims and objectives; whilst in another situation the 'operations' of a *programme* could be a set of workstreams to help achieve the programme's aims and objectives. And not only this, the ESCO model can be applied *within* particular projects and programmes too: for example, part of the 'support' part of a major programme could include a whole programme of activity in itself, which might also be conceptualized using the ESCO model; two examples here could be a procurement process, or a training and development programme, both of which could have their own executive, support, communications and operations arrangements within the context of the overall programme. In summary, being a generic model of purposeful activity, the ESCO model can be applied at all levels of management activity and at the same level several times perhaps. Also, different versions of the model might be created for two organizations involved in the same project or programme, as we now explain.

Multiple models for the same project or programme

In applying the image of a temporary organization, it is important to highlight two further points about the ESCO model: firstly, more than one model might be created for the same project or programme, for example, one image might be created for the client organization and another image might be created for the prime contractor. Both models are images of a temporary organization, the difference being that the former represents the project activity of the client organization and the latter represents the project activity of the contractor organization. And this leads to the second point which is that the ESCO model can also be applied to the actual organizations themselves, for the purposes of understanding how the 'parent' organizations relate to the actual project or programme. For example, for a major project involving a client organization and a prime contractor, four models might be created in relation to the project: two of them could be used for understanding the base organizations, and the other two could be the temporary project organizations.

A useful link to other management concepts and models

To end this chapter, it is important to highlight one final point about the value of the ESCO model: not only does it provide a useful framework for thinking about projects and programmes as temporary organizations, it also provides a useful link to other management concepts and models. For example, in using the ESCO model, one might start considering leadership models in relation to the E part, internal service models in relation to the S part; marketing models in relation to the C part; and operations management models in relation to the O part. In effect, by taking this perspective, many of the concepts and approaches in general management and other relevant disciplines now become relevant to projects and programmes.

Strengths and Limitations

Strengths of the organizational perspective

1. Prompts thinking not just about the organizational aspects, but also the idea of seeing projects and programmes as whole organizations.

2. Focuses attention on organizational entities and inter-organizational relationships rather than the processual aspects of projects.

3. Enables multiple organizational images to be created of the same project or programme, but from different perspectives, for example, client and contractor.

4. A useful perspective for understanding the links between the parent or base organization(s) and the project, programme or portfolio.

5. Enables the use of other management concepts and models to be used in the management of projects, programmes and portfolios.

Limitations of the organizational perspective

1. Not the only way of thinking about the organizational aspects. The ESCO model is just one particular model and other models are available.

2. No single image of a project, programme or portfolio. Different images for different individuals and organizations, for example, client and contractor.

3. Focuses attention on organizational entities rather than the processual aspects of projects, for example, the flux of events. Potential for reification.

4. Provides limited guidance on how to approach the more detailed organizational aspects of projects. A guiding framework only.

5. Neglects the social and political aspects of projects, but can help direct attention to these, for example, relations between the ESCO elements.

*[Images] create insight. But they also distort. They have strengths. But they also have limitations. In creating ways of seeing they tend to create ways of **not** seeing.*

Gareth Morgan

The art of progress is to preserve order amid change, and to preserve change amid order.

Alfred North Whitehead

Chapter Nine

Image 7:
Projects as Change Processes

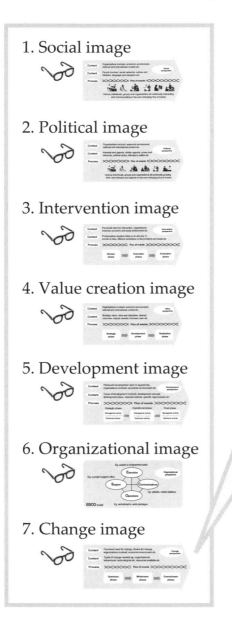

1. Social image

2. Political image

3. Intervention image

4. Value creation image

5. Development image

6. Organizational image

7. Change image

Change Perspective

Chapter Structure

Image Definition

Relevance and Importance

Five Example Aspects

Image Summary

Strengths and Limitations

Image Definition

The CHANGE IMAGE is a framework for seeing projects as change processes, covering aspects such as the context and rationale for change, the perceived scope and content, and the different phases of planned change from the 'up-stream' phase through to the 'downstream' phase.

Relevance and Importance

To get a sense of the current thinking in any field, or the 'hot' topics as some people like to call them, a useful guide is the conference and seminar circuit, and project management is no exception. Indeed, one of the 'hot' topics in project management in recent years has been change management, with some people asserting that *"all projects are change projects"* and *"project management IS change management"*. From this standpoint then, the relevance and importance of seeing projects and programmes as change processes hardly needs stating, and this is certainly the case for projects and programmes like the one briefly described below.

Strategic Change Programme

The Royal Liver Group is made up of Royal Liver Assurance (a 164-year-old Mutual Friendly Society) and other business units. In 2007 a strategic change programme was initiated to restructure the business in response to the changing market environment and future challenges.

The Royal Liver Change Programme illustrates a class of projects known generally as organizational change projects or business transformation programmes, for which the change perspective is clearly very important. Indeed, numerous examples can be linked to this broad class of projects, including most projects and programmes involving IT. However, a few words of caution are needed here: phrases such as "all projects are change projects" effectively pigeonhole projects into categories, which can often preclude the use of other important perspectives. Hence, the focus here is not on change as a *type* of project, namely organizational change projects, but on change as a *perspective*, from which to view and consider the change-related aspects of *all* projects and programmes. This means the change perspective can be applied to not just organizational change projects, but also to other projects and programmes that are not primarily concerned with change; for example, applying a change perspective to engineering projects and construction projects can be very productive indeed, yielding important insights for action that might not otherwise be considered.

Five Example Aspects

Applying this chapter's change image to Royal Liver's Strategic Change Programme, the sorts of aspects that might be considered are:

- What is the *context and rationale* for the changes required within Royal Liver?
- What is the *scope and content* of the required changes within the company?
- What has been the approach so far to the *upstream phase* of the programme?
- What are some key considerations for the *midstream phase* of the programme?
- What should be the approach to the *downstream phase* of the programme?

As with previous chapters, these five questions highlight the five example aspects to be considered, which of course are not the only aspects that could be considered from a change perspective. However, since they apply to most projects and programmes, these are the aspects that we have chosen to focus on, as summarized below.

Aspect 1: Context and Rationale
The context refers to the environment in which change takes place (for example, the social, political, economic and organizational context) and why change is needed, for example, why some proposed changes are believed to be necessary and desirable.

Aspect 2: Scope and Content
This aspect refers to what changes are believed to be necessary and who will be affected for instance. Examples of changes that can be made through projects and programmes include organizational changes, behavioural changes and technological changes.

Aspect 3: Upstream Phase
The upstream phase of the change process refers to the initial activities of any planned change, covering activities such as understanding the context and rationale for change, appreciating and responding to concerns, and laying foundations for the work to follow.

Aspect 4: Midstream Phase
The midstream phase of the change process refers to the main activities of any planned change, covering activities such as understanding the current state in more detail, designing the desired state, prototyping, consultation and implementation planning.

Aspect 5: Downstream Phase
The downstream phase of the change process refers to the final activities of any planned change covering activities such as implementation, reviewing progress and resolving problems, refining processes and systems, and learning from the experience.

As explained in the Introduction to Part 2, this next part of the chapter presents each of these five aspects over two pages, the left-hand page providing a real example (for example, the Royal Liver Programme) and the right-hand page offering some observations for the reader to reflect upon in relation to their own knowledge and experience. Beyond these five aspects, we then summarize the change image as a whole, and briefly state some of the strengths and limitations of this final perspective.

Example Aspect 1: Context and Rationale

DEFINITION

The context refers to the environment in which change takes place (for example, the social, political, economic and organizational context) and why change is needed, for example, why some proposed changes are believed to be necessary and desirable.

REAL-WORLD EXAMPLE

Royal Liver Group Strategic Change Programme

The Royal Liver Group consists of Royal Liver Assurance (a mutual life company with £3.5bn of assets) and a number of manufacturing and distribution businesses in the UK and Ireland. The life assurance business has traditionally been the most profitable but changes in both the market and regulatory environment have resulted in it no longer being possible to sell traditional with-profits life policies, and is known internally as 'sunset' business, in contrast to the manufacturing and distribution business which are known internally as the 'sunrise' businesses. The resulting 'closed book' situation shows the number of policies under administration declining at an average of 10% per annum directly impacting the society's revenue stream. The sunrise businesses cannot mitigate this revenue loss because of their different cost/margin ratios. The net effect is that by 2011 the Royal Liver Group will need to reduce its costs by 33% and to achieve this it will need to make significant changes across the whole organization. In essence, this is the strategic context and rationale for change.

Strategic Change Programme   👓 change perspective

Context	Market and regulatory changes, declining business, need to reduce costs by 33%
Content	Various changes required across the company: organizational, people and systems
Process	⨉⨉⨉⨉⨉⨉⨉⨉⨉ **Flux of events** ⨉⨉⨉⨉⨉⨉⨉⨉⨉⨉

Phase 1: 2007-08	➡	Phase 2: 2008	➡	Phase 3: 2008-10

Illustrative only

REFLECTIVE OBSERVATIONS

Important to start with the context and rationale

In seeing any project or programme that is principally concerned with change, a useful starting point is the *context* and *rationale* for change, which for the Royal Liver Group, turns out to be relatively straightforward; in short, there is a strategic imperative to evolve the company with its currently challenged business model into a profitable one involving the company's new 'sunrise' businesses as mentioned above. And the principal challenge now for Royal Liver is how to achieve this transformation within the required timeframe, whilst continuing to provide existing services to members in a volatile market environment.

Introducing the change image of projects

Not only does the diagram opposite illustrate the Royal Liver example, it also illustrates this book's change image of projects, which like the intervention, value and development images, is essentially a three-phase process, but with the focus on change, as shown below.

Change image of projects   👓 change perspective

Context   Perceived need for change, drivers for change, social and political environment and so on

Content   Types of change needed (for example, organizational, behavioural, technological), resources available

Process   ⟩⟩⟩⟩⟩⟩⟩⟩⟩⟩⟩⟩⟩ Flux of events ⟩⟩⟩⟩⟩⟩⟩⟩⟩⟩⟩⟩⟩

   Upstream phase ➡ **Midstream phase** ➡ **Downstream phase**

                                                                        Illustrative only

---

As the image shows, when looking at a project or programme from a change perspective, there are three important parts to consider: a *context* part that focuses on aspects such as the rationale for change; a *content* part that focuses on the types of changes needed; and a *process* part consisting of three main phases: an upstream phase, a midstream phase and a downstream phase. The actual reality of course is much more complex, as shown by the flux of events, and hence the image is only a *guiding framework* for thinking about projects and programmes, and not a description of the actual reality. Moreover, there are other change management models that can be used with this core image and some of these could be used to help think about the activities of each phase, like the example model below.

An example framework for thinking about the change context

Authors Julia Balogun and Veronica Hope Hailey provide a useful framework called the *Change Kaleidoscope* in their book *Exploring Strategic Change.* As an example model to use with this book's change image, the kaleidoscope model is particularly useful because it highlights many important aspects that might not otherwise be considered – see below.

Change Kaleidescope

*The **change kaleidescope** contains an outer ring concerned with the organisational strategic context, a middle ring concerned with the features of the change context, and an inner ring which contains the menu of design choices open to change agents ... The contextual features ... do not carry equal weight in all organisations ... This is why the diagnostic framework is called a kaleidoscope ... The framework is often used within companies to raise staff awareness of the implications for change, to stimulate debate about difficult areas and to encourage managers to consider what design choices are appropriate to the context of their organisation.*

Source: Exploring Strategic Change *by J.Balogun and V.Hailey 2nd edition (2004). FT Prentice Hall. Reproduced with kind permission*

Example Aspect 2: Scope and Content

DEFINITION

> *This aspect refers to what changes are needed in the situation of concern and who will be affected for instance. Examples of changes that can be made through projects and programmes include organizational changes, behavioural changes and technological changes.*

REAL-WORLD EXAMPLE

Royal Liver Group Strategic Change Programme

Context — Market and regulatory changes, declining business, need to reduce costs by 33 per cent

Content — Legacy servicing, future state finance, governance, knowledge and skills, IT strategy

Process — Flux of events

Phase 1: 2007–08 ➡ Phase 2: 2008 ➡ Phase 3: 2008–10

5 linked workstreams

Legacy servicing

Future state finance development

Governance development

People and communications development

IT strategy delivery

Illustrative only

REFLECTIVE OBSERVATIONS

Continuing with the Royal Liver example, a major challenge for the programme executive has been deciding on the *scope* and *content* of the programme in order to achieve the longer term objectives of the business. For example, one view is that the change programme should just be limited to cost reduction activity, which would limit the scope and content to certain areas of the business; however, there is another view that the future business model could provide additional growth through Royal Liver offering its services to other Mutual Life companies with similar problems, which could also have implications for the scope and content of the programme.

At present, the scope of the programme extends to restructuring the Group's systems and processes in a way that the company will be able to operate within certain cost constraints, whilst simultaneously supporting growth businesses in the highly regulated financial services sector. As the diagram shows, the scope and content of the programme consists of five linked workstreams: legacy servicing, future state finance, governance (including board and internal audit), people and communications and IT strategy. Moreover, each workstream is directed by a member of the senior management team who leads a business change team and is accountable to the organization's executive.

The PSO concept for thinking about scope and content

Anyone familiar with the literature on project management and change management will know there is a plethora of concepts and models for thinking about the management of change through projects and programmes. However, one model in particular that is useful for approaching the scope and content of any planned change is the PSO model provided by Erling Andersen *et al* in *Goal Directed Project Management*. This was introduced at the end of the development chapter and is also described in the extract below:

> *the most common failing in project work is to focus too strongly on the technical content. In typical organizational development projects the situation is the reverse. These are solely concerned with developing people in the organization and relationships between them. There is too little emphasis on developing systems (for example, work processes and procedures) which will support the changes required in the organization. ... It is essential in [any change-related project or programme] that there be a balance between development of the 'system' (the 'object' to be constructed) and development of people and organization.*[1]

Experience shows that the PSO concept is a useful concept for thinking about the different content areas of any project or programme involving change. As the Royal Liver example shows, the programme's five workstreams involve changes in all three areas of P, S and O: the *people* and communications workstream, three *organizational* workstreams concerned with legacy, finance and governance, and an IT strategy workstream to review the *system* changes that are needed. As Erling Andersen *et al* point out, any system changes '*must always be accompanied by planned development of the affected personnel and the organization's relationships, responsibilities and authorities.*'[2]

Getting a number of PSO things right at the same time

Interestingly, research carried out by management consultancy company McKinsey also supports this notion of a PSO-type approach to projects and programmes, as highlighted in an article written by the management journalist Simon Caulkin. Whilst the language of PSO is not used by McKinsey or Caulkin, and although as Caulkin points out, McKinsey has an interest in seeing organizations change, their observations are still insightful as the following extract shows:

> *ALL CHANGE! The traditional cry of the London bus conductor at Tottenham Court Road seems to have become the working slogan of every organization in the land. According to consultants McKinsey, at any time up to 15 of the FTSE100 are 'transforming' themselves and a further 50 changing in less extreme ways. At the same time, there seems almost no part of the public sector immune from being turned around or inside out. ... The need for constant change is now so accepted that few people question it. But the results of all this frantic activity should give pause for thought. McKinsey's research underlines just how high the stakes are. ... Despite the poor average results, successful change, it says, is a matter of getting a number of things right at the same time: a rigorous programme architecture, emphasis on both short-term performance and long-term corporate health, high aspirations, embedding gains in processes in procedures, changing employees' behaviour and transforming leadership. None of these is optional, McKinsey insists. They have to work together as a 'bundle'. Conversely, the minute something is thought of as a silver bullet, it stops being part of the solution and becomes part of the problem.*[3]

Simon Caulkin, The Observer

Example Aspect 3: Upstream Phase

DEFINITION

> *The upstream phase of the change process refers to the initial activities of any planned change covering activities such as understanding the context and rationale for change, appreciating and responding to concerns, and laying foundations for the work to follow.*

REAL-WORLD EXAMPLE

Royal Liver Group Strategic Change Programme

Context Market and regulatory changes, declining business, need to reduce costs by 33 per cent

Content Legacy servicing, future state finance, governance, knowledge and skills, IT strategy

Process *Flux of events*

Phase 1: 2007–08 12 week evaluation exercise

Legacy servicing

Future state finance development

Governance development

People and communications development

IT strategy delivery

Phase 2
May–Oct 2008

Phase 3
2008–10

Illustrative only

REFLECTIVE OBSERVATIONS

Establishing the context and rationale for change

Having set out the context and content of the Royal Liver programme, attention now turns to the three process phases starting with the *upstream phase*, which is the first stage of any planned change. For Royal Liver, this first phase is particularly important because the programme is impacting every part of an organization that has existed for over 150 years; in short, the five workstreams will impact almost the entire Royal Liver operation. Against this background, the first phase involved a 12-week period of challenging this history and establishing the need and urgency for change. Facilitated by external consultants, the whole exercise sought to involve as many people as possible from the business in order to understand the context and challenges ahead. In doing this, numerous meetings and workshops were held and eventually the 'wake up call' was heard by most people, and the organizational vision, capacity and commitment to change was established. As authors Dean and Linda Anderson point out in their book *Beyond Change Management*, it is difficult to overstate the importance of this first phase, for it is here that *'the climate, commitment and runway for the entire change are established'.*[4]

Example activities that might be relevant to the upstream phase

As already stated, there is a plethora of concepts and models for thinking about the management

172

of change through projects and programmes, and not surprisingly, many of these are directly concerned with the *process* of change, and how to manage this process from end to end. The problem, however, is that no two change management models are ever *exactly* the same, and they are often presented as prescriptions rather than prompts, which is the point made by Dean and Linda Anderson in *Beyond Change Management*. Not only this, their own model, the *Change Process Model*, offers a useful prompt for thinking about the upstream, midstream and downstream phases of any change-related activity, which is why we use it here and in the next two aspects for thinking about the three main phases. Here is what they say about their model:

> the Change Process Model, in all its comprehensiveness, is simply designed to support you as you consciously ask which of its many activities are critical for your transformation's success. ... In any given transformation effort, we suggest that you consider all of what is offered in the model and then select only the work that is appropriate to your change effort.[5]

In other words, the role of the *Change Process Model* is not to prescribe what *should* be done, but to prompt various questions about what *might* be done within particular projects and programmes. To illustrate this, the model shown below illustrates some example activities that might be considered for the upstream phase of any change-related activity.

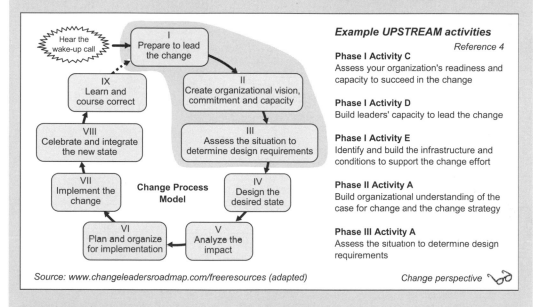

Source: www.changeleadersroadmap.com/freeresources (adapted)   Change perspective

In applying this model it is important to note the following:

- Phases I-IX span all three of our phases: upstream, midstream and downstream.
- The five example activities from Phases I-III relate to this chapter's *upstream phase*.
- The five example activities are suggestive of *what* might be done, rather than *how*.
- Although the activities might be inappropriate, they might still trigger *ideas* for action.

Finally, notice the change perspective icon in the bottom right-hand corner, which is just a reminder that the *Change Process Model* is not a model of the actual reality, or a prescription for action, but a *guide to thinking* about the complex realities of initiating change. And this is not all, for we also need to consider the midstream and downstream phases.

Example Aspect 4: Midstream Phase

DEFINITION

> *The midstream phase of the change process refers to the main activities of any planned change covering activities such as understanding the current state in more detail, designing the desired state, prototyping, consultation and implementation planning.*

REAL-WORLD EXAMPLE

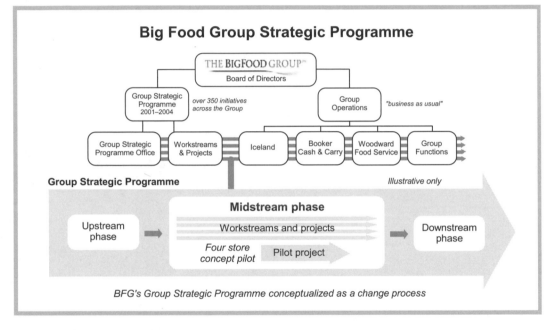

Big Food Group Strategic Programme

BFG's Group Strategic Programme conceptualized as a change process

REFLECTIVE OBSERVATIONS

A different view of the Big Food Group programme

Moving on from the Royal Liver example, the first thing to notice about the example above is how the change process image is a different view of the BFG programme to that shown in Aspect 3 of Chapter 8: in that chapter, the programme was conceptualized as a temporary organization, whereas in this chapter, the programme is seen as a process of organized change; in *Images* terms, they are two different views of the same programme. Hence, for the background to this programme, the reader should refer back to Chapter 8.

Importance of piloting changes in the midstream phase

In this chapter, the Big Food Group Strategic Programme provides a useful illustration of the *midstream phase* of the change process, particularly the aspect of piloting changes before wider implementation. For example, within the Big Food Group, the belief that a 'one size fits all' approach to 750 Iceland stores needed to change, and therefore a four store concept model was developed ranging from a 'core' store offering through to a 'convenience' store offering.

However, a full implementation of the four store types would have entailed a 3-year refurbishment programme involving more than 200 stores per annum and a capital investment in excess of £200m. Hence, within the workstream structure of the overall programme, a pilot project was initiated to assess the four store types in a number of areas determined by demographic analysis. Each was carefully planned and KPIs were established to evaluate each store concept, with the result that when the full refurbishment programme actually commenced, one of the four concepts was dropped because it could not be made to work from a commercial perspective.

Example activities that might be relevant to the midstream stage

Thinking more generally now about the midstream phase of change-related initiatives, it is important to emphasize again that there is no single or correct approach that can be simply followed step by step. That said, as explained earlier, models such as the *Change Process Model* can suggest activities that might be relevant, or at least *ideas* that might be relevant, to a particular project or programme. To illustrate this further, the model below shows a selection of activities from the *Change Process Model* that might be considered for the midstream phase of any change-related initiative.

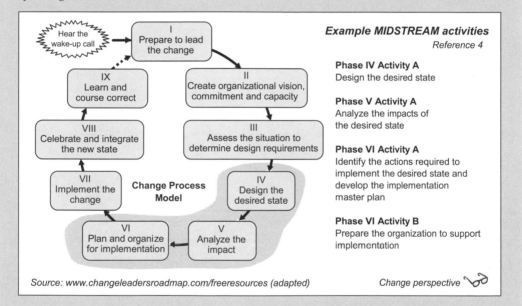

Source: www.changeleadersroadmap.com/freeresources (adapted)   Change perspective

Looking at phases IV and V, a good example of these two phases is the pilot project shown opposite, which was an important part of the programme prior to the implementation of the new store formats (phases VI and VII above). In writing more generally about the midstream phases IV–VI, the authors make a number of important observations summarized in the extract below:

> *the midstream stage of change is when the actual design of the desired state occurs. The design is developed, clarified, tested and refined. Its impact is studied, and plans are created to pace and coordinate its implementation accurately. All of the conditions, structures, systems and policies decided in the upstream stage are tailored and established to help prepare and support the organization for implementation. More readiness is built through participation, and the organization's capacity to succeed in the change is further developed.[6]*

Example Aspect 5: Downstream Phase

DEFINITION

The downstream phase of the change process refers to the final activities of any planned change covering activities such as implementation, reviewing progress and resolving problems, refining processes and systems, and learning from the experience.

REAL-WORLD EXAMPLE

Warburtons SAP Programme

Warburtons SAP Programme   👓 change perspective

Context — 2000: Warburtons' customers now mostly the supermarkets rather than independents. 24x7 business operation with increasing requirements for continuous replenishment

Content — Example changes: creation of a shared service centre to manage payroll for all sites, introduction of centralized purchasing, and replacement of legacy IT systems with SAP

Process — ✕✕✕ **Flux of events** ∞∞∞∞∞∞∞∞∞∞∞→

Upstream phase	Midstream phase	**Downstream phase**
- rationale	- development	Creation of a business review team to review and resolve business issues with SAP. Actions taken included the implementation of changes to reduce the usage of SAP and various changes to work processes to facilitate more local decision making.
- changes	- installation	
- planning	- handover	

Illustrative only

Based on reference 7.

REFLECTIVE OBSERVATIONS

Importance of the downstream phase

Turning now to the *downstream phase* of this book's change process model, the first thing to notice about the Warburtons example is how it contrasts with the value creation model shown in Aspect 5 of Chapter 6. As that chapter shows, from a value creation perspective, the final stage of the SAP programme is seen as the *realization phase*, whereas from this perspective, the final stage is seen as the *downstream phase*, which is a different concept. Although the two images are strongly linked, conceptually and practically, they represent different images of the same programme, and seeing the programme from this chapter's perspective highlights various aspects that might not otherwise be considered.

For example, one of the strengths of the Warburtons programme was the recognition that the centralization of purchasing was *'massively overambitious'* creating *'too much change too soon'* and hence the early formation of a business review team to review and resolve the business issues that were emerging with the implementation of SAP.[7] In summary, this turned out to be a major strength of the programme.

Activities such as installation and handover are not the end point

Part of the value of seeing projects as change processes is that it highlights an important question about the *end point* of projects and programmes, for example, when should a project to implement a new IT system be ended? According to the traditional lifecycle view of projects, the project ends when the new system has been installed and handed over to the users. However, as shown in previous chapters, the image here is essentially a system development image, which is different to the change image being presented here. As the model opposite shows, from a change perspective, activities such as installation and handover are not the end point at all; in fact, they are not even part of the *downstream phase* from this perspective, but rather the back end of the *midstream phase.* And for good reason too, because experience shows that most new initiatives rarely get everything right first time. This does not imply weakness in any way, just a pragmatic acceptance that some things are likely to go wrong, and/or, some things might need changing to accommodate different people's needs and requirements. In summary, planning for this sort of thing in advance and communicating with the relevant stakeholders is an important activity for any project or programme concerned with change.

Example activities that might be relevant to the downstream stage

Like the upstream and downstream phases, it is important to emphasize again that there is no correct approach to this phase either; however, as already explained, one can still be guided by models such as the *Change Process Model*, as shown below.

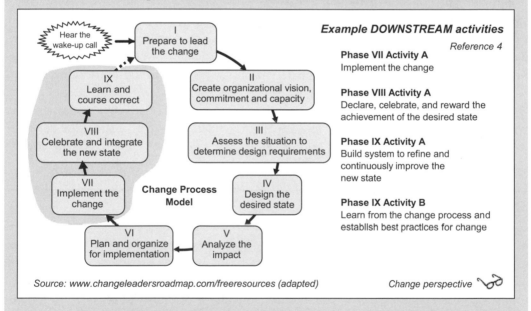

Source: www.changeleadersroadmap.com/freeresources (adapted)   Change perspective

Looking at phase VIII in the model above, a good example of 'integrating the new state' is the activity shown opposite of resolving business issues with the implementation of SAP. Experience shows, however, this sort of activity is frequently initiated at the *end* of a project when problems arise, whereas the message here is that this can be planned from the *start*, and not only this, it might also be seen as a *service* to users, for which we might then apply a service perspective to design this service. But this is not something we are going to expand on here, for this is as far as we go in looking at projects from different perspectives! Hence, we turn now to the final part of this chapter to summarize the change image as a whole.

Image Summary

Having introduced five aspects to consider from a change perspective, we turn now to this book's change image which encapsulates these five related aspects. As stated previously, our aim is not to be prescriptive or all-encompassing, but rather to offer a practical image of projects that the practitioner can use in a variety of different situations. Indeed, like all the images in this book, this particular image can be applied in many different ways, ranging from the occasional use of the whole image or just selected aspects, through to using it in a structured process, or as part of a common language with which to see and talk about the complex realities of a project or programme. These example uses are covered in Part 3 *Applying the Images* but for now it is important to briefly summarize the change image of projects.

Projects as change processes

In essence, the image here is that of *projects as change processes*, by which we mean a planned process to achieve feasible and desirable change. Very importantly, we do not mean a highly structured process of stages, steps and tasks, just the image of an organized process to achieve some feasible and desirable change, in other words, a *starting point* for thinking about projects from this perspective. Moreover, there are two reasons for choosing this particular image of change: firstly, it reflects the planned nature of projects, and secondly, it is particularly relevant to projects and programmes known generally as organizational change projects. Of course, there are other images of change that could be used and many of these might yield useful insights; however, like all the other images in this book, our first concern here is with conceptualizing whole projects and programmes, and for this we need practical images that map the perceived boundaries of projects and programmes. This is why, then, we opt for the change process image shown opposite.

As Figure 9.1 shows, this book's change image takes the view that all planned change initiatives involve three interrelated parts: *context, content* and *process*; the context part covers the *why* of change, the content part covers the *what* and the process covers the *how*. Moreover, a useful way of thinking more about the process part is to frame it in three main phases: an upstream phase, a midstream phase and a downstream phase. In reality, it is all one process of course and the parts are nothing like as separate as the model might suggest. However, as a guide to action, the image provides a useful starting point for approaching any project or programme from a change perspective. Moreover, being a generic model, it doesn't prescribe or stipulate any particular approach to change, and it can be used with other models and frameworks; suggested examples here could be the *PSO model* for thinking about the content part, and the *Change Process Model* for thinking about the process part. However, the really crucial aspect to notice here is how the change image differs to say the image of a development process or a procurement process;

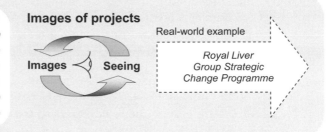

Images of projects

Social image of projects
Political image of projects
Intervention image of projects
Value creation image of projects
Development image of projects
Organizational image of projects
Change image of projects

Images — Seeing

Real-world example

Royal Liver Group Strategic Change Programme

Change image of projects

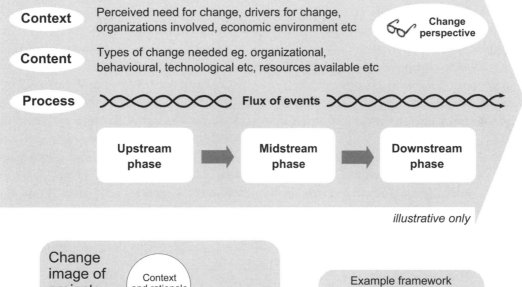

Context — Perceived need for change, drivers for change, organizations involved, economic environment etc

Change perspective

Content — Types of change needed eg. organizational, behavioural, technological etc, resources available etc

Process — Flux of events

Upstream phase → Midstream phase → Downstream phase

illustrative only

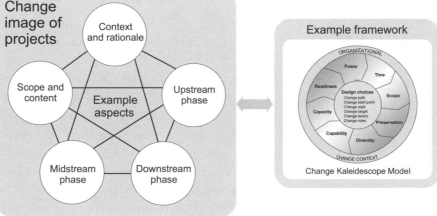

Change image of projects

Context and rationale

Scope and content

Example aspects

Upstream phase

Midstream phase

Downstream phase

Example framework

ORGANIZATIONAL

Power
Time
Readiness
Design choices
Change path
Change start-point
Change style
Change target
Change levers
Change roles
Scope
Capacity
Preservation
Capability
Diversity
CHANGE CONTEXT

Change Kaleidescope Model

Figure 9.1   A change image of projects

conceptually, the image of a change process is not the same as a process to develop a new product, or a process to procure a new facility. This might seem obvious perhaps, and in practice all three images are likely to be relevant in their own way, but these conceptual images should not be mistaken for the actual reality of projects; in this book, they are simply abstract models of purposeful activity, based on different perspectives, to help make sense of the complex realities of projects.

Finally, notice how the change image has strong links with the other images in this book: for example, how the *context* part relates to the social and political images, how the *content* part relates to the intervention and value images, and how the *process* part relates to the development and organizational images. In fact, all seven images are likely to be needed for any project or programme that is primarily concerned with change. And notice too how the change image can be applied to other projects and programmes that are *not* primarily concerned with change: for example, imagine a new aircraft programme tasked with delivering 100 aircraft in a much shorter timeframe than previous programmes; the knock-on effect could be that the company will have to change workforce attitudes, working practices and current IT systems. From a change perspective, although the programme is not primarily concerned with change, there is clearly a *context* for change, and also a number of *content* changes that need to be made to help achieve the programme's objectives, for example, changes to working practices. Now, whether the *process* implied by this forms part of the programme itself, or a separate change initiative perhaps, depends on the situation, but what the example shows is how the *same* programme needs to be seen *both*, as a development process, *and* as a change process, if the objectives are to be achieved. This does not mean the whole programme needs to be seen as a change process, only that the programme needs to incorporate, or at least be supported by, some change-related activity to help achieve the main objectives. As explained in Chapter 2, a guiding principle in applying these images is the principle of *both/and* rather than *either/or*.

Change projects or change as a perspective?

To end this chapter, we return to the claim that *"all projects are change projects"*, which seems to suggest another image of projects called 'change projects'. But is this a useful image? The short answer is obviously yes and it might seem ironic that the question is even posed when so many organizations are engaged in change projects. In short, the point here is whether one sees change as an *end* in itself, or as a *means* to creating value and benefit, or improving problematical situations, or developing new products and services. If seen as a *means*, then the image of a 'change project' becomes more problematical, which is why we focus more on change as a *perspective* rather than as a *type* of project. That said, however, if one sees it as another image of projects, then the answer of course is *both/and* rather than *either/or*.

Strengths and Limitations

Strengths of the change perspective

1. Focuses directly on the phenomenon of change in project environments, as opposed to the development of a product, system or facility.

2. Directs attention to some of the significant aspects and challenges involved in trying to bring about feasible and desirable change.

3. Highly applicable to organizational change projects and also other types of projects that are not directly concerned with change.

4. Applicable throughout the lifecycle and easy to use in conjunction with the other perspectives, for example, the social and political perspectives.

5. Easy to apply with other frameworks and models, and strongly supported by various concepts and models in the change management literature.

Limitations of the change perspective

1. Directly concerned with change and therefore less concerned with the specifics of development or the creation of value for example.

2. Can lead to change being seen as an *end* in itself, rather than the *means* to something else, for example, business or social improvement.

3. No one 'best way' to think about change and no one 'best model' of change management. However, there are many to choose from!

4. Planned change can be much less effective than continuous change, for example, grand initiatives versus continuous improvement.

5. Effective use of the change perspective needs to involve the use of other perspectives, for example, the social and political perspectives.

*[Images] create insight. But they also distort. They have strengths. But they also have limitations. In creating ways of seeing they tend to create ways of **not** seeing.*

Gareth Morgan

Part 3
Applying the Images in Practice

Practice has a logic which is not that of logic.
Pierre Bourdieu

Introduction to Part 3

Now that we have covered the seven core images, we turn now to how they can be used in practice, not as seven separate images, but as a pragmatic framework that can be used in different ways in different situations. And to do this we need to start with a model of the *practice context* in which all practitioners have to operate, for it is this reality, and this book's *image* of that reality, that we need to understand first in order to get the most out of the images and frameworks covered in Part 2.

Framing the practice context

Like the images chapters, we begin with a real example to help illustrate the kind of reality that practitioners have to work with in project environments. Consider once again the example used in Chapter 5: some years ago, the lead author was asked to oversee a consultancy project for a company that produces specialist products for the car industry. The aim of this apparently straightforward project was to determine a new system for improving communication between two of the company's manufacturing sites. Upon visiting the first site, it was found that no one knew anything about the project, and nor was communication between the two sites seen to be an issue. Similarly at the second site, communication was not seen to be an issue either, and it also transpired that the MD was unaware of the administrative fee that was coming out of his budget. Only a week into the project and the author found himself having to deal with a complex situation. Now, this is only one example of course, and some situations are less extreme, but what it shows is that practitioners operate *not* within the lifecycle process, as many PM textbooks seem to suggest, but rather in the messy world of *complex situations* and an ever-changing flux of events that is continually unfolding through time. And as any experienced practitioner knows, there are no 'right' answers in these situations, and they arise not just at the front-end of projects, but also during later phases too, as shown in Figure P3.1 below.

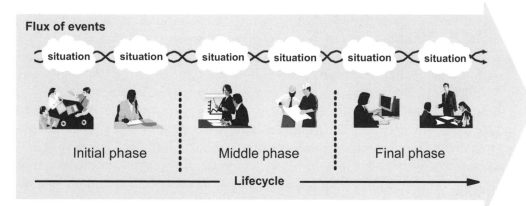

Figure P3.1   This book's image of the practice context

This, then, is how we see the context in which all practitioners operate, but notice in Figure P3.1 that the lifecycle idea is still shown alongside the flux of events. This is because although the actual reality is always a flux of events, the lifecycle idea remains a useful concept to apply with the flux image, in that any project or programme can still be thought of as passing through a number of different 'phases' or 'stages' in the flux. As we stated in Chapter 2, we deliberately work with this 3-phase model partly because of its general applicability and also because it links directly to the four three-phase images in Part 2: *intervention, value, development* and *change*. In short, depending on which images are being used, the three generic phases in Figure P3.1 take on different meaning, prompting various considerations in relation to the project in question. For example, if the *value* image is being used to help guide a business transformation project, the three phases in Figure P3.1 could be seen as the strategic, development and realization phases, each with their own possible implications for action; and alongside this, if the *development* and *change* images are also being used, then various implications will flow from taking these perspectives too. In other words, the *generic lifecycle model* in Figure P3.1 can be framed and reframed in many different ways according to the type of project or programme being carried out and other situational factors. In summary, Figure P3.1 is the *root image* of projects that we start from in using the different images in real situations.

Applying the images in practice: Chapters 10–14

The first thing to say is there is no 'right' set of images to use in any situation for it depends on the role of the practitioner and the organizational standpoint from which the situation is being seen. For example, a project sponsor may only use the social and political images to help make sense of a situation, whereas a team leader may use the development, organizational and change images. But notice the commonality here: all practitioners have to think and act in *situations*, and it is this that leads us to identify three distinct types of use: *selective use, structured use*, and *shared use*. To summarize each one: *selective use* refers to the occasional use of certain images for making sense of a situation or project, *structured use* refers to a more systematic use of the images for crafting the action needed in a situation, and *shared use* is the idea of two or more people using the images as a sort of common language for collectively approaching their own projects and the action needed. In summary, each type of use is just a different way of using the images to help make sense of the complexity of a situation and the action needed going forward. These three types also provide the structure for Part 3: each one is covered separately in Chapters 10 to 12, and then to show how the images have been used in real situations, Chapters 13 and 14 provide two case examples, not as 'the' way to use the images in practice, but as two more examples for the reader to reflect upon in relation to their own approach to making sense of projects in real situations. Figure P3.2 opposite summarises the key points from this introduction to Part 3.

Applying the Images

2. Seven core images ...

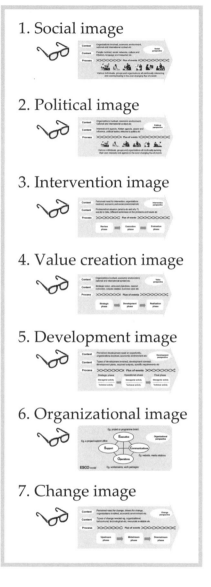

1. Social image

2. Political image

3. Intervention image

4. Value creation image

5. Development image

6. Organizational image

7. Change image

Intellectual world / real world distinction

1. Starting point ...

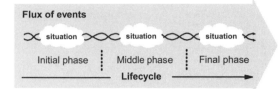

3. Applying the images ...

❏ For use in making sense of real situations involving projects

❏ For use in crafting the action needed in real situations

❏ Use depends on the situation and the practitioner's role and interest

❏ No 'right' set of images to use and *both/and* rather than *either/or*

❏ Three distinct types of use:
- selective use
- structured use
- shared use

P3.2   Applying the images in practice

187

Attention flows of its own accord.
Attention may also be directed deliberately.

Edward de Bono

Chapter Ten

Selective Use of the Images

Introduction

This chapter opens with an example to show how the images can be selectively used by people in different roles to help make sense of their own situations and the action needed. In essence, the idea of selective use is about deliberately 'calling upon' different images as and when needed, and we illustrate this by showing how they can operate in a similar way to Edward de Bono's Six Thinking Hats®. Also included in this chapter are some general guidelines and some brief reflections for the reader to think about in relation to their own approach to thinking about projects.

Illustrative Example

This example demonstrates not only the selective use of certain images in relation to a certain project, but also how the chosen images strongly depend on the practitioner's role and organizational context. Consider how the different people involved in the scheme below might perceive and approach the project in different ways.

Battle of Orgreave site to become civil service office campus
Terry Macalister, *The Guardian* Newspaper

Orgreave, South Yorkshire, the infamous site of violent confrontation between picketing miners and the police during the Thatcher years, is to be the home of a revolutionary new "government office campus" under a £140m scheme outlined yesterday by UK Coal and property development group, Helical Bar.

The two listed companies have formed a joint venture to develop a 660,000 sq ft site on the former coal mining and coking plant and are already in discussions with two government departments about moving staff. Up to 4,000 civil servants could be moved there under plans being proposed by UK Coal, which wants to create a hub of public sector organisations, supported by private IT and outsourcing firms.

The wider development planned for Orgreave and the Waverley area, near Rotherham, is expected to create 6,000 jobs. There would be 4,000 new homes, a range of community facilities such as health centres and a park. Construction is due to start in spring 2009 and the campus should be ready by the autumn of 2010.

The move underlines the way the country's largest domestic coal mining group is trying to generate income from developing disused collieries.[1]

Although labelled a 'scheme', the proposed development is also clearly a 'project' in the sense there is a declared task to develop a government office campus at a cost of £140m by the autumn of 2010. Now, what is important in relation to applying the images is how it will mean different things to the different people and organizations involved, and hence why the use of the images always depends on the context in which they are used. For example, if we assume the senior management of the joint venture see it primarily as a development project to generate income for the two companies, then the value and development images could be very important; whilst for the senior civil servants tasked with moving two departments to a new location, important images could be the political and change images. In other words, their use clearly depends upon the organizational standpoint from which the development is being viewed, which also means the project is *both* a property development project *and* an organizational change project because of the different organizations involved. To illustrate this further, included below are other some example images that could be used by the different people and organizations involved.

Senior management of the joint venture

Since the project is a joint venture between UK Coal and Helical Bar, another useful perspective could be to see the joint venture as a *temporary organization*, named and framed around the Executive/Support/Communications/Operations (ESCO) model. Indeed, as the following questions show, just this model alone could provide a useful framework for thinking about the different parts of the organization. For example, how might the *executive* part be organized? What *support* will be needed? How will the joint venture *communicate* both internally and externally? How should the main *operation* be organized and which parts of the work will be subcontracted? Such questions, of course, are purely illustrative of the kind of thinking prompted by the ESCO model and further questions could be asked by using additional management models as explained at the end of Chapter 8.

Senior civil servants

Looking at the scheme from the Government's perspective, another example image could be the development perspective which could be used to consider another view of the project. For example, there could be a concern that there is too much focus on developing the *campus* and not enough on the *services* to be provided from the campus; in other words, there is too much focus on the *how* and not enough on the *what*. And the action here could be to initiate a more thorough review of the services to be provided and the infrastructure needed to support these services.

A building contractor

For a contractor interested in bidding for the work, two important perspectives could be the organizational and development images: for example, using the ESCO model, what should their executive structure be for meeting the requirements of the tender? Secondly, because of the way the contractor 'reads' the particular situation, it could be necessary in the tender document to separate out the managerial activity from the technical activity to show how the contractor would manage the work.

Senior management of UK Coal

Finally, for UK Coal *'which wants to create a hub of public sector organisations, supported by private IT and outsourcing firms'*, three example images could be the social, political and development images for thinking about the interests and agenda of the organizations involved, the social networks they operate within, where power and influence is perceived to lie in the particular situation, and how the work will be organized to develop the hub idea.

To summarize then, notice how the use of the images always reflects the interests and agenda of those involved, and hence why there is no one 'best way' of using them in real situations. Moreover, as stated in Part 1, although practitioners already consider many of these aspects, they often do so *subconsciously,* which is not always the most effective approach. The point here is that in *consciously* selecting certain images and models such as the ESCO model, these aspects can be thought about more deliberately, which can often lead to *more* aspects being considered within *shorter* timeframes. And in this respect, the images can be used in a similar way to Edward de Bono's Six Thinking Hats®, as the next section now shows.

A Framework for Selective Use

A useful way of visualizing the seven core images is to think of them as seven 'lenses' which can be used in real situations as and when required, just like Edward de Bono's Six Thinking Hats® which can be *'easily put on and taken off'* in different situations. Here is what de Bono says in his book *The Six Thinking Hats*®:

> *what I am putting forward in this book is a very simple concept which allows a thinker to do one thing at a time. ... The concept is that of the six thinking hats. Putting on any one of these hats defines a certain type of thinking. ... The six thinking hats allow us to conduct our thinking as a conductor might lead an orchestra. We can call forth what we will. ... It is the sheer convenience of the six thinking hats that is the main value of the concept.[2]*

A summary of the Six Hats is shown in Figure 10.1 which shows them in no particular order and the sorts of aspects that each hat generally focuses on. There is also a rationale for the colours used which de Bono explains in his book.

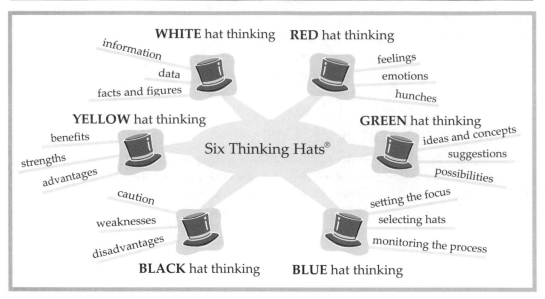

Figure 10.1   The Six Thinking Hats®

Very importantly, it is not a prescriptive method that has to be followed in a certain way, it is a pragmatic framework of different perspectives that can be called upon as and when needed in different situations. As Edward de Bono points out at the end of his book: *'I am not suggesting that at every moment in our thinking we should consciously be using one hat or another. This is quite unnecessary.'* The key aspect is using them as and when needed, and exactly the same principle applies to the seven perspectives in this book: like the hats, they are best thought of as 'lenses' that can be deliberately 'put on and taken off' as and when needed, to help make sense of the different aspects of projects in real situations, as shown in Figure 10.2.

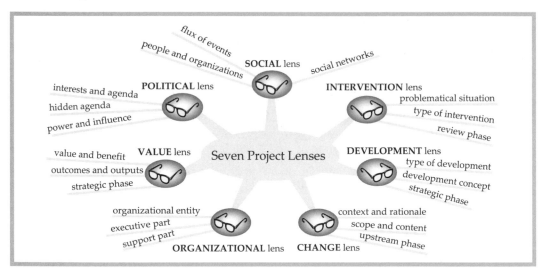

Figure 10.2   Seven lenses for making sense of projects

Just as de Bono states in another book called *Teach Your Child How to Think* that the six hats framework is *'an attention-directing tool, because [each hat] directs attention towards certain aspects'*, the same is true of the framework in Figure 10.2: it too is an attention-directing tool, because each lens directs attention towards certain aspects of projects and not others. Notice too the aspects shown are the first three aspects from Chapters 3 to 9, which are the sorts of aspects that might be considered when using each particular lens. To use Gareth Morgan's words, each lens is both a *way of seeing* and a *way of not seeing*, which is why multiple lenses are needed. In summary, Figure 10.2 is simply a framework to illustrate how the images can be used as a set of lenses for making sense of the complex realities of projects. The next section explains how these lenses can be used in different ways in different situations.

Different Types of Selective Use

Just as there are different ways of using the images, the same is also true of each type of use, and this section briefly lists some of the ways in which the lenses framework in Figure 10.2 can be used in real situations.

One or more lenses only

The idea here is that of using one or more lenses to facilitate an open discussion about a situation or project, but without directing people to consider any particular aspect, or even mentioning that a framework is being used. The only 'steer' provided by the user of the images is one or more lenses and then the discussion begins. For example, questions about a new project could be: *"What for you are the important **social** aspects?"* and *"What for you are the important **political** aspects?"* Then, as the discussion unfolds, other lenses could be called upon to steer the discussion further, but again without drawing on any of the example aspects in this book. Generally, the purpose here is to allow for an open discussion rather than directing it according to a particular image or framework.

One or more lenses, one or more aspects

With this type of selective use, the process is more directed using any of the lenses and aspects from Part 2. For example, a practitioner involved in shaping a future project could deliberately use the value image to help conceptualize some possible outcomes and outputs, which could then be discussed with the client. Or in another situation, a practitioner could use the intervention image to challenge a proposed project, arguing that instead of carrying on with the project, those involved should review the situation first to determine the best way forward, and this may or may not include the proposed project.

One or more lenses, one or more frameworks

This is similar to the previous type, except that a practitioner might also call upon a particular framework or model to help reflect upon certain aspects of a project. For example, the practitioner who is deliberately using the value image to help conceptualize some possible outcomes and outputs for a project, might also use the first- and second-level relationship model in Chapter 6. Or instead of using a model, they might craft some ideas based on the idea that *the goal of a project is not to create value for customers but to mobilize customers to create their own value from the project's various offerings.* Whether it's just a single concept or several frameworks, what matters most is that they are used as *prompts for thinking* rather than *prescriptions for action,* as explained in Chapter 2.

One or more lenses, all five example aspects

The idea of this final example is about calling upon certain images and using all five aspects of each image to help think about a particular project or programme. Two examples here could be: (i) the use of the development image in a review, which could lead to the whole image being used as a guide to action and changes being made to the project; and (ii) deliberate use of the ESCO model to help conceptualize a particular programme and some of the actions needed going forward, for example, links with the parent organization, governance, support, communications requirements and so on.

In summary, these are just some of the ways in which the seven core images can be selectively used in real situations. And the key point here is that they are *knowingly* selected, meaning that just like the Six Thinking Hats®, they can be deliberately called upon as and when the situation demands. But is it really possible to do this given the limited time people have for thinking in practice? This is a crucial point to end on before we turn to the second main type of use.

Reflections on Selective Use

Is it feasible to use the images in the midst of action?

Whilst it might be desirable to use different images, frameworks and concepts in the midst of action, some might question whether this is really feasible. *"We don't have time to think"* they might say, *"our job is just to get the job done and deliver what is required."* Unfortunately, this is rather misguided in that thinking and doing are *not* two separate domains, as the next few points clearly show. For example, as Edward de Bono says in one of his books: *'It is a particularly silly aspect of culture that separates thinkers from doers. Thinkers are not supposed to do. Doers are not supposed to think.*

... That a doer should stand up and proclaim his pride in not thinking reflects either upon his luck or the poor image that thinking possesses.'[3] The late Richard Normann also writes about this in his book *Reframing Business* in a chapter about the thinking capabilities of people in organizations, in particular their conceptualization capability, as he explains in the extract below:

those who say that they don't theorize and that their actions are not based on conceptual thinking are simply unaware of their own process. ... Reflection, conceptualization and theorizing are not inherently in opposition to rapid response and on-the-spot action orientation. Exactly the opposite is true. With our Western modes of thinking, which analytically distinguish between thought and action, we tend to think that an orientation towards conceptualization would exclude an orientation towards action, but we now have enough evidence and sufficient 'rational' theories to realize that such a view is incorrect. ... The distinction is illustrated [opposite]. Obviously, lack of both conceptualization and action will lead nowhere. Strong focus on conceptualization but lack of action orientation is often too slow and leads to 'analysis paralysis'. The organization which does not reflect and conceptualize what it does but is only geared to encouraging action will become what I think of as 'the hysterically hyperactive' organization, with compartmentalization, politics, and lack of aggregation and

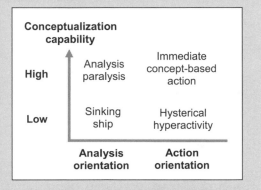

Source: *Reframing Business* by Richard Normann. Publisher: John Wiley. Reproduced with kind permission

*structuring of knowledge as a result. ... **I like to characterize the situation when action is based on pre-reflection and the advanced building of concepts.***[4] *(emphasis added)*

To answer our original question then, it certainly is feasible to use the different images to help craft immediate concept-based action and an example of this was the office campus initiative at the start of this chapter.

In summary, the idea of deliberately using different hats and lenses in the everyday flux of events is a strong practical alternative to the JUST DO IT approach, in that once they have been internalised, they just become part of one's approach to making sense of projects. And, of course, once everyone else in the team knows the lenses, they have a *common language* with which to approach their projects.

When there is a decision to be taken, the first question to ask always is: when does this decision need to be made? That's when you take the decision.

John Cleese

Chapter Eleven

Structured Use of the Images

Introduction

Turning now to the second type of use, this chapter is similar to the previous chapter in that we begin with a real example first to illustrate how the images can be used in practice, except that the focus now is on using the images in a more systematic way to help get from a situation to some agreed action. In other words, in terms of getting from A to B, the idea of structured use is essentially about using the images to help get from a situation S to some agreed action A, using a particular framework we introduce later in the chapter. And like the previous chapter's framework, there are various ways of using this framework which we also cover, along with some final reflections for the reader to think about in relation to their own approach to projects.

Illustrative Example

The example we use is the consultancy project mentioned in the Introduction to Part 3, where only a week into that project there was a complex situation to deal with. As we explained, both manufacturing sites saw no reason for the project, as it was currently defined, but they were still prepared to consider some kind of intervention that could benefit the business. Briefly, how this situation came about was that a new chairman of the company perceived a need for improved communication between the two sites and decided a project was needed to identify a new system for improving communication. Unfortunately, however, what seems to have been overlooked was the fact that both sites were operating as profit centres and therefore had no incentive to improve communication, and hence saw no need for the project.

> *At the front end of project definition ... we often have quite messy, poorly structured situations where objectives are not clear, where different constituencies have conflicting aims.*[1]
>
> Peter Morris

So, what was the approach in getting from the situation to an agreed project with the client? In essence, the team's approach was to deliberately 'learn' their way to an agreed project through a structured process using some of the images in this book. An illustrative summary of this process is shown in Figure 11.1.

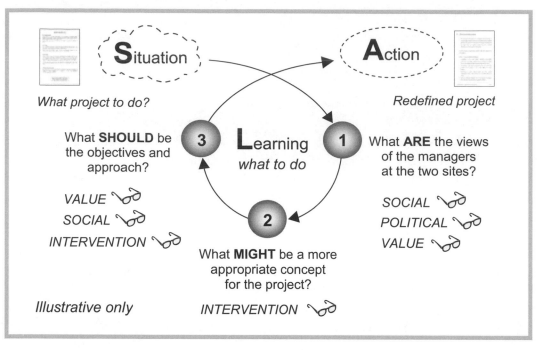

Figure 11.1   An example of structured use

As the diagram shows, there were three stages in learning what to do: (1) finding out what the different views were amongst the people in the situation; (2) drafting a new project concept based on the intervention image of projects; and (3) discussing this concept with the people involved in order to agree the objectives and approach. Other images were also used in the process, notably the social, political and value images, and by the end of 2½ weeks, the team had learnt their way to a new project that was acceptable to the client. Moreover, a certain framework was used to help guide this process, which is not immediately apparent in Figure 11.1, simply because its application here is just one of the many ways in which it can be used in real situations. In fact, in this particular situation, the key word 'learning' was not used at all with the client, this was just the team's concept of what they needed to do to get to an agreed project with the client. And because there was limited time to do this, which is always the case in real situations, this is why a framework was used to help guide the process of getting from S to A.

A Framework for Structured Use

Known as the *situation-learning-action framework,* or the 'SLA cycle' for short, this is a framework that provides help in getting from a complex situation, like the one just described, to some agreed action involving a project or programme. The framework is derived from the well-established approach to tackling complex situations known as Soft Systems Methodology (SSM),[2] but is less detailed than SSM and is specifically designed for projects. We call it the situation-learning-action cycle to emphasize the idea that getting from a situation S to some agreed action A, through a process of organized learning L, is just one 'cycle' of action that will lead to a new situation in the flux of events, and hence the cycle can begin all over again. In other words, the SLA cycle is a generic framework that can be used many times during the life of a project or a programme, and in this sense, is strongly linked to our three-phase model of the lifecycle. In the initial phase, for example, possible uses of the SLA cycle could be: shaping and agreeing a new project or programme (as in the consultancy project example); initiating a project or programme that could include tailoring an approach such PRINCE2™ or Managing successful Programmes (MSP)™; or planning the action needed to bid for a new contract for example. However, before we consider these in more detail, there are two important aspects that need to be explained first.

Situation to action, NOT problem to solution

The first key aspect to highlight is that, in terms of getting from A to B, the SLA cycle is very deliberately 'situation to action' and not 'problem to solution', and there are two reasons for this. Firstly, 'situation to action' reflects more closely what managers and other practitioners actually do in complex situations. As Donald Schön and Peter Checkland point out, the textbook image of *deciding* on *solutions* to *problems* simply doesn't reflect what people actually do. A more accurate description is they make *judgements* about the *action* needed in *situations*, and as further situations 'arise', they make further judgements, and so the process goes on. Now, as stated earlier, most practitioners do this subconsciously in the main, and some might not even think of it quite in these terms, but this generally is what practitioners do in real situations, and hence why the SLA cycle is named and framed the way it is. Secondly, since much of the *action* of projects and programmes has to be shaped and agreed along the way, and such a process always starts from a particular *situation* in the flux of events, it is clearly more appropriate to think 'situation to action' than 'problem to solution'.

Finally, there is just one other point to make about the idea of starting from a situation, which is that regardless of what might be presented at the start of a 'cycle', it is useful to think 'situation' first, not just because this is what people work within, but also because of one crucial feature that is common to all real-world situations, namely that they are always seen differently by the various people involved. As any practitioner knows, no two people ever see a situation in *exactly* the same way, which is why the idea of *learning* what to do in these situations is another key idea, as we now explain.

Learning what to do, NOT solving a problem

To explain what we mean by 'learning' in the SLA cycle, it is useful to consider first a couple of other uses of the word 'learning', as in the following two examples: learning about how a car engine works, and learning what went wrong in a failed project; in short, neither of these illustrate the idea of learning in the SLA cycle. In essence, what the L means is someone deliberately *learning* their way to action in a situation, or groups of two or more deliberately *co-learning* their way to action, with the aid of a facilitator perhaps, or using the SLA cycle as a common language. In all cases, it is essentially the process of getting from 'situation to action', and hence why it is named 'learning what to do' and not 'solving a problem'. Note that the user(s) of the cycle might not use this language with the people in the situation, as indicated earlier, but it is important to remember that the mindset in using the SLA cycle is fundamentally that of deliberately learning what action is needed.

Linked to this idea of learning is another idea which captures the essence of the SLA cycle which is the idea of *knowing what to do when you don't know what to do.* In a project situation, for example, even though the action needed might be unclear (for example, what project to do, or what to do next), we *do* know what to do in this situation, which is to organize a process of learning what to do, as we now explain. Basically, since every situation is unique and the time available for thinking and discussion is always limited, the idea of the SLA cycle is to organize the *process of thinking,* not in a prescriptive way, but in a pragmatic way that reflects the reality of the situation. In this sense, *knowing what to do when you don't know what to do* means deliberately activating a learning process in the situation (that is, the first what to do), to help get from the current situation to some agreed action (that is, the second what to do). And how this might be done is shown in Figure 11.2.

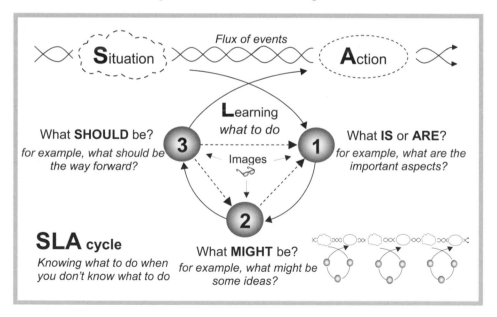

Figure 11.2   The SLA cycle as a framework for structured use

Generally, in using the SLA cycle the first thing to establish is how much time there is to get from S to A and then work back to decide how best to organize the process in the actual situation. So, for example, a practitioner with a couple of weeks to help initiate a new project might hold some initial meetings to find out more about the situation (what IS or ARE?), then draft some ideas for discussion (what MIGHT be?), and then present these ideas for discussion to help decide on the action needed (what SHOULD be?). Alternatively, a three person team with only an afternoon to decide how to approach putting a bid together, for example, could work through all three questions in the same afternoon. Regardless though of how much time is available, those involved consciously know what they are doing, as they have a framework to guide them in working out what to do. Of course, things can also change at any time, for example a meeting might be cancelled or some new requirements might emerge, but this just means the approach is modified accordingly.

One other useful thing to do at the start is to quickly establish, in very general terms, the complexity of the situation under review, in order to decide how best to organize and operate the SLA cycle within the time available. And a useful framework for this is the matrix shown in Figure 11.3, which shows four different types of situation based on the familiar dimensions of *what to do* and *how*. As the framework shows, type 1 is clearly the most straightforward, followed by type 2 situations (like the examples above), through to types 3 and 4, where 4 is the most complex, covering new projects and programmes, and also situations in which there are concerns about an existing project or programme, for example, is it still the right project to be doing? Also, note that in type 2 situations, although only the *how* is unclear, the core idea is still learning what to do, since the *how* at this level can also be seen as *what to do* at the next level. Clearly, this matrix is only a prompt for thinking, and once some initial sense has been made of the situation, the task then is to work through the three questions of the SLA cycle using relevant images.

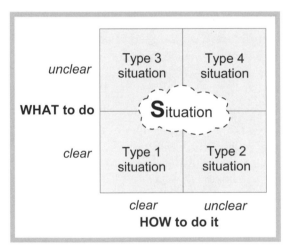

Figure 11.3   Different types of situation

In one sense, it is helpful to see the three questions shown in Figure 11.2 as three main 'stages' in getting from the situation to agreed action, as shown by the sequence of unbroken arrows in Figure 11.2; however, they are not 'stages' in a method or technique sense, firstly because of the iteration that takes place and also because the SLA cycle can be enacted in many different ways over different timeframes. Also, real-life situations are simply too complex to follow a method or technique but one can still use some guiding principles in these situations, and that is what the three questions essentially are: *guiding principles* to help get from S to A. And each principle can be supported by any of the images and models from Part 2 as we now explain.

Stage 1: What IS or ARE?

Fundamentally, the focus here is on learning more about the situation, for example, what is the situation according to the other people involved? What are the key aspects from their perspective? What have been the main events leading up to this situation? Who knows who in the situation? and so on. Also, from a political perspective, what are the interests and agenda of those involved? And what other aspects seem significant? For example, where does power lie in the situation? Clearly, such questions are only illustrative of the kinds of questions that might be asked at this stage and of course any of the other images can be used here too. Note too there is a link here with the selective use of the images, in that as the inquiry process unfolds with new aspects 'calling' for attention, different images and frameworks can be 'called upon' as and when needed. Moreover, once various aspects have been identified, another useful thing to do at this stage could be to visualize the situation as a whole, using a tool called *Rich Pictures*,[3] an example of which is shown in Figure 11.4. As Peter Checkland points out at the bottom of Figure 11.4, pictures are a much better medium than prose for showing the relationships between things in a situation, which is a view supported by Dan Roam in his book *The Back of the Napkin: Solving Problems and Selling Ideas with Pictures*.[4]

Stage 2: What MIGHT be?

Turning now to the second stage of the SLA cycle, the focus here is on generating and developing ideas, suggestions or proposals to help learn what action is needed in the situation under review. For example, in a type 4 situation where it might be unclear what project or projects need to be carried out, the intervention image could be used, where the idea might be to carry out a review first before deciding on what needs to be done and why. Similarly, other images might be used as a guide to action, or to develop ideas for discussion, and other frameworks can be used here too, as explained in Part 2. Whatever images and frameworks are used, however, the mindset at this stage is always *what might be* and not *what should be*.

Stage 3: What SHOULD be?

The final stage of the SLA cycle involves assessing the ideas from the previous stage by once again using the different images and also other perspectives such as risk, cost and so on, before finally reaching an accommodation about the action needed. In practice, the whole cycle is likely to involve several iterations, as shown in Figure 11.2, which is why this is not a stage in the method or technique sense as explained earlier. Also, the word 'accommodation' is important here, which comes from the underlying approach of SSM, which sees an accommodation not as a consensus, where everybody agrees on everything, but rather an agreement that people can 'live with' enabling action to be taken. And reaching such an agreement marks the end of the cycle, which means the 'technical work' of the project or programme can now start.

Rich Pictures

Example picture of the Coalfields Heritage Initiative Kent – see page 136.

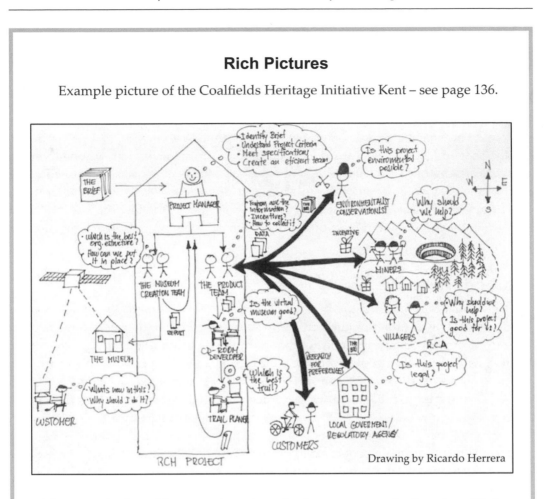

Drawing by Ricardo Herrera

The complexity of human situations is always a complexity of multiple interacting relationships. A picture is a good way to show relationships; in fact it is a much better medium for that purpose than linear prose. … In making a Rich Picture the aim is to capture, informally, the main entities, structures and viewpoints in the situation, the processes going on, the current recognized issues and any potential ones. … we have to remember [though] that however rich they are they could be richer, and that such pictures record a snapshot of a situation which will itself not remain static for very long. Wise practitioners continually produce such pictures as an aid to thinking.[5]

Peter Checkland

Figure 11.4   Rich Pictures

Different Types of Structured Use

Individual practitioner use

Basically, the idea here is that of the practitioner approaching a real situation using the SLA cycle and deliberately using various images and frameworks in the process. Examples here could be: shaping a particular project or programme, responding to an invitation to tender, preparing a business case, developing a risk management plan, writing a project plan or carrying out a strategic review of a project. Moreover, as was mentioned at the start of the chapter, a practitioner can do any of this without making it known that a structured framework is being used. To use the analogy of a 'toolkit', the SLA cycle and the seven images are simply part of the practitioner's toolkit for approaching complex situations.

Group facilitation use

The other main type of structured use is where the SLA cycle and the images can be used for facilitating group inquiry processes in situations, in other words, for helping a group or project team learn its way from a complex situation to some agreed action. Example situations here could be the same as those above, except that the role of the practitioner now is about facilitating the *process,* rather than doing much of the work him or herself; and it is this process that can be structured using the SLA cycle with the various images and frameworks. For example, such a role could be played by a project manager, a programme manager, a team leader or a project support officer and so on, or it might be performed by one or more people external to the project. Also, this kind of role requires other facilitation skills that are beyond the scope of this book and several references on group facilitation are given in Appendix E (see Chapter 9).

Whilst this type of approach can be used at any stage of a project or programme, it is particularly relevant to the *front-end* of projects, since the only thing that exists at this stage are the ideas and images in people's heads; and since the time available at this stage is always limited before some 'doing' needs to start, a facilitation approach can often be very effective. Moreover, one approach in particular that can work well is where a facilitator runs some initial workshop(s) to discuss people's views and ideas on the situation (what IS or ARE?), then drafts some relevant ideas of their own for discussion with the group (what MIGHT be?), and then reconvenes with the group in some later workshop(s) to discuss the ideas to help reach an accommodation about the action needed (what SHOULD be?). There are two key aspects to notice here: firstly, the workshops are just part of the overall process of the group learning their way to action; and secondly, the example illustrates the importance of individual work in the context of group facilitation, in this case the work of the facilitator in stage 2 of the process. This point about combining group discussion with individual work is very important and the SLA cycle offers a practical way of doing this as we just explained: basically, one can think of stages 1 and 3

The limitations of teamwork

Andrew Cracknell, Financial Times Magazine

IT WAS MY BOSS, A HARD-EYED MAN OF MONEY, WHO STOOD in front of me and said, "You see, there's no 'I' in 'Team.' I'm afraid you're just not a team player." I didn't know whether to smack him for his condescension or hug him for the compliment. At the time, I was a copywriter in a reasonably large advertising agency, charged with doing the one thing for clients they could not do for themselves – generate ideas. … Of course there are situations in which teamwork is essential. A surgeon relies upon a well-drilled, well-motivated team, as the captain of a racing yacht must rely on a crew. … [However] it's not in every circumstance that several heads are better than one. How many heads was Mozart lacking?[6]

www.graham-carter.co.uk

Figure 11.5   The limitations of teamwork

as the group discussion stages, and stage 2 as the stage for drafting ideas in the light of stage 1, which are then used as the basis for discussion in stage 3. An interesting take on the importance of individual work was provided by Andrew Cracknell in an article in the *FT magazine* in April 2005, which also included an excellent illustration by Graham Carter, and both of these are shown in Figure 11.5. The message of the article for projects is very important: effective group process requires both group discussion *and* individual work, and hence why it is important to think of any workshop or meeting event as just *part* of an overall process. In the example used earlier, stages 1 and 3 were the group stages and stage 2 was the individual stage in which the facilitator prepared some relevant ideas for discussion.

Mixed use with other approaches

The other type of structured use to briefly mention is 'mixed use' which is simply the idea of using the SLA cycle in conjunction with other frameworks and approaches such as PRINCE2™, MSP™, plan-do-review, the Define, Measure, Analyze, Improve, Control (DMAIC) process for six sigma projects, or any in-house framework for managing projects. For example, the SLA cycle could be used to tailor PRINCE2™ in a particular situation through the kind of process just described, whereby the framework of PRINCE2™ could be tailored in stage 2 and the draft ideas then discussed in stage 3 to decide how best to approach the project. Or another example could be to use the SLA cycle to craft an approach for reviewing a particular programme by tailoring a review framework such as Office for Government Commerce's (OGC) Gateway™ Process. These are just two more examples of using the images in a structured way and there are others that we could mention. But instead of focusing further on these, we turn now to some final reflections on this second type of use.

Reflections on Structured Use

The complexity and status of real-world situations

Since this chapter and the other chapters in Part 3 are about using the images in real situations, it's important to say a few words about why such situations are complex and also something about their existence which is hardly ever mentioned. Returning to the consultancy project example, the situation was complex because the people involved each had a different view of the project, and not only this, the two manufacturing sites saw no reason whatsoever for the project; in fact, for the two manufacturing sites, there was no situation at all. What this shows is that not only are *problems* perceived in different ways, but so too are *situations*, and hence as Peter Checkland points out below, we should beware of giving 'situations' a status they do not deserve:

> *these concepts and this kind of language – of 'situations', 'issues', 'problems' – are very commonly used in everyday talk, but they are subtle concepts, and we need to beware of giving them a status they do not deserve. We must not reify them; they do not exist 'out there', beyond ourselves, as we can assume 'that beech tree' and 'that dog scratching itself' do. 'This situation', and 'this problem' indicate dispositions to think about (parts of) the flux in particular ways, and they are themselves generated by human beings.[7]*

This explains why the S in the SLA cycle is deliberately 'situation' rather than 'problem' to allow for these different views to be understood in getting to the action. And it is this phenomenon of the multiplicity of views that constitutes much of the complexity in situations, as the following extract points out:

> *complexity is not just a matter of there being many different factors to bear in mind … of possible decisions and events. Complexity is also generated by the very different constructions that can be placed on these factors, decisions and events.[8]*

As a definition of complexity, this is insightful because it highlights not only the multi-faceted nature of situations (that is, the many factors to bear in mind), but also the fact that they are *constructed* in different ways by the various people involved. In other words, real-world 'situations' suddenly go from being *complicated* to being *complex*, because of the different *mental constructions* that people place on them. So, given this reality, what else might we suggest to help deal with this complexity in project environments?

Distinguishing between 'content' and 'process'

It was explained earlier that a useful way of understanding the SLA cycle is to think of it as *knowing what to do when you don't know what to do*. As we explained earlier, even though what to do might be unclear in a situation, we *do* know what to do, which is to *think about the thinking* needed in the situation. The underlying idea here is to mentally distinguish between the perceived *content* of a situation, and the *process* of engaging with that situation, so that conscious attention can be given to the process and not just the content. Other writers also highlight the importance of this distinction, for example Karl Albrecht in his book *Practical Intelligence*:

> *understanding the difference between **content** and **process**, particularly in a group situation, is one of the simplest, most powerful, and least understood secrets of practical*

*intelligence. At least 95 per cent of humans are utterly distractible by the information that arises in a discussion and quite oblivious to the process that's going on. When group meetings get confused, derailed or deadlocked, or they fail into conflict, the cause is more likely to be a failure of **process consciousness** rather than not having the needed information or not having the intelligence to make use of it. ... If you have a highly developed sense of **process consciousness**, you can think on both levels at the same time: you can observe, react to – **and guide** – the process and its content at the same time.*[9]

Because of the widespread use of the word 'process', it is important to note here that we are *not* referring to business processes, procurement processes, change management processes, risk management processes and so on. What we are referring to are the *thinking processes* of individuals and groups, and how these processes can be consciously organized in complex situations using the SLA cycle. And a real example of this is provided in Chapter 13 with more reflections on the cycle.

This just leaves one other idea to mention about 'process' that has links to all the ideas above. Earlier in the chapter, we explained that in using the SLA cycle, a key thing to establish at the start of the process is the time available for getting from S to A, and to then organize the process accordingly. This time aspect is very important as we now explain.

Not making decisions until they have to be made

The last point to make is that in getting from S to A, don't make a decision about the action needed until the final decision needs to be made. In other words, deliberately hold back from deciding what to do until a final decision is needed, or a final proposal needs to be submitted. A thought-provoking take on this is provided by the comedian John Cleese, whose thoughts were summarized in the *New York Times* in February 1999:

> *[speaking at a conference in January 1999] Mr. Cleese said ... "When there is a decision to be taken, the first question to ask always is: When does this decision need to be made? That's when you take the decision." After all, he explained, until that point, "new information, unexpected developments and – perish the thought – better ideas might occur." THE pressure on managers at all levels to act quickly is enormous, he said. "Although taking decisions very fast looks impressive, it is in fact not only show-off behaviour, but actually a bit cowardly. It shows you'd rather give the impression of decisiveness than wait to substantially improve your chances of coming up with the right decision."*[10]

Cleese explained these were not his ideas, but the ideas of Guy Claxton whose book *Hare Brain, Tortoise Mind* also prompted him to say *"just occasionally I get that feeling that somebody has said something important"*. The ideas in Claxton's book are indeed important and are very applicable to the SLA cycle in complex situations, for example, not rushing the process and making decisions until they have to be made. Also, since this process is about *learning* what to do in complex situations, it seems appropriate to mention one of Claxton's other ideas on learning, which presents a serious challenge to those who always favour quick decision making:

good learners don't always learn fast. The ability to hang out in the fog, to tolerate confusion ... is another vital aspect of resilience and thus of learning power: slow is often smart. Good learners, those able to get to the bottom of things and come up with solutions that are truly effective rather than superficially convincing, are emphatically not fast answerers.[11]

Whether it be a practitioner learning their way to action in a real situation or a group co-learning their way to action, the ability to hang out in the fog until something needs to be finalised and agreed is an important aspect of this second type of use. In Claxton's words, one should trust the 'tortoise' to play its part in the social process of working out the action needed in human situations.

Looking ahead now to the third type of use, so far we have concentrated mainly on *individuals* using the ideas and images in real situations, but what if *groups* of two or more could apply these ideas together in conversations and discussions? What if the whole group or team has a strong sense of *process consciousness* and not just the facilitator or leader? This is the idea behind the third and final type of use.

Language sets everyone the same trap; it is an immense network of easily accessible wrong turnings.
Ludwig Wittgenstein

Chapter Twelve

Shared Use of the Images

Introduction

So far in Part 3, the focus has been on individual practitioners using the images in different situations, either selectively as shown in Chapter 10, or in a structured way as shown in Chapter 11. In this chapter, we focus on groups of two or more people using the images as a shared framework for prompting and steering their discussions in the everyday flux of events, as in the example below:

[Person A] "From a development perspective, here are two possible concepts …"

[Person B] "It seems to me, from a change angle, the first one is more achievable …"

[Person C] "I agree, but politically, it might still be necessary to achieve the second …"

Although purely illustrative, this example shows a team using the images framework to discuss some new initiative, with each person deliberately 'calling upon' different perspectives to help steer the discussion. Since they all know the perspectives, they use the images framework as a ***common language*** for thinking and talking together about projects, and this is the idea that we focus on here. And the reason for this is simple: much of the work on projects involves people *thinking and talking together*, in meetings and workshops for instance, and experience shows that using a common language can make a significant difference to this process. Indeed, part of the reason projects flounder is the lack of a shared language for conducting group discussions in the everyday flux of events; for example, if everyone has a different interpretation of words such as 'value', 'development' and 'change', and they are not aware of this, then the potential for misunderstanding is obviously much greater and only limited progress will be made. Our suggestion here, as the example shows, is to use the images framework as a common language, which includes not only the language of the images from Part 2, but also the language of the Situation-Learning-Action (SLA) cycle from Chapter 11, which can also function as part of this shared language. And like the last two chapters, we start with an illustrative example first of a project team engaged in a discussion, and then present the underlying framework, followed by some practical suggestions and general reflections at the end.

In a nutshell, managers live in a rhetorical universe … The first step in taking a fresh perspective towards management is to take language … seriously.[1]

Robert Eccles and Nitin Nohria

Illustrative Example

To illustrate the idea of using the images as a common language, including the ideas of selective use and structured use, we use the example in Chapter 7 of the Coalfield Heritage Project. For this project, imagine a scenario in which the team is meeting for the first time to discuss the action needed to initiate the project and imagine they only have an afternoon to do this; also, all four members use the images framework as a common language when working together on projects. Summarized below is an illustrative transcript of their half day discussion.

Developing an action plan for initiating the project: ½ day discussion

See page 136 for a brief description of the project.

 [Project Manager] "Since we need to agree an action plan for the initiation phase by the end of the afternoon, I suggest we use the SLA cycle and agree some rough timings for each stage … We can always revisit these during the afternoon … So, looking at the current situation: what ARE the various aspects that we need to consider?"

[Person A] "I suggest we list the people and organizations first and then capture the key considerations for each of these …" [20 min later] [Person B] "It seems to me, from a development perspective, there are three deliverables …" [Person A] "I agree, but what is less clear are the desired outcomes of the project …" [Project Manager] "That is my impression too and I suggest we now look at the situation as a whole by doing a rich picture." [45 min later, Project Manager] "It feels to me we've mapped the situation as much as we can and we need to consider now what MIGHT be the actions that flow from this"

 [Person B] "I suggest we frame the actions using the Executive, Support, Communications and Operations (ESCO) model, since many of the actions needed seem to relate to the four parts of the model …" [20 min later, Person A] "So far, we've not looked at the project from a change perspective and this could be a major change for some of the museum staff …" [Project Manager] "Yes, let's do that now …"

[15 min later, Project Manager] "It feels like we've covered all the possible actions and we need to agree now what the actions SHOULD be from here on. To do this, I suggest we group the actions into the following areas … and then agree who should do what and by when …"

[45 min later, Project Manager] "This feels like a reasonable plan to me and we'll review it again next week … thanks for your input this afternoon."

Illustrative only

It is important to note that the example opposite is purely illustrative of the kind of discussion that a team could have using the images as a common language; had more time been available to produce the action plan, say 2 or 3 days, then the team could have approached the task in a different way, possibly through some meetings and individual work along the lines discussed in Chapter 11. And notice too the role of the project manager: whilst he or she is facilitating the discussion process, this is different to the facilitation approach in Chapter 11, in that the whole team is aware of the process and the need to co-manage it within the time available. As the example shows, although there is a lead facilitator, others are also helping to prompt and steer the discussion, in a way that is sensitive to the views of others, whilst also ensuring the main task is achieved. In doing this, people can suggest things without causing others to think *"Why are we now discussing this?"* or *"How have we suddenly got on to this?"* In other words, there is an unfolding logic to the discussion which is explicit and purposeful, and whilst some people might not agree with this logic, they can still contribute to the discussion, and suggest other directions to go in. Also, in this kind of discussion, power over the process is more evenly distributed than other types of discussion, where certain people dominate because of their role and personality. In summary, this is the kind of discussion that people can have using a common language, and the value of this can be very significant. However, for it to be effective, it also requires people to adopt certain behaviours in the process, such as suspending judgement and accepting that it will be messy at times, which we briefly cover in a later section. In the next section, we illustrate the concept in more general terms.

A Framework for Shared Use

To illustrate the concept generally, Figure 12.1 shows a nominal group of three people periodically thinking and talking together using the images framework as a common language. How and when this framework is used depends entirely upon the people involved: in some conversations, it could be that only one or two of the perspectives are called upon, whilst at other times, the group might conduct a whole discussion using the images framework, like the example opposite. And just to reiterate, this includes not just the language of the seven lenses, but also the technical language of the SLA cycle, namely words such as 'situation', 'learning' and 'action', and the three questions of: 'What ARE?', 'What MIGHT be?' and 'What SHOULD be?' Including this as well means the framework provides not just a common language for talking about the different aspects of projects, it also provides a shared language for talking about the *process*, as in the example opposite when the project manager says: "*Since we need to agree an action plan for the initiation phase by the end of the afternoon, I suggest we use the SLA cycle and agree some rough timings for each stage.*" Since all the other team members understand the SLA cycle and the ideas behind it, they have a shared language for talking about the process as well as the content. This

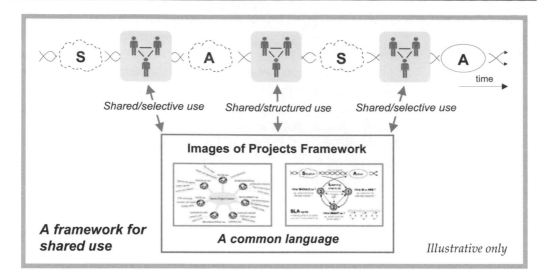

Figure 12.1   The seven lenses and SLA cycle as a framework for shared use

distinction between content and process was highlighted in Chapter 11 and the extract used from Karl Albrecht's book *Practical Intelligence* is worth repeating again here:

> *understanding the difference between **content** and **process**, particularly in a group situation, is one of the simplest, most powerful, and least understood secrets of practical intelligence. At least 95 per cent of humans are utterly distractible by the information that arises in a discussion and quite oblivious to the process that's going on. When group meetings get confused, derailed or deadlocked, or they fail into conflict, the cause is more likely to be a failure of **process consciousness** rather than not having the needed information or not having the intelligence to make use of it. If you have a highly developed sense of **process consciousness**, you can think on both levels at the same time: you can observe, react to – **and guide** – the process and its content at the same time.*[2]

Moreover, as Albrecht points out, this applies not just to individuals, it can also apply to groups, an idea which he regards as *'the most powerful possibility of all'*, when the whole group have a strong sense of process consciousness:

> *when the members of a group can consciously observe and manage their own thinking process, they can usually arrive at better decisions, more quickly, and more humanely than they otherwise would. … process consciousness enables a group to focus their mental energies more effectively.*[3]

This essentially is what our illustrative example sought to show: how a project team can jointly observe, react to and guide their own thinking process and its content at the same time, by using the images framework as a common language. And it is this idea that we too regard as the most powerful possibility of *Images of Projects*. This is because of one simple fact already mentioned, which is that projects and programmes are created and sustained through people *thinking and talking together*, and it is this that makes the common language idea the most powerful possibility of all. That said, there are limitations to this of course, notably the influence of power and politics, and we return to this briefly at the end of the chapter. The potential however to improve the quality of group discussions through the use of a common language is very significant and to illustrate this further we briefly mention two more examples in the next section.

Different Types of Shared Use

The two examples here build directly on the two main types of selective use and structured use in that we see the joint use of certain images as *shared/selective use,* and a more structured use of the images by a group as *shared/structured use*. We make this distinction simply to illustrate further the idea of using the images framework as a common language and to show how these two examples relate to other ideas elsewhere which advocate a similar approach.

Shared use of the lenses framework (selective use)

In Chapter 10 on selective use, it was explained how the seven images can operate in a similar way to Edward de Bono's Six Thinking Hats®, in that just as certain hats can be 'put on and taken off' in conversation, the same applies to the seven lenses shown again in Figure 12.2. Like the six hats, the seven lenses can be used in two ways essentially: they can be used by individuals to work on their own tasks, which was the focus in Chapter 10, and they can also be used by groups as a shared language for discussing the different aspects of projects. And it is this shared use that is the more significant mode of use, as Edward de Bono points out with his own framework of the Six Thinking Hats®:

Figure 12.2   The seven project lenses

> *it is obvious that the framework will be most useful if all the people in an organization are aware of the rules of the game. .... The concept works best when it has become a sort of common language.*[4]

Shared use of the SLA cycle (structured use)

The other example of shared use is illustrated through the example of the Heritage Project team who deliberately structured their discussion using the language of the SLA cycle and used various images and models (for example, the ESCO model) to help prompt and steer the process. Moreover, this also illustrates another idea that relates to shared/ structured use, namely the idea of *dialogue,* which is attracting increasing interest in some organizations. In writing about this in *The Creative Thinking Plan,* Guy Claxton and Bill Lucas state:

> *dialogue is more than conversation, argument or discussion. ... [it] is more a mood or a quality of conversation than a specific technique, though there are ways in which this mood – which is very different from the more normal feel of a discussion – can be encouraged. Everyone is familiar with the mood of dialogue. You feel it in a heart-to-heart conversation with an old friend. You occasionally catch it in a meeting in which suddenly everyone is sitting forward in their seats, totally engaged and bound together in a spirit of communal enquiry. Everyone is aligned: listening, learning, contributing, and willing to look with fresh eyes and to hold up their own taken-for-granted beliefs and opinions to challenge. People are living on the edge of their understanding, genuinely willing to be perplexed, to admit confusion, to dare to look underneath their reassuring 'position' to the greater complexity these positions are often designed to conceal and contain. ... Dialogue is basically a set of ground rules that encourages this mood shift to occur ... Often a facilitator is needed, at least to begin with, ... Gradually [however] the members of the group allow themselves to become genuinely puzzled and engaged, to reveal their uncertainties, to hear the resonance with other people's uncertainties, and to join a journey of exploration that is both meaningful and collaborative.*[5]

To a large extent, this is what the Heritage Project team were doing in talking about the action needed to initiate the project: they engaged in a *dialogue* about the project and used the images framework to facilitate this process. Moreover, because the team was using the SLA cycle to help *learn* what action was needed, they were also engaged in what might be termed a *learning conversation,* which is illustrated in Figure 12.3. In combining the ideas of the SLA cycle with the idea of dialogue, this offers a potentially powerful approach for talking together about projects, but it also presents a serious challenge to practitioners, as William Isaacs points out in his book *Dialogue and the Art of Thinking Together:*

> *dialogue represents a way of working that while perhaps embedded in the genes of our ancestors is new to us. Most people lack real experience of it. We are unused to speaking together openly and consciously, particularly in high-stakes, without any intention of somehow possessing for ourselves something of the outcome of these exchanges. ... We do not know how to participate in such a way that we have not planned in advance what*

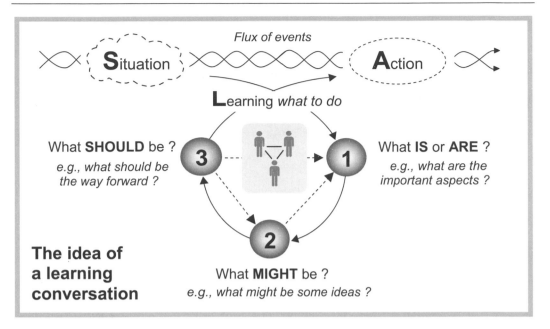

Figure 12.3   The idea of a learning converstaion

we are going to say, or where we are deliberately inquiring into. We come prepared, well stocked with thoughts, perhaps having sought to prepare others as well. And when the going gets tough, we fall back on argument and debate.

One implication of this is that as our experience with dialogue increases, we discover that the words we have to express ourselves are ill equipped to capture what we feel. For many of us, our language reflects the "machine age" in which we live. This is particularly reflected in the business culture. There we "force" issues, "drive change," "roll out" efforts to expand. ... Our language has become fragmented. We speak to reinforce our positions. We can see this same tendency to fragment in the fact that we have many words that seem to mean something different to everyone you ask. Words like **process** *and* **system** *mean so many different things to different people that they might as well be in different languages. ... To the extent that we remain caught in the language of the machine age, we will always be mired, unable to soar, unable to think. Changing the way we speak will shift how we think.*[6]

Much of the language in project and programme management still remains caught in the machine age, which is why we advocate the use of a richer language based on the idea of multiple perspectives. We would suggest that changing the way we speak about projects and programmes, through the deliberate use of multiple perspectives in organized learning conversations, can not only shift how we think about them, but can also make a significant difference to the outcomes in the longer term.

Reflections on Shared Use

Still multiple interests and agenda

Earlier we used a quote from Edward de Bono's book *The Six Thinking Hats®* in which he states: *'The framework will be most useful if all the people in an organization are aware of the rules of the game.'* Whilst this is helpful in explaining the common language idea, it can also be read as if there is just a single 'game' to be played within organizations, which is clearly not the reality and not what de Bono means. As any experienced practitioner knows, there are multiple 'games' played within organizations, linked to the different interests and agenda of those involved, or 'language games' as the philosopher Ludwig Wittgenstein would call them, as explained in the extract below from *The Great Philosophers*:

> *new ideas about language and meaning [have been] articulated most significantly in the posthumously published Philosophical Investigations. In this work, Wittgenstein set out to show that language gains its meaning from the way in which it is used … Linked to this idea is the notion of a 'language-game'; the ways and contexts in which words are used depends upon the 'game' being played. The idea of the language-game is linked to specific activities.*[7]

Interestingly, this both supports and challenges the idea of using the images as a common language: it supports the idea of a group needing to work with a shared framework (since words mean different things in different contexts), but it also illuminates the reality that people will be continually engaged in other 'language games' linked to other interests and agenda. Not only this, it suggests that this type of use is likely to be of most value to groups who share the same objectives for a project, such as a client team or contractor team for example. When those involved, however, are more of an aggregate group than a close-knit team, this third type of use is much less appropriate. That said, it is still the case that much of the work on projects and programmes is about people *thinking and talking together* and it is interesting to note that it is *this* process that is now of increasing interest to researchers, as the last point here explains.

The social process of thinking and talking together

As mentioned in Chapter 3, the social process is a complex subject area and there is a plethora of literature that extends way beyond the scope of this book. There is one body of work, however, that is worth mentioning here, since it not only offers another perspective on people thinking and talking together, but also recent Project Management Institute (PMI)-funded research based on this perspective identifies some important implications for practitioners. Developed by Ralph Stacey, the ideas are known collectively as *complex responsive processes of relating (CRPR)* and the main idea is the concept of 'relating'. As he points out in the extract below, this is essentially what people are doing all the time in the social process of everyday life:

organizing is human experience as the living present, that is, continual interaction between humans who are all forming intentions, choosing and acting in relation to each other as they go about their daily work together. ... there is a process of interaction, or relating, which is itself a process of intending, choosing, and acting. No one steps outside it to arrange it, operate on it or use it, for there is simply no objectified "it". There is only the responsive process of relating itself.[8]

Based on this relating idea, CRPR offers a way of understanding the complexity of the social process, including for example the intricacies of conversations that usually go unnoticed in the ebb and flow of everyday life. Moreover, CRPR is now attracting the interest of project management researchers, notably a PMI-funded research team led by Dr Svetlana Cicmil and Dr Terry Cooke-Davies, who explain how CRPR shifts the focus away from the management *of* complexity, to management *in* complexity, and the implications of this profound shift for managerial practices and competencies. Writing about this in the *Project Management Journal* in June 2007, the team state that:

this concept provides some important propositions related to management knowledge and competencies, which refocus attention away from managerial intervention "from outside" promoted by the conventional body of project management knowledge, toward the ability of practitioners to engage in these processes of conversational and power relating, and reflexivity in thinking about one's own complex processes of relating with others.[9]

As another social image of projects, the image of complex responsive processes is a helpful perspective in that it reinforces the point that there is only *one* process that all practitioners are immersed in when working on projects, namely the social process of *people **relating** through thinking and talking together*. And it is this process that the images framework is designed to enrich and facilitate through groups of people using it as a common language.

Like de Bono's Six Thinking Hats®, the images of projects framework works best when it has become a sort of common language.

"We seemed to have covered a lot of ground in this workshop, has there been something operating in the background?"

Member of BSR Project Team

Chapter Thirteen

Case Example 1:
Initiating a Major Retail Project

Introduction

Now that we have covered the three types of use, this chapter and the final chapter provide two examples of how the images have actually been used in real situations, together with some reflections on these experiences to reinforce the ideas in previous chapters. The logic behind this is that since these experiences helped to form the ideas in this book, it seems appropriate to include two examples to show how the ideas have actually been used in practice. The first example, which is the subject of this chapter, shows how the ideas were used in a one-off situation to help initiate a project for Tesco Stores Ltd, which was a complex situation because of the different views within the project team about a major new development. Then in the next chapter we provide a more complex example to show how the ideas and images were used to help initiate a major research project over a period of 6 months, where the lead author who was responsible for the project had no formal authority.

For this chapter, the sections are organized as follows: the chapter begins with a brief introduction to Tesco's Branch Specific Ranging (BSR) project and a summary of the flux of events leading up to the situation of concern in February 1996. This was also the start of MW's involvement in the project and the next section presents his initial reading of that situation from several different perspectives. In short, MW's brief was to help the team develop a conceptual model of BSR for a one-store trial and this was to be done through a 2-day workshop scheduled for April 1996. Against this background, the next two sections explain how the workshop was planned and facilitated using some of the images and ideas from earlier chapters, together with a summary of the main events and what happened next. Finally, at the end of the chapter, there are some reflections on how the ideas helped in this situation and how they link back to earlier chapters.

Background and summary of events: Aug 1995–Feb 1996

Tesco Stores Ltd is the UK's leading food retailer with operations now in Europe, Asia and North America. Building on the success of its Clubcard initiative in the early 1990s and other customer-focused initiatives, Tesco's growth strategy in the 1990s was to embark on a major retail development programme involving new store concepts such as Tesco Express, Tesco Metro and Tesco Extra. To help achieve this, a new strategic project called

Branch Specific Ranging (BSR) was initiated by the Tesco Board in August 1995, aimed at ranging Tesco's stores much more specifically to the local areas in which the stores were trading. For each store, this would mean taking into account aspects such as the local competition (current and anticipated) and the local demographics, in order to identify the optimum non-core product range for each store. Also included within the scope were non-food items such as clothes and white goods, and household services such as dry cleaning. Following the Board's approval in 1995, a cross-functional team was formed with representatives from the various divisions of the company, including commercial, retail and IT; basically, since the project was going to affect nearly all of Tesco's operation, it was necessary to have representation from all the relevant divisions. By early 1996, however, the project team were struggling to develop an agreed conceptual model of BSR; two workshops had been held in November 1995 and February 1996 and there was now a growing concern that the project was fast becoming an IT project rather than a business project involving IT. Moreover, with another workshop planned for April 1996 and a one store trial scheduled for June to September 1996, there was now an urgent need to develop a prototype model for the one store trial.

A Complex Situation

In response to this situation, the lead facilitator on the project, known as RD from here on, decided to seek some external help with developing the conceptual model of BSR. Moreover, he also decided that the approach for developing this model should be Soft Systems Methodology (SSM), and since neither he nor the team had any experience of using this approach, RD selected MW to help facilitate the April workshop. And it was during his first meeting with RD, that MW soon started to sense this was a complex situation as summarized in the box below.

Reading the situation from different perspectives

Key considerations:

- From a SOCIAL perspective, the BSR project team was a cross-functional team of people from different parts of the company, and all had their own views on BSR linked to their own divisions and responsibilities. This was evident from the documents produced so far from the previous workshops. Furthermore, many of the documents showed there to be differing views on how BSR should be implemented, and hence a major challenge for the next workshop was how to bring these views together into an overall model that could be evaluated in the one store trial.

- From a POLITICAL perspective too, the situation was complex in that the team was expecting significant progress to be made on the development of the conceptual model at the April workshop. Since this had been the aim of the second workshop in February 1996 and only limited progress had been made, the next event was politically important for the team. In terms of the project's schedule, it was important for the next workshop to develop the model, otherwise the one-store trial could not go ahead.

- From an ORGANIZATIONAL perspective too, the situation was complex in that the BSR project was central to the new store development programme, and the project itself was being sponsored by one of Tesco's board directors. Moreover, in terms of the Executive, Support, Communications and Operations (ESCO) model, the project was being supported by an internal consultancy group called the Business Support Group, and it was important for MW to understand this group's link with the executive and operational elements of the project.

In looking at the project documentation produced by the team so far, there was also uncertainty about whether the BSR project was one project or a number of projects, and it seemed to MW that a more useful approach could be to see it as a programme of projects that could develop as the work progressed, rather than one large project. From this perspective, the next workshop could then be seen as part of a project to evaluate the business case for BSR, which would also include the one-store trial scheduled to start in June 1996. At their next meeting, MW and RD agreed this should be the way forward and RD confirmed the main requirement for the April workshop was to produce *"a model agreed by all that can be taken forward"* (source: RD's meeting notes). They also agreed that the approach of SSM should remain 'hidden' in the background so as to avoid discussion about the underlying approach and the risk of getting deflected from the primary task of developing the model. With these aspects in mind, MW set about planning the two day workshop.

Planning the Workshop

In planning the April workshop, the task was to create a workshop framework that would help the project team *learn* its way to an agreed model of BSR and the action needed to prepare for the forthcoming trial; and the team had 2 days in which to develop this model, with facilitation support from MW and RD. With this concept in mind, MW set about crafting a framework to guide the workshop discussion, and the box on the next page lists some of the key considerations in crafting this framework.

Planning the workshop using different perspectives

Key considerations:

- From a DEVELOPMENT perspective, the technical activity of the workshop was to develop a prototype model of BSR, and since the requirement was for a *conceptual model* of BSR (that is, a kind of 'to-be' model that could be tested before wider implementation), the chosen modelling approach was SSM, as already mentioned. The detail of this approach, however, is beyond the scope of this book, which is why from here on we use the three core principles of the SLA cycle (which are derived from SSM) to describe how the workshop was organized.

- WHAT IS or ARE? Bearing in mind the team's different views on BSR, it seemed sensible to spend the first morning discussing how the various team members viewed BSR in relation to the following questions: (i) what are the *current problems* with Tesco's ranging practices? (ii) what is the *essence* of BSR from each team member's point of view? (iii) what are the team's views on the *wider aims* of BSR? (iv) what could be some problems in *operating* BSR? and (v) what could be some problems in *moving to* BSR? In short, the perspectives being applied here were the VALUE, DEVELOPMENT and CHANGE perspectives, and the purpose of this initial work was to capture these views to help develop the model of BSR.

- WHAT MIGHT BE? Following discussion of questions (i) to (v), the group could then be directed to consider some ideas for *what might be* a relevant model of BSR, and for this MW would create a model before the workshop to use as a starting point for discussion. The assumption here was that rather than try and develop a prototype model from scratch, it would be better to start with a model based on the team's work to date, and then develop this further in relation to the points raised in the morning. Note: the generic model would be created using the conceptual modelling techniques of SSM (referenced in Appendix E).

- WHAT SHOULD BE? Following a brief introduction to the generic model, the team would then be directed to consider how this model should be developed in relation to their responses to questions (i)–(v), leading hopefully to a model that could be evaluated in the forthcoming trial. Finally, the group would be directed to consider the trial itself, and here again MW would use a draft model to initiate a discussion amongst the team about the action needed to prepare and conduct the trial. And once these actions had been discussed, this would be the endpoint of the workshop.

Based on the ideas opposite, MW drafted the workshop framework and produced the two generic models that were to be used as starting points for discussion. Moreover, with the workshop now only a week away, MW agreed to fax these ideas to RD for discussion over the phone, after which any changes would be made, and RD would then produce the materials for the workshop. In the event, only minor changes were made to the workshop framework and RD agreed to produce a schematic version for use as an agenda for the two days – see Figure 13.1. Also shown in Figure 13.1 is the SLA cycle which was the underlying framework for the workshop.

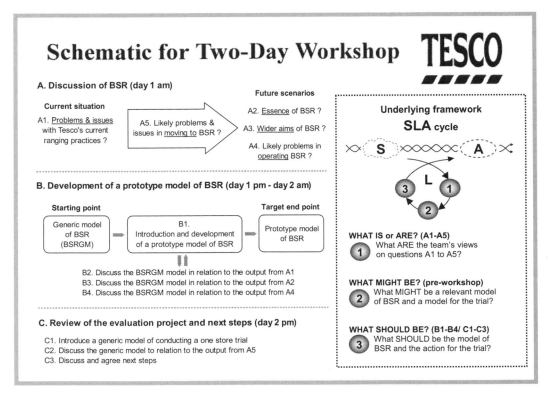

Figure 13.1   Schematic for 2-day workshop

By this stage, MW and RD had consciously learnt their way to a workshop plan and the intention now was to help the BSR project team learn its way to an agreed prototype model for BSR. To explain what happened next, the next section briefly summarizes the April workshop and the events that followed.

Summary of the Workshop

The workshop was held at Tesco's management centre in Hertfordshire and 12 people attended from different parts of the company, including the store manager of the Didcot store in Oxfordshire which had been chosen for the trial. In opening the workshop, the project manager outlined the background and aims for the 2 days and RD explained how MW had been chosen to help with the project. Following these introductions, MW then introduced the framework for the 2 days by talking through the schematic shown in Figure 13.1 and this was agreed by the project team to be a sensible structure. With this, the workshop then commenced with a general discussion of BSR to set the scene for the main discussion to follow.

Discussion of BSR (A1–A5)

During the first morning, the general discussion of BSR generated many observations about Tesco's current ranging practices, some possible problems in operating BSR, and the likely problems in moving to BSR. All of these points were recorded on flip charts and displayed on the walls of the room for use later in the workshop. It was explained by MW that the purpose of this stage was simply to capture these points for discussion later in the afternoon. Other points were raised in relation to the aims and objectives of BSR, including the view that BSR should become a core competency for Tesco. To summarize this part of the workshop, the first morning was spent understanding how the different team members perceived Tesco's current ranging practices, where they wanted to be and why, and what they saw as the problems and issues in getting there (re: the CHANGE perspective). And not surprisingly, given their different roles within the project, there were many different perspectives on all these aspects, and it was important to capture these for consideration later in the day.

Development of a prototype model of BSR (B1–B4)

After lunch on the first day, attention turned to the development of the prototype model and MW explained the suggested process: a generic model (created before the workshop) would be introduced as the starting point for discussion and the team would then develop this model through a structured comparison with the points raised in the morning. For example, having identified a range of possible problems in operating BSR, the team might seek to develop the model further by designing in features to deal with some of these anticipated problems. MW talked through the generic model and the team felt this was a good starting point for discussion. Moreover, to help facilitate this discussion, RD created a large wall chart version before the workshop, which proved to be particularly useful in helping the team to discuss and adapt this model in relation to what had been discussed in the morning. Throughout the afternoon of day 1 and the morning of day 2, various aspects were added, changed and refined in relation to many of the points raised in the morning; for example, by relating the model to the likely problems of operating BSR (question A4 in Figure 13.1), various changes were identified which had not been foreseen by the team which represented important learning for the project. Throughout this stage, a lot of effort was spent developing the model with everyone contributing ideas, counter ideas and on-the-spot evaluations of possible implications for Tesco's supply chain. By lunchtime on the second day, the model was sufficiently detailed for a one-store trial to proceed, based on the team's view that they had incorporated most of the relevant points from the initial discussion of BSR.

Review of the evaluation project and next steps (C1-C3)

Following the development of the prototype model, the team's attention was then directed towards the evaluation project and the next steps after the workshop. The important question now was: How should the prototype model be taken forward? To help answer this question, MW had prepared another generic model to use as a starting point for discussion and a similar process was enacted with MW and RD facilitating the team's discussion of what needed to be done to prepare for the trial. Like the BSR model, the trial model helped to identify a number of important aspects that had not been foreseen and a number of these emerged by relating the model to the discussion on day 1, specifically question A5 in Figure 13.1. By this stage all of the planned work had been done and after the workshop a full set of notes was produced from the flip charts in preparation for the forthcoming trial, including the following note written by the project manager to the team: *"Thank you very much for all your input to the workshop. I thought the output from the 2 days was excellent, covering a lot of ground and giving us a very good start for mapping out the work required over the forthcoming months to implement the one store trial"* (Tesco memo, 11th April 1996).

With regard to the events that followed, the trial was held in the summer of 1996 which led Tesco to extend the trial to several other stores in late 1996. Following a series of successful trials, the company implemented BSR across a range of selected stores, and since then BSR has now become standard merchandising practice across the company. Reflecting back on the events now, it is clear that the April workshop made an important contribution to the project and much of this was due to the commitment and contributions from the project team, and the excellent facilitation support provided by RD. However, what was also significant was the role played by the SLA cycle and some of the images in this book, as the final section now explains.

Reflections on the Case Example

At the end of the workshop, RD conducted a review of the 2 days and one of the comments was: *"We seemed to have covered a lot of ground in this workshop, has there been something operating in the background?"* This was a perceptive remark and yes there was something operating in the background – the SLA cycle and certain images – and this is what we reflect upon here to reinforce some of the points made in earlier chapters.

An organized way of getting from situation to action

As explained in Chapter 11, the SLA cycle is an organized way of getting from a situation to some agreed action, not in a technique-like way, but in a way that is tailored to the situation under review. As Figure 13.1 shows, the three principles of the SLA cycle were applied as follows: firstly, the morning of day 1 was spent learning about the different team members' views on questions A1–A5 (what ARE?); secondly, before the workshop, MW created two models to use as starting points for discussion (what MIGHT be?); and thirdly, these were then used to help develop the prototype model and to prepare for the one store trial (what SHOULD be?). In other words, the whole process was deliberately organized to help the team learn their way to an agreed model for the one store trial, and it is this aspect of a *consciously organized process* that is fundamental to understanding the SLA cycle.

Situation to action, NOT problem to solution

Another key aspect from Chapter 11 is that the SLA cycle is always about getting from a situation to action, not problem to solution, and not only this, the focus is always a *perceived* situation, as Peter Checkland reminds us in the extract below:

nothing is intrinsically 'a situation'; it is our perceptions which create them as such, and in doing that we know that they are not static; their boundaries and their content will change over time. Some of the situations we perceive, because they affect us in some way, cause us to feel a need to tackle them.[1]

Applying this to the BSR example, there was clearly a perceived situation in early 1996 that the BSR project was fast becoming an IT project and action was needed to help move things forward; this was certainly RD's perception of the situation and it soon became MW's perception following his initial discussions with RD. And this essentially was the starting point of MW's involvement. And notice too the endpoint of MW's involvement, action not solution, which comprised both the prototype model and the action needed to prepare for the trial. This was not a solution, it was just the *action* needed to move things forward to the next stage.

Learning for action, NOT solving a problem

The other key aspect to mention again about the SLA cycle is the idea of 'learning' which comes directly from the learning cycle idea in SSM, which Peter Checkland usefully summarizes in the following extract:

[the SSM learning cycle is] a cycle of learning which goes from finding out about a problematical situation to defining/taking action to improve it. The learning which takes

place is social learning for the group ... though each individual's learning will be, to a greater or lesser extent, personal to them.[2]

Applying this to the Tesco example, the social learning for the group was the BSR project team *learning* its way to an agreed prototype model of BSR and the action needed to prepare for the trial. Furthermore, each member of the project team also learnt a lot about their particular role within the project and how it was going to affect their division. And all of this was done in an *organized way*, which links to the earlier idea of consciously organizing the process to allow for this kind of learning to take place, and also because of the limited time available.

The importance of 'social learning' in group situations

The idea of 'social learning' also relates to the ongoing creation of social reality which is particularly relevant to projects because of the different people and organizations involved. As the Tesco example shows, the actual reality of any project is not the lifecycle process, but a social and political process of people continually interacting with each other in an ever-changing flux of events. From a social process perspective, there is no single and separate reality 'out there', but rather everyone's own realities all continually evolving and changing through time, as Peter Checkland points out in the extract below:

social reality is the ever-changing outcome of the social process in which human beings, the product of their genetic inheritance and previous experiences, continually negotiate and re-negotiate with others their perceptions and interpretations of the world outside themselves.[3]

In the Tesco example, all that existed at the start of the BSR project were differing ideas and perspectives amongst the people involved about the concept of BSR; in other words, 'BSR' and the 'one-store trial' were not things 'out there' that existed independently of the people involved, they were ideas and images in people's heads that needed to be negotiated and renegotiated through group discussion. And this is what the SLA cycle helped the team to do, to negotiate and renegotiate their differing ideas and images in an organized way, thus enabling a model of BSR to be created and the one-store trial to go ahead. In summary, the SLA cycle is based on the view that all human situations are *subjectively experienced* and this subjectivity needs to be taken *seriously* if effective action is to be taken.

A writer may try his best to draw a map of how things are, that will be equally valid for all; but all he can really do is to paint a picture of what he sees from the unique and transient viewpoint which is his alone.

Sir Geoffrey Vickers

Chapter Fourteen

Case Example 2:
Managing a Major Research Project

Introduction

Three weeks into a new job in September 2002, the lead author attended a meeting of the Centre for Research in the Management of Projects (CRMP) at University College London. Just before entering the meeting, he was told that a possible action from the meeting could be to submit a funding application for a new research initiative in project management. Moreover, it was also suggested that he should *"take the lead on this,"* and yet paradoxically he had no idea what 'this' was about. By the end of the meeting, the expected action became a recommended action, and MW was now faced with the challenge of taking this initiative forward. Months later, it would evolve into something called *Rethinking Project Management* and this chapter shows how the first phase of this project was managed using the ideas and images in this book.

In contrast to the previous chapter which focused on the use of the images in a one-off situation, the aim of this final chapter is to show how the images can be used over a prolonged period of time to help deal with the challenges faced. Clearly, this is just one example and there is no suggestion here that this is 'the' way to use the images in practice; as explained in Chapter 10, there is no one 'best way' of applying the images, for it depends on the practitioner and their particular role and interest. However, what this example does seek to show is how the images can provide a useful aid to managing projects and programmes in the ever-changing flux of events. As Peter Checkland points out, to 'manage' anything in practice, the practitioner has to deal with a complex and ever-changing flux of events, and this was certainly the reality that the lead author (MW) faced in managing this complex initiative.

Now, some people might rightly ask if this is an appropriate example to illustrate the images in action, and some might even question whether the initiative was really a 'project' at all? The response to this is simple: for the funding body, this was most definitely a 'project', and for MW too, it was a project that needed careful managing from various perspectives. For example, it was *public money* that was being used to fund this initiative, and hence an important perspective was the value perspective to help think about the value that might be created from this particular project. And not just this, the fact that this initiative was to be carried out in a university setting meant it was also challenging *politically*, for as Henry Kissinger once said: *"University politics are so vicious precisely because the stakes are so small."*[1] In summary, being a more complex example, this chapter provides a useful case example to finish on.

Background and summary of events

As we stated in the Introduction, it was Keynes who said that people who described themselves as practical men, proud to be uncontaminated by any kind of theory, always turned out to be the intellectual prisoners of the theoreticians of yesteryear. Whether we agree or not with Keynes' assertion, it does remind us that all practical activity in any professional field is based on some theory or knowledge, irrespective of whether the practitioner is aware of this or not. Although this covers both *personal knowledge* and *published knowledge*, it was the published knowledge in project management that *Rethinking PM* was concerned with, that is, mainstream ideas and techniques taught to practitioners and students. Given the growing critiques of these ideas and techniques, the objective of the *Rethinking PM* initiative was to identify the areas in which new knowledge is needed to support practitioners working on today's projects and programmes.

Funded by one of the UK research councils – the Engineering and Physical Sciences Research Council (EPSRC) – *Rethinking PM* was funded as an 'EPSRC network' for which the objectives are generally twofold: (1) to create a community of people interested in reviewing an important research area; and (2) for that community to develop a future research agenda through a series of meetings and workshops, held usually over 2 years. To do this, a lead university is normally expected to identify those interested in participating in the project, and then apply for funding to carry out the work. The funding covers the travel and accommodation expenses of the academic participants, administrative support (for example, a network coordinator) and the development of a website for use by the network participants.

And this briefly is what happened with *Rethinking PM*: for the first 6 months of the project, MW set about creating a group of academics and practitioners interested in 'rethinking' mainstream PM ideas. And alongside this, with support from the group, MW gradually developed the funding proposal that was submitted in April 2003. Four months later, in August 2003, the project was formally approved, marking the end of the first phase of the project. Interestingly, however, this was only the *start* of the project for EPSRC, whereas for MW, this was now the start of the *second phase* in the three-phase lifecycle model, which usefully shows how the same 'project' is always constructed differently by the different people and organizations involved (re: Aspect 2 in Chapter 3). Staying with MW's model of the project, the main activity of the second phase was the meeting programme which started in March 2004 and ended in January 2006. Seven meetings were held in different locations in the UK and the main substantive meetings were closely aligned with the interests and perspectives of the participants, focusing on seven areas of concern: *projectification, managing multiple projects, actuality of projects, dealing with uncertainty, managing business projects, the profession and practitioner development.* Moreover, it was decided that seven meetings would not be enough to develop the required output and that significant between-meeting activity would be needed. Consequently, a considerable amount of activity was carried out between the meetings, resulting in a series of working papers covering the perceived issues and themes arising from each meeting, as well as the main findings emerging from the project as a whole.[2] And since January 2006 was the official end date from EPSRC's perspective, this also marked the end of the second phase for MW, and the task now was to disseminate the main findings to PM researchers and practitioners. For MW, this final phase was very important, as it was here that the work of the project needed to be shared with PM researchers and practitioners, and for this several publications were produced and various presentations were given to different audiences.

In summary, a large number of people contributed to the *Rethinking PM* initiative and the outputs produced only emerged because of the collective effort of so many people across the three phases of the project. The box below summarizes the three phases.

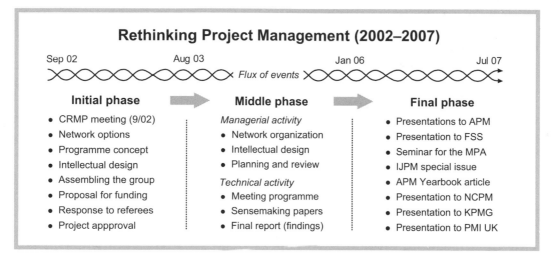

Figure 14.1   The three phases of Rethinking PM (2002–07)

From here on, this chapter is about MW's experience of managing the first phase of this initiative using the images in this book. Without question, this was a project that had to be managed from *multiple perspectives*, as this chapter will show. Right from the initial meeting in September 2002 when 'it' all started, through to a final industry presentation in July 2007 (when he judged 'it' to have ended), the reality experienced by MW was always that of a complex and ever-changing flux of events, and hence was approached using the images in this book. More importantly, these images were found to be *useful* in dealing with the challenges faced, which in a practical field such as project management, should be the 'test' of any practical framework. In summary, MW had to manage the initiative in some way, and it was found that the images framework provided a useful framework, as this chapter will now show.

Initial Phase (Sep 2002–Jan 2003)

The situation in September 2002

From MW's perspective, the story of *Rethinking PM* starts in September 2002 when he attended his first meeting of the Centre for Research in the Management of Projects, a joint research group between UMIST (now part of the University of Manchester) and University College London (UCL). Just before entering the meeting, he was told that a possible action could be to submit a research proposal for an EPSRC network in project management, and moreover, it was suggested that he should *"take the lead on this,"* and yet paradoxically he had no idea what an EPSRC network was. Not only this, he entered the meeting wondering what "taking the lead" might mean in the context of a group he had only recently joined. Just 3 weeks into a new job and it felt like a major challenge was starting to emerge in the unfolding flux of events! Attended by over 20 people, the main concern of the meeting was that project management was still not being recognized by the funding councils as an important research area, despite the increasing growth in project work across many sectors. For many of those present, it simply wasn't on the 'radar screen' of EPSRC (a phrase repeatedly used in the meeting), and to help change this, CRMP should submit a research proposal for a 'network' in project management. In essence, the logic seemed to be that if EPSRC funded a new research network, and this was successful, there would be more chance of obtaining further research funding in the future. No specific objectives were agreed for the network, only that a proposal needed to be submitted to the research council within approximately 6 months. The meeting ended with MW feeling that he was now in a complex situation that needed to be approached in an organized way from this point on.

Understanding the situation and the broader context (what ARE?)

After the CRMP meeting, MW met with UMIST's Head of CRMP who explained the basic idea of an EPSRC network and suggested some names of other PM academics who might be interested in participating. Being new to the PM community and not having any experience of writing research proposals, MW found these suggestions helpful and duly set about researching more into EPSRC networks. Guided by the EPSRC website, his next task was to start contacting people for expressions of interest and it was here that he started to think more seriously about the social and political aspects of the task in hand. Operating in unfamiliar territory, both in respect to EPSRC networks and the CRMP research group, MW was acutely aware of the environment he was now operating in, and the need to continually 'read' the social and political aspects of the developing situation. In many respects, this was a new 'game' that MW was now playing and previous experience had taught him that academics were not always the easiest to play ball with!

SOCIAL and POLITICAL perspectives

Key considerations:

- After nearly 2 months in the flux of events since the CRMP meeting in September 2002, it felt to MW that one aspect in particular 'calling' for his attention was the recent history of CRMP, and also what the relationship seemed to be between the two groups at UMIST and UCL. This was felt to be important because the network proposal was to be a joint submission from UMIST/UCL, and he needed to understand the history of CRMP (as best he could) before putting any ideas forward to the two groups. This was done mainly by studying various documents and talking to people within the Project Management Division at UMIST.

- Another significant aspect 'calling' for his attention during this time was the apparent tribalism within the Project Management Division at UMIST, which he was starting to sense through discussions with its members and listening closely to their language in staff meetings. Like CRMP, there was a history to this division, which MW needed to try and understand before developing the proposal to EPSRC. This was not unusual in that most academic departments are usually more tribal than team-oriented, and it was important to try and understand this tribal context as much as possible.

- Another key consideration for MW at this stage was identifying which other people and organizations to contact, and how best to do this by phone, email or preferably through a meeting. In short, from MW's perspective, the initial social interaction with these people needed very careful handling, for without the support of these people, there would be no network.

Although the proposal was to be a joint submission from UMIST and UCL, it was felt that certain academics in other universities might also be interested in supporting the bid as named 'co-investigators' in the proposal. These were the first people to be approached by MW and it soon became apparent there was strong support for this initiative; 2 months in and the idea of a network in project management was clearly of interest to the people contacted so far. For MW, the initial aim here was to seek expressions of interest before circulating any specific proposals on what the network might focus on and how it might work.

Options and ideas for discussion (what MIGHT be?)

With support for the idea, the task now was to draft some options for what the network might focus on and what it might hope to achieve in the longer term; in other words, for MW, it was important now to see it as both a *development process* and a *value creation process*, and to start drafting some ideas from these two perspectives, which could then be used as the basis for discussion, (re: stage 2 of the Situation-Learning-Action (SLA) cycle.)

DEVELOPMENT and VALUE perspectives 👓

Key considerations:

- From a development perspective, the key consideration for MW at this stage was WHAT was the network going to develop and WHY? In other words, in terms of this book's development image, a central concern for MW was the *development concept* of the network (re: Aspect 2 in Chapter 7): in essence, what should this concept be? Starting with EPSRC's own perspective on this, the general concept of an EPSRC network was twofold: (1) to create a community of people interested in reviewing a research area; and (2) for this group to develop a research agenda to inform future research in the chosen area.

- Clearly, then, there was a development concept of sorts, but whilst this was helpful, there were still important questions to deal with, for example, what should the network focus on? And what exactly was a 'research agenda'? For MW, looking at this from a development perspective, the research agenda represented the 'output' of the network, and yet in classical PM terms, there was no 'specification', or even guidelines, for the required output.

- And *how* should this 'research agenda' be developed? Since the concept was about developing a research agenda *to inform future research,* this was another major concern for MW because the approach itself would be very important if the research agenda output was going to be of any value to researchers.

- And finally, MW had another concern in looking at the network from a value creation perspective: in short, what would be the value of this network to practitioners, as opposed to researchers? From a value perspective, MW felt that it was important to try and shape the initiative in a way that might also be of interest and value to practitioners, so that they too might benefit from the work of the network. Providing the network met the requirements of the funding body, this was felt to be entirely justified on the basis that project management is first and foremost a practical activity, involving *both* theory and practice, and the whole initiative seemed to offer a good opportunity for practice to inform theory, and theory to inform practice.

Based on these concerns and considerations, MW began drafting some ideas and options in November 2002 for what the network might do and how it might work; in short, three options were drafted, two serious contenders, and a third option that was unlikely to receive funding from EPSRC. Taking forward the two main contenders, the first option was to focus just on the front-end of projects and programmes, based on recommendations from previous research projects that this was an important area for future research; and the second option was a much broader concept to review the PM field as a whole, to see how mainstream theory about projects (for example, the lifecycle concept) should be developed in relation to the developing practice across different industry sectors. Named *Rethinking Project Management*, this was the preferred option for MW for two reasons: firstly, it seemed to fit better with the operation of an EPSRC network, and secondly, it offered more scope for a larger group of people to be involved. Moreover, because this was only a *concept* for discussion at this stage, and not the final proposal, it was important to think about a possible programme of activity that could operate within the general structure of an ESPRC network.

DEVELOPMENT perspective

Key considerations:

- Having formulated the concept of *Rethinking PM*, it was important to develop some draft ideas on HOW the 'rethinking' task could be carried out. In other words, from a development perspective, what would the *process* be for carrying out this task? And because it was a 'rethinking' task, the process that needed to be thought about was an *intellectual process*, in other words, the 'technical process' of rethinking mainstream PM ideas, as opposed to the social process through which the work would be carried out.

- Moreover, since the concept was to 'rethink' mainstream PM ideas, the logical output of this process – mainstream PM ideas 'rethought' – could then be seen as the 'research agenda' output of the network; however, at this stage, MW had no idea what the structure of this agenda might be. Rightly or wrongly, he chose to focus on the inquiry process of *Rethinking PM* and assumed that the research agenda output would emerge as the work progressed. At this stage, then, what was needed was a defensible framework of activity to guide the network meeting programme.

- Three other considerations were important here: (1) what was being 'rethought' was mainstream PM ideas, not current practice; (2) the concept of 'rethinking' would mean extending and enriching these ideas, not abandoning them; and (3) as well as the meetings, the programme would also need to include a significant amount of between-meeting activity to help produce the research agenda output.

Discussion of the options (what SHOULD be?)

Initially, all three options were discussed with the Head of CRMP at UMIST and the third option was soon discarded in favour of the front-end option and the broader option of *Rethinking PM*. Whilst the broader option was the preferred option, it was stressed that this was an ambitious proposal and would need careful writing before any submission was made to EPSRC. Heeding this advice, the next step for MW was to discuss the two options with the Head of CRMP at UCL.

SOCIAL and POLITICAL perspectives

Key considerations:

- Since the proposal was to be a joint submission from UMIST and UCL it was important to share the two options with the Head of CRMP at UCL who had agreed to act as one of the co-investigators. MW also felt that he needed to meet with him personally to allow for a richer discussion rather than just emailing a document and trying to discuss it over the phone. Also, as the next point explains, MW had another reason for wanting to meet with him.

- Since both options were linked to this person's research interests, especially the *Rethinking PM* option, MW was keen for him to be involved in the network, not least because it was to be a joint submission, but also because of his intellectual contribution to the field so far, and the knowledge and experience he would bring to the network discussions. Taking time out to meet with him personally, rather than phone or email, was MW's way of trying to secure his interest and involvement.

In December 2002, the two met and there was a memorable moment in the meeting when the Head of CRMP expressed interest in the *Rethinking PM* option, stating this would be something he would be interested in participating in. For MW, this was a highly significant moment in the unfolding flux of events, for it was at this moment that he 'felt' there was now a clear direction and this was the option to focus on. There was no formal or systematic evaluation of the two options, just a strong 'sense' this was the way to go, based on all the work that had been done so far. Continuing on with the meeting, MW explained the draft meeting programme for *Rethinking PM* and the UCL Head of CRMP suggested some other industry sectors that the network might look at and some companies that might be involved. These were helpful suggestions and it was agreed that MW would now write a draft proposal which he would circulate for comments. The direction was now set for *Rethinking PM* and the task now was to write the proposal to EPSRC to obtain funding for the initiative.

Initial Phase (Jan–Aug 2003)

In January 2003 MW completed a first draft of a six-page case for support required by EPSRC as part of the proposal submission. Also included in this was the meeting programme which embodied the intellectual process already described. Mindful that these were only ideas for discussion and not the finished product, MW circulated the draft proposal to the other academics who had agreed to act as co-investigators, and others who had expressed interest in taking part. Socially and politically, this next stage in the flux of events was very important, as the next box explains.

SOCIAL and POLITICAL perspectives

Key considerations:

- Although from a development perspective, MW had worked out a possible framework of activity, he was also acutely aware that in reality the network would be a social and political process, involving various people with differing interests and perspectives. Seeking feedback on the proposal, therefore, was very important at this stage, for without the input and support of these people, there would be no network. Moreover, MW was also aware that most of the people he was contacting at this stage already knew each other, in other words, he was interacting with a social network that already existed. And the implication of this was that even though most of this interaction would take place either over the phone or by email, clear and consistent communication was needed with all those involved. For example, MW would regularly copy emails to people to keep them informed.

- As well as seeking feedback, another key consideration was the need to emphasize to people that there would be further opportunity to shape the framework at the first meeting. In other words, for MW, the primary task at this point was less about 'writing a proposal' and much more about 'creating a network of people' interested in taking part in a new research initiative.

- Seeing it also as a political process, MW was aware that he had limited power and influence in this situation, for example, he had no formal authority over people and was new to the academic community in project management. Tactically therefore, key considerations in approaching people were rational persuasion, consultation and the building of a group with a common cause. In summary, MW judged that the social network that was now forming, and visible to people through the various email exchanges, would itself be a major influence on people's decision to participate.

After circulating the draft proposal, it was clear from people's comments that there was strong support for both the overall concept and the proposed programme, which many expressed through a letter of support that would eventually be included in the final submission. Moreover, it was not just academics who expressed their support for the network, so too did a number of senior industry people, including the Executive Director of the Major Projects Association (MPA), the Chairman of the Association for Project Management (APM), and the Managing Director of Human Systems Limited. Sensing that a network was now 'forming', MW was also starting to sense the enormity of the challenge that lay ahead; it was one thing to write a proposal to EPSRC, quite another to develop a research agenda with a diverse group of people all with differing interests and perspectives! However, the immediate task was to finalise the submission to EPSRC and in April 2003 eight copies of the proposal were sent off consisting of the official proposal form (below), a track record document, a six-page case for support, the proposed meeting programme and 23 letters of support.

At this point, the normal procedure for EPSRC is to send the proposal out for referees' comments, before it is finally assessed at an internal panel where the final decision is made. This was duly done and in June 2003 MW received copies of the referees' comments, together with an invitation to respond, stating that: *"Your response will be put to the panel to assist it in ranking the proposal."* Instructed also that: *"Any response longer than [one page of A4 would]* **not** *be put to the panel,"* MW responded to the referees' comments in June 2003, and in August 2003, was officially informed that the project had been approved.

EPSRC OFFER LETTER:

Standard Research GR/S64363/01

"The EPSRC is offering a grant towards the cost of the above **project** *subject to the terms and conditions …" (emphasis added)*

Eleven months on from September 2002, and *Rethinking Project Management* was now an official project with funding from EPSRC.

Some Reflections on Phase 1

Projects are many things at once!

The first thing to mention from this account is how the example illustrates the phenomenon that projects are many things at once. For just as Gareth Morgan states that *'any realistic approach to organizational analysis must start from the premise that organizations can be many things at one and the same time,'*[3] the same is true for projects: any realistic approach to managing projects must, we believe, also start from the premise that projects are many things at once. For example, from September 2002 onwards, the EPSRC network initiative was simultaneously: a social process, a political process, a development task, and also for MW, a value creation process, given that he saw the 'value' of this initiative to be a very important aspect. As Morgan states in his book: *'Though managers and organization theorists often attempt to override this complexity by assuming that organizations are ultimately rational phenomena that must be understood with reference to their goals or objectives, this assumption often gets in the way of realistic analysis. If one truly wishes to understand an organization it is much wiser to start from the premise that organizations are complex, ambiguous, and paradoxical.'*[4] And this essentially was the premise that MW started with in September 2002: that this initiative was going to be complex, ambiguous and paradoxical, and why, therefore, he decided to approach it in an organized way from different perspectives.

Conscious use of different perspectives

Taking MW's account of this first phase, any experienced practitioner might well reflect on how is this different to what they already do in their own practice? To help answer this, we turn again to Gareth Morgan's book in which he states: *'One of the beauties of the [Images] approach is that it builds on what many people already do quite naturally. ... [by applying multiple images] we are invited to do what we do naturally, but to do so more **consciously**.'* (emphasis added).[5] And herein lies the difference: the invitation of the *Images* concept is to do what we already do, but to do so more *consciously* through the use of different images and frameworks, in order to help tackle the realities being faced. In other words, since projects are complex and one's experience is always limited, the practitioner deliberately chooses to work with different images of projects as part of his or her approach, in order to explore the insights and the implications for action which flow from these, and all in a way which combines with their own knowledge and experience.

When do projects actually start?

According to the mainstream image, a project starts with a well-defined objective to develop something to specification, cost and time; however, with the EPSRC initiative, there was no specified objective at the start, only that a proposal needed to be submitted to EPSRC to try and influence future funding decisions. But *what* was the proposal to focus on and *how* should it be developed? And *who* should be involved and *when* and *where* should the work be carried out? These were all questions faced by MW at the start of the initiative, which from a mainstream PM perspective, could suggest that MW was not yet dealing with a 'project'. And yet from a social process perspective, it could be argued that any new initiative starts as soon as people begin *talking* about 'it', even though they might not see 'it' as having already started, as was the case with this initiative. In other words, for many people, projects only start when the 'action' starts, and yet as the social image shows, the action is 'in' the interaction itself, and hence initiatives start when people begin *talking* about them. Or maybe even further 'upstream' in the flux of events, when the MD has an idea in the bath?

Importance of decision making at the front-end

Just as the upstream part of the flux of events is important for understanding how past events and decisions account for the present, so too is the downstream part for reminding the practitioner of how future events and decisions will be shaped by decisions taken in the present. In the case of the network initiative, MW was acutely aware that the decisions and judgements he was making at this stage would have a significant influence on the events to follow, which was yet another reason why he approached the initiative from multiple perspectives. For example, *value for money* considerations were important for MW, which is why the value perspective was important to apply alongside the development perspective; after all, this was public money that was being applied for, and the decisions here would have a significant influence on what could eventually be achieved. As the late Sir Geoffrey Vickers points out in his book *The Art of Judgement*:

> those who are engaged in a course of decision making soon become aware that each decision is conditioned not only by the concrete situation in which it is taken but also by the sequence of past decisions; and that their new decisions in their turn will influence future decisions.[6]

A good example of this was provided in 2007 by Sir John Rose, Chief Executive of Rolls-Royce Plc, who paid tribute to the contribution of his predecessors: *"We owe a huge amount to the people who were making the decisions 20 years ago – and if they hadn't made them, we wouldn't be feeling so cheery. And the decisions we are taking now will affect not only my successors, but their successors."*[7]

Final Reflections on the *Images* Concept

Having now reached the end of this book, we end with an important extract from the book that inspired us to write *Images of Projects*. At the end of *Images of Organization*, Gareth Morgan writes about what inspired him to write his own book:

I believe that some of the most fundamental problems that we face stem from the fact that the complexity and sophistication of our thinking do not match the complexity and sophistication of the realities with which we have to deal. This seems to be true in the world of organization as well as in social life more generally. The result is that our actions are often simplistic, and at times downright harmful. ... I believe that we are active in constructing our worlds; that we can benefit from greater awareness of the processes through which this occurs; and that we can become simultaneously more reflective and more proactive in shaping the way social reality unfolds.[8]

*We too believe that some of the fundamental problems faced by practitioners stem from the mismatch between the complexity of real-world situations and **how they are thought about** by the people involved. And like Gareth Morgan, we too believe that we are active in constructing our worlds; and that we can, over time, learn to become more reflective and more proactive in the way we think about these situations, particularly in the world of projects where this kind of thinking is a crucial craft skill. In short, this is the worldview behind **Images of Projects.***

****

Appendices

Appendix A   Example Matrix of Perspectives and Tools

Listed below are many of the tools featured in this book and also some examples referenced in Appendix E. A shaded box indicates the suggested 'default' perspective.

Example tools HOW \ Perspectives WHAT	Social perspective	Political perspective	Intervention perspective	Value perspective	Development perspective	Organizational perspective	Change perspective
Flux of events image	■	•	•	•	•	•	•
What is the pig? illustration	■	•	•	•	•	•	•
Social network diagram	■	•	•			•	•
The dialogue model[1]	■	•	•			•	•
Complex responsive processes model[2]	■	•	•			•	•
Cultural web model	■	•	•	•	•	•	•
Iceberg metaphor	■	•	•				
Tribal interests model	•	■	•	•		•	•
Personal interests model	•	■	•	•		•	•
Power and influence framework	•	■	•	•	•	•	
Political tactics framework	•	■	•	•	•		
Attitude to politics framework	•	■	•				•
Rich Pictures	•	•	■	•	•	•	•
Types of intervention matrix			■				
Different models of consultation[3]			■				•
Effectiveness, efficacy & efficiency[4]			■	•	•		•
1st and 2nd level relationship model				■		•	
Outcomes-outputs-resources triangle				■	•	•	
WHY/WHAT/HOW analysis	•	•	•	■	•	•	•
Benefits dependency network[5]				■	•		
CATWOE analysis[6]	•	•	•	•	■	•	•
PSO model			•		■	•	•
Milestone plans[7]			•		■		•
Stage gate models			•		■		•
ESCO model						■	
Positioning framework for the PBO[8]						■	
Organizational capabilities model[9]						■	
Responsibility charts[10]			•		•	■	•
Change kaleidoscope model			•				■
Change process model			•				■

Appendix B   Theory Behind *Images of Projects*

Although *Images of Projects* draws on the work of many people, the book's main ideas are based on the ideas of five eminent contributors to the management field, namely Gareth Morgan, Peter Checkland, Donald Schön, Edward de Bono and Guy Claxton. Neither fad nor fashion, these people's ideas are about the *process of thinking* in real situations, and they are either very *insightful* in what they illuminate, and/or very *practical* in what they offer to practitioners. Not only do they provide the theoretical foundations for *Images of Projects*, they also underpin many of the practical ideas in this book, and a brief summary of their work is given below.

IMAGES OF ORGANIZATION (1986)

Gareth Morgan

Research focus: making sense of organizations

Brief summary: according to Gareth Morgan, one of the crucial skills of effective practitioners is the ability to 'read' situations with various scenarios in mind and to craft the actions that seem appropriate to the situation of concern. Many develop this skill intuitively, through experience and natural ability, and for this reason, it is often seen to be an innate skill. Morgan takes the view that all practitioners can develop this crucial skill, to varying degrees, and the *Images* concept is about developing (or enriching) this skill for managing in organizations.

SYSTEMS THINKING, SYSTEMS PRACTICE (1981)

Peter Checkland

Research focus: the use of systems thinking in management situations

Brief summary: Peter Checkland's unique contribution has been to change the way we can think about, and approach, complex situations in organizational settings. By combining systems thinking with an innovative programme of rigorous practice-based research over 30 years, he and his collaborators developed the approach of *Soft Systems Methodology (SSM)*, which enables managers of all kinds to deal with the complex realities of the situations they face. This 30-year programme is arguably the most significant and productive programme of *action research* ever undertaken in the broad field of management.

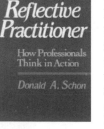

THE REFLECTIVE PRACTITIONER (1983)

Donald Schön

Research focus: how practitioners actually think in action

Brief summary: unfortunately, the title of Schön's seminal book often invokes a view that it is about practitioners stepping back to learn from their experience, when in fact the subtitle is much more representative of what the book is about: *how practitioners actually think in action*. In essence, Schön's book offers a profound insight into how effective practitioners actually deal with complex situations through experience and intuition, and likens the process to a form of artistry, which he believes can be developed through education and development.

LATERAL THINKING FOR MANAGEMENT (1971)
Edward de Bono

Research focus: how the mind works and tools for thinking

Brief summary: the work of Edward de Bono is well-known throughout the world and is based on the view that *'thinking is the ultimate human resource'* and is fundamentally a skill that can be developed. His approach to developing skill in thinking centres on the deliberate use of attention-directing tools such as the Six Thinking Hats®. Moreover, whilst he has written many books over the years, including *I am Right, You Are Wrong* (1990), all of his work is based on a very insightful model of how the mind works, presented in *The Mechanism of Mind* in 1969.

HARE BRAIN, TORTOISE MIND (1997)
Guy Claxton

Research focus: cognition, intuition and learning

Brief summary: after reading Guy Claxton's seminal book, the British comedian John Cleese said of it *"just occasionally I get that feeling that somebody has said something important."* One of the key messages of the book is that practitioners need to allow more time for the 'tortoise mind' to play its part and to stop hare brain 'bullying' tortoise mind into making quick decisions or snap judgements. In other words, people can become more effective by thinking less in situations and allowing the tortoise to play its role before decisions are made. As Cleese points out, know when the decision needs to made and only then make the decision.

Appendix C   An Article on the Pragmatism of Richard Rorty

Although completely unrelated to this book and the five books above, the following article encapsulates the philosophical stance of *Images of Projects* and its emphasis on a *pragmatic* approach towards working on projects. Originally published in the *Financial Times*, the article is reproduced here with kind permission.

Why Rorty's search for what works has lessons for business
John Kay, *Financial Times*, June 19th 2007

What mattered to Richard Rorty was not the search for what is true, but the search for what works. And that is what economists can learn from him. The test of a model, a way of thinking, or a theory, is not truth, but usefulness.

When a student of business and economics wants to ponder the conceptual foundations of these subjects, Richard Rorty, who died on June 8, is the modern philosopher I recommend. This suggestion would have surprised Rorty. He was the archetypal American liberal, with no time or regard for the world of business and finance. His most important work, published 30 years ago, was *Philosophy and the Mirror of Nature,* which debunked the notion that scientists could succeed in a search for the mirror of nature, the truth about "The Way the World Is".

Rorty was not a relativist who believed that all opinions were equally valid. He called the leftwing postmodernists of American humanities departments, who parroted phrases from the continental European philosophers he admired, creeps. Rorty was a modern representative of the American pragmatic tradition, associated with John Dewey and William James. By claiming that philosophical distinctions mattered only if they made a difference to practice, Rorty distanced himself from recent analytic philosophy. What mattered to him was not the search for what is true, but the search for what works. The test of a model, a way of thinking or a theory is not truth but usefulness.

Many of Rorty's philosophical critics claimed he was attacking a straw man, arguing that no one really believes they know, or might know "The Way the World Is". But I have met people who believe they know "The Way the World Is", in executive suites, on trading floors and in investment banks. I know consultants who are employed to report on "The Way the World Is". To be sure, there is an element of pragmatism in their approach. What better demonstration of their insight into "The Way the World Is" than their exalted positions and extravagant bonuses?

The academic search for truth, for scientific rather than commercial knowledge of "The Way the World Is", has different motives. The modern economist is driven by physics-envy. Physicists have the best claim to hold a mirror to nature: their models have proved so useful that no one would think about heat, pressure or motion in any other way. Many people claim this is because these theories are true.

The pragmatic Rorty argued that to say the theories are true adds nothing to the observation that the models are useful. This claim, applied to hard science, is a subject of continuing disagreement. But Rorty's perspective is surely right for complex and fluid situations whose outcome depends on human interaction. The soldier's war stories give insight into "The Way the World Is", but in a very different way from the models of quantum physics. No individual soldier – no general – ever sees the whole picture; no one can ever, in this sense, hold a mirror to nature. The best accounts will eventually come from the military historian or the novelist who pieces together – and manufactures – a narrative from fragments of information and experience. There can be many such accounts, some better than others, none representing a unique correspondence with the truth.

And so it is with business and finance. I have often given an account of an event in business history and been confronted by a participant who offers an account of "The Way It Was". But all he offers is an account of the way it was for him. Even an aggregation of such accounts can provide only a partial and controversial description of the whole. Economists often assert that economic theory says this or predicts that. But economic theory will never hold a mirror to nature. Good economic arguments are specific to their context. There are no universal economic laws, only trends and tendencies.

Yet business journalists continue to believe that chief executives can tell them "The Way the World Is" at their companies. Professional modellers imagine that by adding ever more realism and complexity to their black boxes, they come closer to describing "The Way the World Is". Visionary leaders imagine they can reconstruct industries through rationalist knowledge of "The Way the World Is".

Rorty's pragmatism can save us from these errors. His philosophy meets his own test: an understanding of it should change how we behave.

Source: www.johnkay.com. Reproduced with kind permission from John Kay.

Appendix D   Underlying Research Approach

Like all books, *Images of Projects* is the product of a particular history and hence it is important to briefly set out the research approach that has been used to develop the book's core ideas and why this approach has been used. In short, since the world of projects is a practical field, the approach used has been *action research*, which in this work meant starting 15 years ago with some ideas (re: the theory in Appendix C), working with the ideas in real situations, and then gradually evolving them through further use in practice, with the eventual result being the images framework on page 29. Moreover, in doing this kind of research, it is important to know what model of action research is being used and in this work the approach used was Peter Checkland's model that he briefly explains below:

> *action research requires involvement in a problem situation and a readiness to use **the experience itself** as a research object about which lessons can be learned by conscious reflection. In order to make this possible it is absolutely essential to declare in advance an intellectual framework which will be used in attempts to make sense of both the situation and the researcher's involvement in it. It is with reference to the declared framework that 'lessons' can be defined. The action researcher thus has two hopes: that the framework will yield insights concerning the perceived problems which will lead to practical help in the situation; and that experiences of using the framework will enable it to be gradually improved.*[1]

The last sentence summarizes how the authors have developed the ideas in *Images of Projects* through a process of deliberate learning from real experiences. For example, the lead author has worked with many organizations and many cohorts of students over the years in tackling various project situations using the ideas, and gradually evolved the ideas by adapting and refining them in relation to these experiences. Of course, in doing this it was not a linear or systematic process, but rather a *cyclic* process of steadily learning what ideas could eventually be transferable to others. And this included plenty of false trails and cul de sacs explored along the way! However, since the action researcher is *conscious* of the ideas being tried out in situations, changes can be made and the learning process can continue. This research model is shown in Figure A1 and is elegantly summarized by Peter Checkland in the extract below:

> *theory which is not tested out in practice is sterile. Equally, practice which is not reflective about the ideas upon which it is based will abandon the chance to learn its way steadily to better ways of taking action. Thus, theory must be tested out in practice; and practice is the best source of theory. In the best possible situation the two create each other in a cyclic process in which neither is dominant but each is the source of the other.*[2]

Figure A1   An action research model

Appendix E   References and Suggested Reading

This appendix lists all the references used in the Overview, Chapters 1 to 14, and Appendices A to D. Suggestions for further reading are also provided and the reader is encouraged to explore other publications not listed here.

Overview

1. Pearce S and Cameron S (1997) *Against the Grain.* Butterworth-Heinemann.
2. Morris P (1994) *The Management of Projects.* Thomas Telford Books.
3. Ibid.
4. Dinsmore P and Cooke-Davies T (2006) *The Right Projects Done Right!* Jossey-Bass.
5. Op. Cit 2.
6. Winter M *et al* (2006) Directions for Future Research Directions for Future Research in Project Management: The Main Findings of a UK Government-Funded Research Network. *International Journal of Project Management,* 24:8, 638–649.
7. Ibid.
8. Morgan G (1997) *Images of Organization.* 2nd Edition. Sage Publications.
9. Morgan G (1998) *Images of Organization: The Executive Edition.* Sage Publications.
10. Pugh D and Hickson D (1996) *Writers on Organizations.* 5th Edition. Penguin Books.

Suggested Reading
Morris P (1994) *The Management of Projects.* Thomas Telford Books.
Maylor H (2003) *Project Management.* 3rd Edition. FT Prentice Hall.
APM (2006) *The APM Body of Knowledge.* 5th Edition. Association of Project Management, UK.
Turner J (1999) *Handbook of Project-Based Management.* 2nd Edition. McGraw-Hill.

Chapter 1

1. Advertisement for Project Manager: Equipment Direct (Ref: RIT1230). *The Guardian,* 2003.
2. Moving the boundaries. Interview with Sainsbury's CIO Maggie Miller by Douglas Hayward. *Financial Times,* 15th October 2003.
3. Maligned, misaligned or both? Article by Andrew Lawrence. *Information Age,* May 2004.
4. Managing Business Change. Presentation by Ian Paterson (Corporate Head of Programme Management at Birmingham City Council). *Best Practice Showcase,* London, June 2005.
5. Successful IT: Modernising Government in Action. *UK Cabinet Office Report,* 2000.
6. Not fit for purpose: £2bn cost of government's IT blunders. *The Guardian,* 5th January 2008.
7. The Challenges of Complex IT projects. Report of *The Royal Academy of Engineering* and *The British Computer Society,* April 2004.
8. Hughes B *et al* (2004) *Project Management for IT-Related Projects.* The British Computer Society.
9. McAfee A (2006) Mastering the Three Worlds of Information Technology. *Harvard Business Review,* November 2006.
10. Senge P (1990) *The Fifth Discipline.* Doubleday Books.
11. de Bono E (1971) *Lateral Thinking for Management.* McGraw-Hill.
12. Ibid.

Suggested Reading

de Bono E (1971) *Lateral Thinking for Management.* McGraw-Hill.

Pearce S and Cameron S (1997) *Against the Grain.* Butterworth-Heinemann.

Senge P (1990) *The Fifth Discipline.* Doubleday Books.

Chapter 2

1. Morgan G (1997) *Images of Organization.* 2nd Edition. Sage Publications.
2. Morgan G (1998) *Images of Organization: The Executive Edition.* Sage Publications.
3. Pugh D and Hickson D (1996) *Writers on Organizations.* 5th Edition. Penguin Books.
4. Op. Cit 1.
5. Battram A (1998) *Navigating Complexity.* The Industrial Society.
6. Pearce S and Cameron S (1997) *Against the Grain.* Butterworth-Heinemann.
7. Op. Cit 1.
8. Anderson D and Ackerman Anderson L (2001) *Beyond Change Management.* Jossey-Bass.
9. Op. Cit 6.
10. Levene R (1997) Project Management. In: *Concise International Encyclopaedia of Business Management,* 578–597. International Thompson Business Press.
11. Turner J (1999) *Handbook of Project-Based Management.* 2nd Edition. McGraw-Hill.
12. Gido J and Clements J (1999) *Successful Project Management.* International Thomson Publishing.
13. BSI (2002). *BS6079-1: Project Management.* British Standards Institute.
14. Fay B (1990) Critical realism? *Journal for the Theory of Social Behaviour,* 20, 33–41.
15. Schön D (1983) *The Reflective Practitioner: How Professionals Think in Action.* Basic Books.
16. Ibid.
17. de Bono E (1971) *Lateral Thinking for Management.* McGraw-Hill.
18. Ibid.

Suggested Reading

Morgan G (1993) *Imaginization: The Art of Creative Management.* Sage Publications.

Pugh D and Hickson D (1996) *Writers on Organizations.* 5th Edition. Penguin Books.

Schön D (1983) *The Reflective Practitioner: How Professionals Think in Action.* Basic Books.

Introduction to Part 2

1. Pettigrew A (1987) Context and action in the transformation of the firm. *Journal of Management Studies.* Volume 24:6, 649–670.
2. Internet: www.connectingforhealth.nhs.uk. Accessed 2008.
3. Ibid.
4. Internet: www.direct.gov.uk. Accessed 2008.
5. Internet: www.communities.gov.uk. Accessed 2008.
6. Internet: www.neighbourhood.gov.uk. Accessed 2008.
7. Internet: www.braunstone.com. Accessed 2008.
8. Internet: www.london2012.com. Accessed 2008.
9. Internet: www.edenproject.com. Accessed 2008.
10. Ibid.
11. DIY? Forget it: get a man in. Article by Julia Finch. *The Guardian* Newspaper, June 26th 2006.

12. Kingfisher Group Annual Report 2007–08. Internet: www.kingfisher.co.uk. Accessed 2008.
13. Internet: www.dover.gov.uk/kentcoal. Accessed 2008.

Chapter 3

1. Checkland P and Poulter J (2006) *Learning for Action: A Short Definitive Account of Soft Systems Methodology and its use for Practitioners, Teachers and Students*. Wiley.
2. Vickers G (1965) *The Art of Judgment*. Chapman and Hall.
3. Checkland P (1994) Systems Theory and Management Thinking. *American Behavioral Scientist*, 38:1, 75–91.
4. Morgan G (1993) *Imaginization: The Art of Creative Management*. Sage Publications.
5. Smith C (2006) *Making Sense of Project Realities*. Gower Publishing.
6. Cross R and Parker A (2004) *The Hidden Power of Social Networks*. Harvard Business School Press.
7. Ibid.
8. Internet: www.brainyquote.com/quotes/authors/h/harold_s_geneen.html. Accessed 2008.
9. Johnson G and Scholes K (2002) *Exploring Corporate Strategy*. 6th Edition. FT Prentice Hall.
10. Senior B (2002) *Organisational Change*. 2nd Edition. FT Prentice Hall.
11. Op. Cit 5.
12. Eccles R and Nohria N (1992) *Beyond the Hype: Rediscovering the Essence of Management*. Harvard Business School Press.
13. Mangham I (1986) *Power and Performance in Organizations: An Exploration of Executive Process*. Blackwell.
14. Humphrys J (2004) *Lost for Words*. Hodder and Stoughton.
15. Morgan G (1997) *Images of Organization*. 2nd Edition. Sage Publications.
16. Vaill P (1989) *Managing as a Performing Art*. Jossey-Bass.
17. Checkland P (1981) *Systems Thinking, Systems Practice*. Wiley.
18. Variant translation of a quote by Diogenes Laërtius in *Lives of the Philosophers* Book IX, section 8. Internet: http://en.wikiquote.org/wiki/Heraclitus. Accessed 2008.

Suggested Reading
Morgan G (1997) *Images of Organization*. 2nd Edition. Sage Publications.
Smith C (2006) *Making Sense of Project Realities*. Gower Publishing.
Patterson K *et al* (2002) *Crucial Conversations*. McGraw-Hill.
Weeks H (2008) *Failure to Communicate*. Harvard Business Press.
Kolb D and Williams J (2003) *Everyday Negotiation*. Jossey-Bass.
Cornes A (2004) *Culture from the Inside Out*. Intercultural Press.
Stacey R *et al* (2000) *Complexity and Management*. Routledge.

Chapter 4

1. Morgan G (1997) *Images of Organization*. 2nd Edition. Sage Publications.
2. Pinto J (1996) *Power and Politics in Project Management*. Project Management Institute.
3. Op. Cit 1.
4. Smith C (2006) *Making Sense of Project Realities*. Gower Publishing.
5. Internet: www.cambridge.org/catalogue/catalogue.asp?isbn=9780521009461. Accessed 2008.

6. Op. Cit 2.
7. Op. Cit 1.
8. Senior B (2002) *Organisational Change.* 2nd Edition. FT Prentice Hall.
9. Yukl G and Falbe C (1990) Influence Tactics and Objectives in Upward, Downward, and Lateral Influence Attempts. *Journal of Applied Technology*, 75:2, 132–140.
10. Harrison F and Lock D (2004) *Advanced Project Management.* 4th Edition. Gower Publishing.
11. Op. Cit 8.
12. Op. Cit 1.
13. Op. Cit 1.
14. Op. Cit 2.
15. Op. Cit 4.
16. Checkland P and Scholes J (1990) *Soft Systems Methodology in Action.* Wiley.

Suggested Reading

Morgan G (1997) *Images of Organization.* 2nd Edition. Sage Publications.

Pinto J (1996) *Power and Politics in Project Management.* Project Management Institute.

Smith C (2006) *Making Sense of Project Realities.* Gower Publishing.

Brandon R and Seldman M (2004) *Survival of the Savvy.* Free Press.

Pfeffer J (1992) *Managing with Power.* Harvard Business School Press.

Hodgson D and Cicmil S (Eds) (2006) *Making Projects Critical.* Palgrave Macmillan.

Chapter 5

1. Winter M (2009) Using Soft Systems Methodology for Structuring Project Definition. In *Making Essential Choices with Scant Information: Front-End Decision-Making in Major Projects.* Edited by Terry Williams, Knut Samset and Kjell J. Sunnevåg. Palgrave Macmillan.
2. Checkland P and Poulter J (2006) *Learning for Action: A Short Definitive Account of Soft Systems Methodology and its use for Practitioners, Teachers and Students.* Wiley.
3. Checkland P and Winter M (2006) Process and Content: Two Ways of Using SSM. Special Issue on Problem Structuring Methods, *Journal of the Operational Research Society.* Volume 57:12, 1435–1441.
4. Ibid.
5. Op. Cit 2.
6. Executive Programme for Prison Service Plus (2007–2008), Manchester Business School.
7. Argyris C (1970) *Intervention Theory and Method.* Addison-Wesley.
8. Oswick C and Grant D (Eds) (1996) *Organisational Development: Metaphorical Explorations.* Pitman.
9. Harvey D and Brown D (2001) *An Experiential Approach to Organization Development.* 6th Edition. Prentice-Hall International.

Suggested Reading

Checkland P and Poulter J (2006) *Learning for Action.* Wiley.

Kahane A (2004) *Solving Problem Solving.* Berrett-Koehler Publishers Inc.

Schein E (1999) *Process Consultation Revisited.* Addison-Wesley.

Hogan C (2002) *Understanding Facilitation.* Kogan Page.

Roam D (2008) *The Back of the Napkin: Solving Problems and Selling Ideas with Pictures.* Portfolio.

Chapter 6

1. Walker S and Marr J (2001) *Stakeholder Power.* Perseus Publishing.
2. de Bono E (1992) *Serious Creativity.* Harper Collins.
3. Normann R (2001) *Reframing Business: When the Map Changes the Landscape.* Wiley.
4. Ibid.
5. Winter M and Szczepanek T (2008) Projects and programmes as value creation processes: a new perspective and some practical implications. *International Journal of Project Management,* 26:1, 95–103.
6. Ibid.
7. IT-Enabled Change: Implementation of SAP at Warburtons. Presentation by Colin Saunders (former IT Director). *Rethinking Project Management Network,* October 20th 2004, Newcastle.
8. Ibid.
9. Internet: www.ogc.gov.uk. Accessed 2008.
10. Cohen D and Graham R (2001) *The Project Manager's MBA.* Wiley.
11. Delivering on Clichés: Accenture's Annual Report Almost Makes Sense – Until You Read it Phrase by Phrase. Article by Lucy Kellaway. *Financial Times,* February 17th 2003.
12. Op. Cit 3.
13. How my party got it so very wrong on apartheid. Article by David Cameron. *The Observer,* August 27th 2006.

Suggested Reading

Dinsmore P and Cooke-Davies T (2005) *The Right Projects Done Right.* Jossey-Bass.

Morgan M *et al* (2007) *Executing Your Strategy.* Harvard Business School Press.

Ward J and Daniels E (2006) *Benefits Management.* Wiley.

Davies A and Hobday A (2005) *The Business of Projects.* Cambridge University Press.

Morris P and Jamieson (2004) *Translating Corporate Strategy into Project Strategy.* PMI.

OGC (2007) *Managing Successful Programmes.* The Stationery Office.

Kelly J *et al* (2004) *Value Management of Construction Projects.* Blackwell.

Chapter 7

1. Andersen E et al (2004) *Goal Directed Project Management.* 3rd Edition. Kogan Page.
2. de Bono E (1971) *Lateral Thinking for Management.* McGraw-Hill.
3. Internet: www.jobs.ac.uk. Accessed 2004.
4. Internet: www.dover.gov.uk/kentcoal. Accessed 2008.
5. Winter M, et al (2006) The Importance of 'Process' in Rethinking Project Management: The Story of a UK Government-Funded Research Network. Special Issue of *International Journal of Project Management,* Volume 24:8, 650–662.
6. Ibid.
7. OGC (2005) *Managing Successful Projects with PRINCE2.* The Stationery Office.
8. OGC (2007) *Managing Successful Programmes.* The Stationery Office.
9. Op. Cit 1.

Suggested Reading

Lowe D (2009) *Commercial Management: Theory and Practice.* Blackwell. (In press.)

Davies A and Hobday A (2005) *The Business of Projects.* Cambridge University Press.

Andersen E et al (2004) *Goal Directed Project Management.* 3rd Edition. Kogan Page.

Maylor H (2003) *Project Management.* 3rd Edition. FT Prentice Hall.
Gardiner P (2005) *Project Management: A Strategic Planning Approach.* Palgrave Macmillan.
DeCarlo D (2004) *Extreme Project Management.* Jossey-Bass.
OGC (2005) *Managing Successful Projects with PRINCE2.* The Stationery Office.

Chapter 8

1. Packendorff J (1995) Inquiring into the temporary organization: new directions for project management research. *Scandinavian Journal of Management,* 11:4, 319–333.
2. The Eden Project Annual Review 2005/06. Internet: www.edenproject.com. Accessed 2007.
3. The ESCO model is derived from: 3. Checkland P (1981) *Systems Thinking, Systems Practice.* Wiley; 4. Wilson B (1984) *Systems: Concepts, Methodologies, and Applications.* Wiley.
5. Internet: www.london2012.com. Accessed 2008.
6. Managing Strategic Change to Recreate Shareholder Value. Presentation by Tony Szczepanek. *Rethinking PM Seminar,* Major Projects Association, October 18th 2006, London.

Suggested Reading

Andersen E (2008) *Rethinking Project Management: An Organisational Perspective.* FT Prentice Hall.
Davies A and Hobday A (2005) *The Business of Projects.* Cambridge University Press.
Deering A and Murphy A (2003) *The Partnering Imperative.* Wiley.
Grimsey D and Lewis M (2004) *Public Private Partnerships.* Edward Elgar.
Boddy D (1992) *Managing Projects: Building and Leading the Team.* FT Prentice Hall.
Turner R (1995) *The Commercial Project Manager.* McGraw-Hill.
Binney G *et al* (2005) *Living Leadership.* FT Prentice Hall.
Goffee R and Jones G (2006) *Why Should Anyone be Led by You ?* Harvard Business School Press.

Chapter 9

1. Andersen E *et al* (2004) *Goal Directed Project Management.* 3rd Edition. Kogan Page.
2. Ibid.
3. Plus ça change: Kremlin 1980 to the Whitehall of today. Article by Simon Caulkin. *The Observer,* April 9th 2006.
4. Anderson D and Ackerman Anderson L (2001) *Beyond Change Management.* Jossey-Bass.
5. Ibid.
6. Ibid.
7. IT-Enabled Change: Implementation of SAP at Warburtons. Presentation by Colin Saunders (former IT Director). *Rethinking Project Management Network,* October 20th 2004, Newcastle.

Suggested Reading

Cameron E and Green M (2004) *Making Sense of Change Management.* Kogan Page.
Anderson D and Ackerman Anderson L (2001) *Beyond Change Management.* Jossey-Bass.
Balogun J and Hailey Hope V (2004) *Exploring Strategic Change.* 2nd Edition. FT Prentice Hall.
Senior B (2002) *Organisational Change.* 2nd Edition. FT Prentice Hall.
Binney G and Williams C (1995) *Leaning into the Future.* Nicholas Brealey Publishing.
Schein E (1999) *Process Consultation Revisited.* Addison-Wesley.
Hogan C (2002) *Understanding Facilitation.* Kogan Page.

Chapter 10

1. Battle of Orgreave site to become civil service office campus. Article by Terry Macalister. *The Guardian* Newspaper, 29th November 2007.
2. de Bono E (1985) *Six Thinking Hats.* Little, Brown and Company.
3. de Bono E (1982) *De Bono's Thinking Course.* BBC Books.
4. Normann R (2001) *Reframing Business: When the Map Changes the Landscape.* Wiley.

Suggested Reading

de Bono E (1985) *Six Thinking Hats.* Penguin.
de Bono E (1982) *De Bono's Thinking Course.* BBC Books.
Albrecht K (2007) *Practical Intelligence.* Jossey-Bass.
Claxton G and Lucas B (2007) *The Creative Thinking Plan.* BBC Active.

Chapter 11

1. Morris P (2002) Science, objective knowledge and the theory of project management. *Civil Engineering Proceedings of the Institute of Civil Engineers,* 150, 82–80.
2. Checkland P and Poulter J (2006) *Learning for Action: A Short Definitive Account of Soft Systems Methodology and its use for Practitioners, Teachers and Students.* Wiley.
3. Ibid.
4. Roam D (2008) *The Back of the Napkin: Solving Problems and Selling Ideas with Pictures.* Portfolio.
5. Op. Cit 2.
6. Team dream. Article by Andrew Cracknell. *Financial Times Magazine,* April 16th 2005.
7. Checkland P (1999) *Soft Systems Methodology: A 30-Year Retrospective.* Wiley.
8. Open University (1985) Managing and Messy Problems. Block 1, Course T244, *Managing in Organizations,* The Open University, Milton Keynes.
9. Albrecht K (2007) *Practical Intelligence.* Jossey-Bass.
10. Talking Management with John Cleese: Soldier of Convention or Agent of Change?; A Rebuff To the Ministry Of Silly Bosses. Article by Adam Bryant. Internet: *www.nytimes.com.* Accessed 2008.
11. Claxton G (1999) *Wise Up.* Bloomsbury.

Suggested Reading

Kahane A (2004) *Solving Problem Solving.* Berrett-Koehler Publishers Inc.
Roam D (2008) *The Back of the Napkin: Solving Problems and Selling Ideas with Pictures.* Portfolio.
Albrecht K (2007) *Practical Intelligence.* Jossey-Bass.

Chapter 12

1. Eccles R and Nohria N (1992) *Beyond the Hype: Rediscovering the Essence of Management.* Harvard Business School Press.
2. Albrecht K (2007) *Practical Intelligence.* Jossey-Bass.
3. Ibid.
4. de Bono E (1985) *Six Thinking Hats.* Little, Brown and Company.
5. Claxton G and Lucas B (2007) *The Creative Thinking Plan.* BBC Active.
6. Isaacs W (1999) *Dialogue and the Art of Thinking Together.* Doubleday.

7. Stangroom J and Garvey J (2005) *The Great Philosophers*. Arcturus Publishing Ltd.
8. Stacey R et al (2000) *Complexity and Management*. Routledge.
9. Cooke-Davies T et al (2007) We're not in Kansas anymore, Toto: mapping the strange landscape of complexity theory, and its relationship to project management. *Project Management Journal*, 38:2, 50–61, Project Management Institute.

Suggested Reading

Wheatley M (2002) *Turning to One Another*. Berrett-Koehler Publishers Inc.

Claxton G and Lucas B (2007) *The Creative Thinking Plan*. BBC Active.

Isaacs W (1999) *Dialogue and the Art of Thinking Together*. Doubleday.

Chapter 13

1. Checkland P and Poulter J (2006) *Learning for Action*. Wiley.
2. Ibid.
3. Checkland P (1981) *Systems Thinking, Systems Practice*. Wiley.

Chapter 14

1. Internet: www.thinkexist.com/quotation. Accessed 2008.
2. Winter M, et al (2006) The Importance of 'Process' in Rethinking Project Management: The Story of a UK Government-Funded Research Network. Special Issue of *International Journal of Project Management*, Volume 24, 8, 650–662.
3. Morgan G (1986) *Images of Organization*. Sage Publications.
4. Ibid.
5. Ibid.
6. Vickers G (1965) *The Art of Judgment*. Chapman and Hall.
7. Rolls's fighting spirit honoured. *The Sunday Times*, February 11th 2007.
8. Op. Cit 3.

Appendix A

1. Patterson K et al (2002) *Crucial Conversations*. McGraw-Hill.
2. Stacey R et al (2000) *Complexity and Management*. Routledge.
3. Schein E (1999) *Process Consultation Revisited*. Addison-Wesley.
4. Checkland P and Poulter J (2006) *Learning for Action*. Wiley.
5. Ward J and Daniels E (2006) *Benefits Management*. Wiley.
6. Op. Cit 4.
7. Andersen E et al (2004) *Goal Directed Project Management*. 3rd Edition. Kogan Page.
8. Davies A and Hobday A (2005) *The Business of Projects*. Cambridge University Press.
9. Ibid.
10. Op. Cit 7

Appendix D

1. Checkland P and Scholes J (1990) *Soft Systems Methodology in Action*. Wiley.
2. Ibid.

****

Index

If you have found this book useful you may be interested in other titles from Gower

Project Manager's Guide to Purchasing
Garth Ward
March 2008   244 x 172 mm   232 pages   Hardback 978-0-566-08692-2

Project Reviews, Assurance and Governance
Graham Oakes
October 2008   244 x 172 mm   288 pages   Hardback 978-0-566-08807-0

Tools for Complex Projects
Kaye Remington and Julien Pollack
February 2008   244 x 172 mm   232 pages   Hardback 978-0-566-08741-7

Training for Project Management
Three volume set
Ian Stokes
January 2009   297 x 210 mm   1000 pages   A4 Looseleaf 978-0-566-08901-5

Go to:
www.gowerpublishing.com/projectmanagement for details
of these and our wide range of other project management titles.

Visit **www.gowerpublishing.com** and

- search the entire catalogue of Gower books in print
- order titles online at 10% discount
- take advantage of special offers
- sign up for our monthly e-mail update service
- download free sample chapters from all recent titles
- download or order our catalogue